"If there is one subject the modern and now postmodern world does not, and perhaps cannot, understand, it is the imagination. We have exiled this weird aspect of consciousness into the dry flatland of the imaginary and the meaningless. We also, frankly, fear it, and for some very reasonable reasons. So when should we trust it? What do we *do* with it? And how does it relate to our social norms and ethical concerns? Does it? Should it? Here is a most practical guidebook for our own imaginal lives, a kind of how-to manual that never dumbs down and always lifts up. The reader senses that she or he is walking through a dangerous but fascinating forest behind a trusted guide. We never quite get out of the forest, but we learn not to be so afraid of the teeming darkness that is all around us, that is in us, and that *is* us."

—**Jeffrey J. Kripal, J. Newton Rayzor Professor of Religion, Rice University, USA, and author of** ***Secret Body: Erotic and Esoteric Currents in the History of Religions***

"An essential and innovative contribution to understanding ethics and fantasy, this beautifully crafted book is a must-read for any serious student of depth psychology. The nuanced endeavor of ethical decision-making can prove treacherous without an in-depth understanding of the psychic factors at play. In his rich exploration of the ethical imagination, Fitzpatrick presents eight guiding principles for understanding the 'ethical gray zone' of the human psyche, shedding vital light on the sometimes harrowing path of individuation."

—**Carolyn Bates, PhD, Jungian analyst and co-author of** ***Sex in the Therapy Hour: A Case of Professional Incest***

"This beautiful book perfectly marries contemporary philosophy, psychological theories, and theological insights to help us talk about the imagination in ethical ways. The result is a work that explains and leads us through the complexities of ethics and one you will go back to over and over for reference. Sean paves a clear path to create an ethical imagination for all who seek to navigate this digital age fully and successfully. It is a unique combination of research, storytelling, and a provocative call to action."

—**Reverend Dr Wismick Jean-Charles, former Vice-President of Academic Affairs of the University Notre-Dame of Haiti and current Vicar General of the Montfort Missionaries**

"While we, and the world, hold ourselves accountable for our behaviors, are we also accountable for the far more autonomous insurgencies of the imagination? Should we feel 'guilty' for what transpires in dreams, fantasies, projections, or do they open an aperture into a developmental dialogue with our fuller humanity? Sean Fitzpatrick undertakes a probing investigation of these questions and presents the reader with a most thoughtful set of lenses and concrete recommendations through which to see these dilemmas, engage them, and feel less separated from the rich complexity of our souls."

—**James Hollis, PhD, Jungian analyst and author**

The Ethical Imagination

What do we do with our fantasies? Are there right and wrong ways to imagine, feel, think, or desire? Do we have our fantasies, or do they have us? In *The Ethical Imagination: Exploring Fantasy and Desire in Analytical Psychology*, Sean Fitzpatrick explores how our obligation to the Other extends to our most intimate spaces.

Informed by Jungian psychology and the philosophy of Emmanuel Levinas, Fitzpatrick imagines an ethical approach that can negotiate the delicate and porous boundary between inner and outer, personal and collective fantasy. Combining both theory and practice, the book examines theorists of the imagination, such as Plato, Coleridge, Sartre, and Richard Kearney, explores stories from contemporary culture, such as Jimmy Carter and New York's "Cannibal Cop", and includes encounters in the consulting room. *The Ethical Imagination* explores how these questions have been asked in different ways across culture and history, and Fitzpatrick examines the impact of our modern, digital world on ethics and imagination. In this original examination of the ethical status of our imagination, this book illustrates how our greatest innovations, works of art, and acts of compassion emerge from the human imagination, but so also do our horrific atrocities. Fitzpatrick compellingly demonstrates that what and how we imagine matters.

Unique and innovative, this book will be of immense interest to Jungian psychotherapists, analytical psychologists, and other mental health professionals interested in the ethics, the imagination, and clinical work with fantasy. It will also be an important book for academics and students of Jungian and post-Jungian studies, philosophy, religious studies, and ethics.

Sean Fitzpatrick, PhD, is the executive director of The Jung Center, Houston, USA, and a psychotherapist in private practice. He received his doctorate in psychology, with a specialization in Jungian studies, from Saybrook University, USA.

The Ethical Imagination
Exploring Fantasy and Desire in
Analytical Psychology

Sean Fitzpatrick

LONDON AND NEW YORK

First published 2020
by Routledge
2 Park Square, Milton Park, Abingdon, Oxon OX14 4RN

and by Routledge
52 Vanderbilt Avenue, New York, NY 10017

*Routledge is an imprint of the Taylor & Francis Group, an informa
business*

© 2020 Sean Fitzpatrick

The right of Sean Fitzpatrick to be identified as author of this
work has been asserted by him/her/them in accordance with
sections 77 and 78 of the Copyright, Designs and Patents Act
1988.

All rights reserved. No part of this book may be reprinted
or reproduced or utilised in any form or by any electronic,
mechanical, or other means, now known or hereafter invented,
including photocopying and recording, or in any information
storage or retrieval system, without permission in writing from
the publishers.

Trademark notice: Product or corporate names may be
trademarks or registered trademarks, and are used only for
identification and explanation without intent to infringe.

British Library Cataloguing-in-Publication Data
A catalogue record for this book is available from the British Library

Library of Congress Cataloging-in-Publication Data
Names: Fitzpatrick, Sean (Psychotherapist), author.
Title: The ethical imagination : exploring fantasy and desire in
analytical psychology / Sean Fitzpatrick.
Description: Abingdon, Oxon; New York, NY : Routledge, 2019. |
Includes bibliographical references and index. |
Identifiers: LCCN 2019013041 (print) | LCCN 2019015240 (ebook) |
ISBN 9781351233071 (Master eBook) | ISBN 9781351233064 (Adobe Reader) |
ISBN 9781351233040 (Mobipocket) | ISBN 9781351233057 (ePub) |
ISBN 9780815378167 (hardback) | ISBN 9780815378174 (pbk.)
Subjects: LCSH: Fantasy. | Psychoanalysis.
Classification: LCC BF175.5.F36 (ebook) | LCC BF175.5.F36 F58 2019 (print) |
DDC 154.3—dc23 LC record available at https://lccn.loc.
gov/2019013041

ISBN: 978-0-8153-7816-7 (hbk)
ISBN: 978-0-8153-7817-4 (pbk)
ISBN: 978-1-351-23307-1 (ebk)

Typeset in Times New Roman
by codeMantra

To Melanie and Daniel

Contents

	Acknowledgements	x
	Preface: images and ethics in the digital age	xii
1	Introduction	1
2	Imagining the imagination	14
3	What do we make of fantasy?	51
4	Imagining ethics	70
5	Eating the liver, killing the tortoise: the ethical and the imaginal	95
6	A dream of the desiring imagination	113
7	The law of the (imaginal) land	133
8	Conclusions	146
	Index	155

Acknowledgements

At least one of the core ideas of this book is not new: the imagination is always on some level collective. And this project has very much been a collective undertaking. It's a truism that we live what we research, and the clumsiness and messiness of the ideas I've worked to shape on the page reflects the clumsiness and messiness of the ways I've lived with the questions you'll find ahead. If I've succeeded in articulating some useful perspectives on the ways our imaginal lives touch and influence each other, it's come fumblingly and at times with suffering, for me and for those who have shared the path with me.

This book began as a dissertation project at Saybrook University. The faculty in the Jungian studies program guided me through four year of essentially writing the same paper over and over again as I worked through this material. Priscilla Murr, Jerry Ruhl, Lynn Cowan, and program chair Alan Vaughan were supportive throughout. Eugene Taylor took the work seriously and served as my dissertation chair until his untimely death. My relationship with Pittman McGehee began in an undergraduate classroom some 20 years ago and continued through Saybrook classrooms until today—he opened the doors of Jungian psychology to me and carried my projections with care and wisdom. And my fellow students in the program, especially Pohsuan Zaide, Derek Martin, John Schuster, and John Price, encouraged me and took the work seriously. I can't thank them enough.

As I began the transition from dissertation to book, Ron Schenk read the manuscript closely and gave me extensive, invaluable notes that framed the rest of the process. Students and colleagues in classes and workshops at The Jung Center of Houston, the Houston Psychoanalytic Society, the Vancouver Jung Society, the Texas Department of Criminal Justice's Sex Offender Treatment Program, and the San Francisco Jung Institute all helped to shape the material. The board and staff of The Jung Center remain incredibly supportive; I could not have done this work without them. I especially want to thank board presidents James Conlan and Scott Fletcher, trustees Travis Broesche, Karen Magee, and Michael Lieberman, and staff members Andrea McLemore, Jen Wilkins, Elissa Davis, Andria Frankfort, and Jyoti Iyer.

The faculty members of the department of religion at Rice University continue to be intellectual beacons in my life. William Parsons directed my master's thesis two decades ago and remains a mentor and inspiration. The late Edith Wyschogrod's kindness and care with the strange Jungian in her classroom made an indelible mark on me; it has been a singular pleasure to find her again on the page as I've worked to come to terms with her colleague and teacher Emmanuel Levinas. And Jeff Kripal's intellectual courage, generosity of spirit, and friendship have been irreplaceable gifts. His invitations to weeklong symposia at the Center for Theory and Research of the Esalen Institute greatly expanded the horizons of the imagination for me.

David and Amanda Moore and their beautiful children have carried me through the most difficult passages of the work. Scott Stanley provided significant guidance as a member of my dissertation committee and became a good friend along the way. Don Williams, Rodney Waters, and Elizabeth Maynard have been boon companions, compassionate and insightful guides as I grappled with the research in the context of my life.

James Hollis remains my most important teacher. His friendship, vulnerability, and unwavering support have made much more than this book possible.

My parents, John and Rita Fitzpatrick, appear in this book. I love them both. I miss my father, who died early in my doctoral work. And I continue to be startled by my mother's courage and the depth of her love.

My wife, Melanie, has suffered this for nearly ten years. Her insight, compassion, and love are bottomless, ferocious. Thank you, thank you, thank you.

Permissions

From THE RED BOOK by C. G. Jung, edited by Sonu Shamdasani, translated by Mark Kyburz, John Peck, and Sonu Shamdasani. Copyright © 2009 by the Foundation of the Works of C. G. Jung. Translation copyright © 2009 by Mark Kyburz, John Peck, and Sonu Shamdasani. Used by permission of W. W. Norton & Company, Inc.

Extracts from Collected Works used with permission from Taylor & Francis and Princeton University Press.

Preface
Images and ethics in the digital age

My generation straddles the digital divide. As a young teenager, I remember walking along Geneva Creek, in the high country near Guanella Pass in Colorado, my father's film camera in my hands. Twenty-four exposures, each one substantial, valuable. I watched the ripples, the pop of sun on water in the thin air. Committed to an aperture, a shutter speed, a perspective and angle. A moment. Then that moment would be sealed away in the case until the roll was complete, taken to a drugstore in suburban Denver, processed and returned. Usually, I earned the money it cost to process and print the film. I could not tell you then, nor could I adequately express now, how important that moment was—what was happening, or what it meant. I was compelled. And I am drawn back to the images again and again.

Thirty years later, the camera in my phone rivals that film camera in power, but without the expense and time. The digital single-lens reflex camera I carry with me many days is immensely more powerful. The alchemy of the darkroom retains its romance, but it is much easier to open my digital images in a photo-editing program on my laptop, where I can make thousands of fine adjustments instantly with no consequences and little cost. Creative freedom with little constraint. Technical limitations are romanticized as necessary to the creative process, but the sheer possibility of digital intervention is dizzyingly empowering.

It is tempting to suggest that the power of the individual image has been diminished by the digital age. The experience of standing with a camera in hand, finger poised on the shutter release, has undoubtedly changed for me on this side of the digital divide. The great photographer Henri Cartier-Bresson, following Cardinal de Retz, described what he called "the decisive moment": "To me, photography is the simultaneous recognition, in a fraction of a second, of the significance of an event as well as of a precise organization of forms which give that event its proper expression" (Cartier-Bresson, 2004, p. 20). This was how I sometimes experienced the photographic act in the film age: a moment of experiential presence that it is difficult to avoid putting into the language of mysticism. Per William James, the mystical experience is noetic, ineffable, transient, and ... well, not exactly passive (James, 1994/1902).

The power to click prematurely and often, to "hose it down," as the University of Texas film professor Steven Mims puts it, changes the experience. The act of capturing can more easily take over the moment. In a single-lens reflex camera, each time the shutter is triggered, the mirror that allows the photographer to see through the lens is pulled away so that the sensor can be exposed, blinding the photographer in the moment of the image's creation. We lose that moment of sensory connection. Every time we press that button, we are disconnected, again and again, seeing only the blackness of our device.

This is the age of the image. The phone I carry in my pocket captures the world around me in neat packages, visual moments that perhaps provoke memory, perhaps degrade it. Depending on your theoretical perspective, either position has its advocates, though the pessimists are the loudest. The fear is that the image has replaced the imagination. Because I can create an immediate digital visual record, the fullness of the experience, and our capacity to continue it, fades.

And, to the pessimists, the pressure of the combined images of the human community seemingly squeezes out any hope of my experience being in any way *mine*. On the cusp of the digital age, Jean Baudrillard felt this coming: "I no longer succeed in knowing what I want, the space is so saturated, the pressure so great from all who want to make themselves heard" (Baudrillard, 1983, p. 152). He augured the opening of the era of a "forced exteriorization of all interiority" and a "forced introjection of all exteriority," which leaves each of us as "only a pure screen, a switching center for all the networks of influence" (p. 153). To Baudrillard, I am nothing but the sum of the images through which greater powers (corporate, political, religious— pick your malevolent force) control me, and my images are immediately, obscenely available to all.

Mark Zuckerberg opened Facebook to the public in 2006. Baudrillard died one year later.

As I wrote this last paragraph, my phone burped up a message I had never seen before: I had formed a new "Memory." It was my photo program, helpfully organizing my photos from a recent weekend away from home and collecting them under the names of the towns I'd visited, and the dates I'd been there. It didn't collect all of the photos. Some algorithm sorted out similar images, perhaps it privileged images I had texted to others or edited, and it highlighted an image of me. This is precisely one of the issues contemporary critics cite when they declare the end of the imagination. Our memories are being created, shaped, and dispensed with by forces outside our control.

I do not believe that the postmodern image has destroyed the imagination, though what we mean by imagination will be worth exploring. Far from it. And of our postmodern hermeneutic tools, depth psychology is uniquely suited to help us navigate the age of the image. Bresson's "decisive moment" resonates with Jung's understanding of the symbolic imagination.

Something more appears through, coincides with, our images when we are present to them.

It is that quality of presence that preoccupies me. Because whether our images have a material analogue—whether we are talking about a photograph/ video/sketch/written narrative or an ongoing or remembered experience (and remembered experiences are ongoing, in their way)—we are present to them, through them, in a relative way. And I feel that the relativity of our presence to our images has an ethical dimension. This is as true of the images we consume as those that emerge in our experience through dreams, reveries, memories. Indeed, that consumption of images has a clear ethical resonance. When we consume, we use up, we eat, we waste. I do not believe that every encounter with an image is a consumption. But many are.

In an eloquent essay on the documentarian Claude Lanzmann (*Shoah*) and the philosopher Emmanuel Levinas (to whom we will look for guidance later), film scholar Libby Saxton (2007) explored a fundamental issue with the images we create. Trained in philosophy, Lanzmann was preoccupied with narrating the Holocaust without representing the irrepresentable, the horror that extends beyond all possibility of conveyance. Lanzmann shot 350 hours of interviews with survivors, perpetrators, and witnesses, and in his completed works he famously included only the filmed testimony, making no effort to recreate or represent the events described by his subjects. Saxton points out, however, that, even for Lanzmann, "the camera mediates otherness and manipulates our look." Lanzmann inevitably marshaled his scrupulously shot narrators in the service of his own argument, objectifying them in spite of his fierce desire not to, making their perspectives secondary to his. And, one might further argue, evoking experiential representations within the imaginations of his audience, by intent and design. Lanzmann's narrators exteriorized their experiences, and we introject them.

The imagination is simultaneously inside and outside, a field in which we all participate, and of which we are largely unaware. In *Secret Body* (2017), the historian of religion Jeffrey Kripal argues that

> We desperately need a new theory of the imagination (or a revived old one), one that can revision the imagination not as simply a spinner of fancy and distracting daydream, but also, at least in rare moments, as an ecstatic mediator, expressive artist, and translator of the really real. (p. 7)

I share Kripal's desire and its urgency. What follows is neither a new or a revived theory of imagination, but an exploration of it, a performance of it, and in some ways an idiosyncratic creation of it, written by a committee of convenience in which "I" (already multiple) am one among Baudrillard's many trying to be heard. How we encounter and relate to those Others who are simultaneously within and without matters. My partner, my son, my family and friends and colleagues and clients all live in my imagination, along with many long gone and many yet to come, many psychically real Others who live in dreams, symptoms, myths, and movements of the soul.

References

Baudrillard, J. (1983). The ecstasy of communication. In H. Foster (Ed.), *The anti-aesthetic: Essays on postmodern culture*. New York, NY: The New Press.

Cartier-Bresson, H. (2004). *The mind's eye: Writings on photography and photographers*. New York, NY: Aperture.

James, W. (1994). *The varieties of religious experience*. New York, NY: Penguin. (Original work published 1902)

Kripal, J. (2017). *Secret body: Erotic and esoteric currents in the history of religions*. Chicago, IL: University of Chicago Press.

Saxton, L. (2007). Fragile faces: Levinas and Lanzmann. *Film-Philosophy*, *11*(2), 1–14. Retrieved from http:/www.film-philosophy.com/2007v11n2/saxton.pdf

Chapter 1

Introduction

What do we do with our fantasies? Are there right and wrong ways to imagine, things we should or should not think, feel, or desire? Is it foolish or wise to believe that our fantasies have enduring personal and collective influence?

In perhaps the most influential sentence on this subject in the Western canon, the writer of the Gospel of Matthew gave us this perspective from Jesus:

> I say to you that everyone who looks at a woman lustfully has already committed adultery with her in his heart. (Matthew 5:28, *New Oxford Annotated Bible*)

That verse had a singular moment of contemporary cultural relevance in 1976, when American presidential candidate Jimmy Carter was interviewed by *Playboy* magazine. After suggesting that "Christ set some almost impossible standards for us," Carter admitted that "I've looked on a lot of women with lust. I've committed adultery in my heart many times" (Scheer, 1976, p. 86). This was a strange, unprompted admission by a political figure with a great deal to lose. Carter continued,

> Christ says, don't consider yourself better than someone else because one guy screws a whole bunch of women while the other guy is loyal to his wife. The guy who's loyal to his wife ought not to be condescending or proud because of the relative degree of sinfulness. (p. 86)

Almost 40 years separates us from what *Time* magazine called an "uncomfortable moment for America" (Top 10, 2013). Carter's well-intended candor reflects the convoluted lines of moral reasoning and perhaps psychological suffering that follow from traditional interpretations of scripture. Jesus appears to have made a moral equivalence between an intrapsychic experience of lust and sexual experiences between adults. In the calculus of sin and salvation, Jesus' new message superseded the Old Testament prohibition on

2 Introduction

extramarital sex. Just wanting it, it seems, also is sinful. The real sin Carter indicted is pride and the tendency to assume positions of moral superiority. If one accepts the initial premise, all of us sin; it is who we are, and this interpretation of Christian teaching implies that we must constantly be at war with ourselves. Who we are is always already unacceptable. How we could possibly change is a mystery. They are "almost impossibly high standards" (Scheer, 1976, p. 86) by which to live one's life.

What is lust? How does it appear? Where is it located? In what dimensions do we track its presence? Contemporary discourses—psychological, biological, philosophical, sociological, theological, literary, economic—register it differently. We are forever removed from the social and linguistic contexts of Jesus' remarks. The techniques of literary criticism foster doubt in the provenance of many of his scripturally recorded teachings. When Carter cited this passage, he imagined its meaning afresh, even as he likely believed himself to be referring to a stable, enduring truth. Carter's words appeared in a publication that is deeply concerned with evoking, celebrating, relieving, and even attempting to fix lust in contemporary discourse in a particular philosophical way. Pages away were images of naked women, photographed and airbrushed into heightened, stylized abstractions, symbolic images of lust, for the sake of lust—the ostensible reasons most readers bought the magazine.

What does this particular passage from Jesus' life—and a president's preoccupation with it—reflect about our myths of the imagination and its ethical status in the contemporary moment? We do not have to locate lust in the imagination; it might be equally useful to talk about it as a physiological experience, in terms that distill a complex phenomenon into clean, quantifiable clinical observations: elevated heart rate, dilated pupils, changes in temperature, increases in the production of fluids. To invoke an abstract concept such as *imagination* could lead us down materialist rabbit-holes. Why use *imagination* when we could talk about specific neural processes? Imagination seems an evocative but imprecise, outdated catchall that specialist inquiry has rendered an antique bit of poetry. Just to know to what it refers is difficult; as illuminated by Iris Murdoch (1986) in a philosophical context, imagination is a tough notion to define. Does it refer to a kind of experience? An action one can take? A complex but ultimately reducible biological process? The German word for imagination, *Einbildungskraft*, means literally the power to create a picture or image. We explore this problem in some detail throughout this work,[1] particularly within the discourse of analytical psychology.

We would be deluded if we were to believe that an MRI machine and decades of detailed neural mapping would provide us anything close to the meaning of our experience of the imagination. The myth of scientism— the naïve belief that scientific inquiry serves not only as a tool but as a comprehensive system of meaning and the ultimate answer to all of our problems—underlies this fantasy that the notion of imagination (indeed, of much psychological language) might be replaced by conceptual vocabulary on a materialist register. Indeed, all of our conceptual systems are imaginal, networks of symbols that have greater or lesser energy the more or less they are found to be valuable in coming to terms with contemporary experience. We will return to this idea; social constructionist thought and broader post-modern epistemological critiques necessarily inform this viewpoint. The starting point for our conversation is the simple observation that, like all discourses, psychology emerged in certain social, philosophical, historical, economic, and political contexts.

Jesus' admonition refers to what he called the "heart" or the symbolic inner nexus and engine of psychic energy. We might understand this heart to be the metaphoric locus of our fantasy of ourselves, or the place in which all human experience ultimately occurs. *Imagination* is without doubt a space constructed in discourse; we imagine imagination into being, and various eras in Western discourse have conceptualized imagination in varying ways.[2] It is a discursive space elaborated in careful detail by the Swiss psychiatrist C. G. Jung and the tradition of writers in analytical psychology that emerged from his thought. Jung wrote that "every psychic process is an image and an imagining" (Jung, 1969b, para. 889), which is a proposition that undergirds his psychology. So analytical psychology takes the imagination very seriously, as is reflected in the title of Avens' (1980) work: *Imagination Is Reality*.

Matthew's Jesus seems to have agreed with Avens' proposition. Intrapsychic experiences are morally equivalent to actions in the world. Jimmy Carter's reading of this is in one sense representative of traditional Christian approaches to the subject.[3] We are responsible for what we imagine, not just for what we do. Jesus' teaching seems to correct an implied inclination toward understanding inner experience as separate from reality. It can be interpreted as suggesting that we have control over our intrapsychic experience. Indeed, it often has been interpreted that way, with harshly punitive implications. It can also be interpreted to suggest that we engage in internal acts that have moral import and spiritual significance.

Though the context is loaded—undoubtedly, Carter at least unconsciously struggled with the conflict between his Christian beliefs and his experience of sexual desire—he is more interested in reading this passage as a warning about pride. Though it would run counter to mainstream readings, we could understand Matthew's Jesus to have emancipated us from the pursuit of moral superiority. If one's imagining an act has the same moral consequence as doing it, we cannot ever be better than anyone else. Across the millennia, Jesus might be winking at us: *Do you seriously believe you can stop yourself from having lustful thoughts? Give it up, buddy. That road leads to obsession and compulsion. No one is perfect.* This last implication is undoubtedly present in Christian moral theory—with the glum addition

4 Introduction

that we must strive toward perfection and are thus existentially shackled to failure.

Christian conceptualizations of the imagination are almost universally grim. Kearney (1988) noted that the Christianity of the Middle Ages took a prevailing attitude of "prudence or distrust" (p. 138) toward products of the imagination. The imagination was understood as the source of sinful illusion or a mortal hubris that risked the blasphemy of assuming God's own power of creativity for humanity. The images we create have the potential to occlude our vision of the divine.

This is only part of our cultural inheritance. Imagination also has been seen as the necessary mediating function between sensory experience and pure thought (Aristotle, Kant), a realm of experience distinct and ontologically superior to reality (Ibn 'Arabi via Henri Corbin), a "synthetic and magical power" (Coleridge, 1984/1814, p. 16), the sine qua non of consciousness (Sartre), and indistinguishable from reality (Derrida). Although we explore both the genealogy of its use in the Western intellectual tradition and its specific appearances in analytical psychology and allied literatures, we must make the obvious, necessary observation that the term *imagination* is itself imagined as a projection screen for our deepest hopes and fears about human nature. This book's treatment of imagination is no different.

The same is true of how we will treat ethics. Although specific ethical codes are the products of cultural and historical moments, and they change—often radically—over time, the notion of ethics would appear to have at least superficial stability across history. Ethics guide us in making decisions about how to behave. Etymologically, *ethic* derives from ancient Latin and Greek words related to the character or disposition of an individual (Ethic, 2014). This movement from a reflection on who individuals fundamentally are, to an articulation of principles by which they might live, is significant, and the tension between them is woven throughout ethical discourse. Codes developed for a collective and applied across all individuals necessarily make poor fits for all situations and all characters. In one of his few direct statements on ethics, Jung (1969a) wrote that "one can hardly think of a single rule that would not have to be reversed under certain conditions" (p. 16). Even the apparently stable category of the ethical, however, has shifted over time and remains a dynamically changing mode of describing human experience. Is it innate or inculcated by society? Is it built on religious foundations or a tool of collective domination by political powers?

The central question of this book is how psychological ethics apply to the imagination. As we explore the nature and potential value of articulating an ethic or ethics of the imagination in this way, we necessarily invent, or perhaps reimagine, our terms. The goal of this project is not to establish a Big Brother of the imagination, nor to outline a neat code by which we could hope to evaluate what is right or wrong in this invented space of the imagination. Instead, we will sketch the complex ways a set of texts have imagined the imagination and ethics. In particular, we will explore how the discourse of analytical psychology reflects contemporary preoccupations with these two ideas, including the way in which the discovery of the unconscious[4] affects the way we imagine ethics. This project is by its nature an attempt to create an ethical imagination even as we critique such an impulse. Our greatest innovations, works of art, acts of compassion emerge from the human imagination, as do our horrific atrocities. *How* we imagine matters.

This conversation repeatedly runs the risk of sliding into nebulous ambiguity. This reflects the researcher's limitations. I also believe it reflects an unavoidable structural necessity. This research discusses interior experience rather than objects readily available for a person to examine. This dissertation is ultimately a fantasy of the imagination or a fantasy of ethics. Materialist rabbit holes abound when one surveys Western philosophical and psychological theory for answers to these questions. So I frame some of these issues with narratives intended to illuminate the real-world implications of these ideas. The therapist's question—where does the client suffer?—motivates this dissertation in profound and undoubtedly unconscious ways. The theoretical answers I hope to explore are driven by personal and clinical experience. If the starting position is that we imagine all of our experience—as Jung suggested—then all of human experience is potentially open for examination. By way of beginning I focus on two composite sketches of narrow experiences of imagination, personal and professional, both of which reflect ethical conflicts related to fantasy.

Personal fantasy

Conflicts of desire are present in all of my psychotherapy sessions, whether I am the client or the therapist. We all want experiences that are not available to us because of lack of resources, overpowering fear, or inner prohibitions. We internalize codes of conduct that organize our experience and instruct us that certain kinds of experience are forbidden; aberrant; or even written under erasure, impossible to acknowledge as experience. Those unacceptable experiences happen nonetheless, and a cornerstone of psychodynamic theory is that what is unacceptable within will emerge regardless of our will to avoid it. Jung (1969a) suggested that the individuation process emerges from the experience of "conflicts of duty" (p. 15) that force us to bring unconscious contents into consciousness.

The intensity of erotic attraction makes conflicts that involve erotic desire particularly charged. Morgan[5] was in a monogamous relationship for five years when she began to experience powerful fantasies about a neighbor she saw frequently during walks near her home. They talked casually from time to time, and the attraction deepened for her on each occasion. She found her waking thoughts increasingly dominated by these fantasies and began to schedule her walks to coincide with times she had encountered him before.

6 Introduction

Her partner, meanwhile, began to experience her as distracted and distant. She felt guilty—she knew she was increasingly preoccupied—but she had less and less interest in spending time with her current partner and sometimes actively avoided him. Her distress continued to increase. She loved her partner, and she could not understand why she found herself imagining her neighbor in such vivid and engaging ways. She also wondered whether she should continue her current relationship if she was persistently fantasizing about someone else. Did the fantasies mean that she should seek out this neighbor? Were they a sign that she needed to leave her partner? Were they selfish wish-fulfillment?

We can talk about Morgan's suffering on biological, social, psychological, political, and religious registers, and Morgan may have experienced her conflicts on those registers. To the extent that she was conscious of these conflicts, she also might have conceptualized them as conflicts *between* those registers. For instance, she might understand her desire for her neighbor to be a product of biological desire, whereas her desire to remain faithful to her partner reflects social norms and religious doctrine. Are the fantasies a simple fact of biology, a natural expression of reproductive instinct? Were they influenced by an increasingly sexualized media that relies on erotic stimulation to attract viewers? Do they reflect a creeping narcissism that is the product of a consumer culture oriented toward stoking desire, satisfying it, then stoking it again? Do demonic forces lurk beneath them: Was there a Wormwood engaged in a metaphysical war for Morgan's soul? What do they say about the quality of her current relationship? Were they a call to greater development or a retreat from it?

Although there are other ways to talk about them, these kinds of dilemmas reflect ethical concerns. What effects did Morgan's fantasies have on her current relationship? This is the *interpsychic* dimension of imaginal ethics; that is, the implications that one's fantasies might have for the lives of others. Certainly, Morgan's fantasies about another partner might precede a decision to leave her current partner. What effects did Morgan's fantasies have on her own process of individuation? This is the *intrapsychic* dimension of imaginal ethics.[6] A deeper question, which reappears throughout these pages, is whether Morgan had any choice about her fantasies. Does she have them, or do they have her? This is the most important question for an ethical sensibility determined to achieve a fixed, reliable understanding of right and wrong, responsible and irresponsible. As we begin this conversation, however, I propose that we will never satisfactorily answer it. We do and do not control our fantasies; we do and do not choose to enter them; we do and do not create them; we are and are not responsible for them. These are central pairs of opposites for us to hold in tension. Perhaps a better way to frame the question is not whether we should have specific fantasies but how we should have them or how we should host them when they manifest in our awareness. For Morgan, the appearance of these fantasies marked a period of psychic suffering that may have opened the possibility of greater consciousness.

Professional obligations

The literature on psychological ethics is dominated by discussions of the development of romantic and sexual relationships between client and therapist. Most professional codes of conduct for mental health professionals prohibit any kind of personal relationship between therapist and client, for a period of time ranging from five years following termination to the entirety of their lives. Some voices, such as Haule (1996), have argued that the nature of therapeutic healing depends on total authenticity between client and therapist. Therapists, in Haule's understanding, must make themselves completely open to what may develop in the therapeutic relationship, including the possibility of beginning a romantic relationship with the client that would lead to a violation of ethical codes and the loss of the therapist's license. Haule's point is that the nature of any therapeutic relationship is necessarily erotic and private and occurs in a domain influenced by, but necessarily separate from, the public space articulated by ethical codes:

> Therapy is an erotic enterprise demanding a kind of union in which both parties undergo a partial dissolution and interpenetration, much as we experience in romantic love. The work itself is not love but takes place within an interpersonal field created and nourished by love. Eros is the ground and life of the work. (p. 85)

Without diving deeper into Haule's (1996) argument, it is worth suggesting that Haule's fantasy of therapy differs from that of the profession's authorities. In the contemporary theory of psychological boundaries,[7] the development of psychic structures is aided by therapists' consistent intention to resist losing sight of their roles as therapists. The therapist is not a friend, lover, business partner, religious guru, or parent. Children raised in environments where clear roles are not present—where caregivers are inconsistent or neglectful and expect the children to meet the parents' relational, economic, or even sexual needs—develop psychic structures that mirror the chaos and permeability of their external relationships. Writing in the Jungian tradition, Feldman (2004) theorized that the creation of imaginal space and the ability to create symbols depends on the way in which infants are touched by their caregivers. The infant's experience of its own skin creates an internal experience of containment that allows stable psychic structures to develop.

This is the briefest sketch of complicated theoretical positions. We can, however, begin to see the complexity of the choices faced by the therapist who works psychodynamically and with an awareness of transference/countertransference dynamics. Haule's (1996) fantasy of a therapy that involves some level of "dissolution and interpenetration" (p. 85) seems at odds with contemporary understandings of the importance of presenting consistent, empathic attention to the client's difference and maintaining one's sense of separateness.[8] When we turn to the vignette from Schwartz-Salant (1989) in chapter 7, we will see how fraught with ethical nuance and difficult choice the discernment process can become.

We can think about imaginal ethics in therapy in many ways, but I briefly suggest three. The most obvious involves the therapist's experience of the client as a figure in his internal experience; that is, a person that the therapist understands to be the client in some substantial way or a character that appears in the imagination.[9] Another dimension involves the way we fantasize the therapeutic process in which we are engaged. This is not simply the theoretical assumptions or list of steps we expect to follow but the way we internalize the space of therapy.[10]

A third involves the psychoanalytic notion of reverie, which had its origins in the work of Bion (1962) and was vividly articulated by Ogden (2004) as a tool for understanding the client and the therapeutic relationship. Reverie includes "our ruminations, daydreams, fantasies, bodily sensations, fleeting perceptions, images emerging from states of half-sleep (Frayn 1987), tunes (Boyer 1992) and phrases (Flannery 1979) that run through our minds, and so on" (Ogden, 2004, p. 158). Ogden understood the therapist's reveries during sessions to provide a rich trove of symbolic information otherwise unavailable to therapist or client. He framed the analytic experience as marked by the appearance of "the intersubjective analytic third" which "stands in dialectical tension with the analyst and analysand as separate individuals with their own subjectivities" (p. 109). The relationship is structured "in a way that strongly privileges the exploration of the unconscious internal object world of the analysand" (p. 109). Therapists'[11] reveries give them access to the client's unconscious in immediate ways that are easy to overlook or willfully repress.

Various ethical concerns arise in each of these three imaginal domains in therapy. In what follows, we will focus on the therapist's fantasies about the client, which cannot help but shape their interactions, as well as imaginal experiences that therapists have in the clinical moment. Ramona, a 54-year-old therapist, worked with Mason, a 25-year-old man, for eight weeks. Mason sought therapy to treat occasional panic attacks and test anxiety that hampered his ability to complete his undergraduate program. During their brief work together, they focused on identifying triggers for his anxiety and panic and learning methods by which to reduce the perceived anxiety. Ramona also found that she had recurring fantasies that Mason, who lived with his divorced mother, would move into his own apartment. She saw him graduating, training to be an attorney in another city, and starting a successful career there. She opened a line of conversation with him about his experience of living at home and encouraged him to investigate other living arrangements. She also suggested that he would be a good candidate for graduate school and wondered what professional path he might have been considering.

Ramona did not, however, spend time reflecting on why those fantasies might have emerged. The urge to encourage his development in specific ways was strong. These fantasies may have reflected Mason's unconscious wishes; Ramona's encouragement of them may in fact be developmentally useful. They also may reflect Ramona's unconscious biases and what we might classically call countertransference. If Ramona had difficulty separating from her own mother when she was Mason's age, we might wonder whether she was projecting her own regrets onto him. We might also wonder whether culturally constructed notions of masculinity might not have influenced Ramona's experience of Mason. Might a separation of Mason from his mother allow a new dynamic of dependence to manifest with Ramona? Might this change just repeat an old pattern of relationship with women rather than liberate him? Ramona's fantasies did not suggest one or another specific course of action. Instead, they called for attentiveness, an attitude of curiosity, and an awareness of the implications of leaving them unexamined. To move into his own apartment might have helped Mason move beyond an unhealthy relationship with his mother. It also might have burdened him financially, affected his schoolwork, and separated him from an important support network. How therapists host their fantasies is of eminent concern to the ethical practice of psychotherapy.

The road ahead

In the following pages, I explore the imagination with an ethical flashlight, a thin beam in an infinite, inky blackness. My goal is not to map the vast terrain; the sands will not hold our tracks. Instead, my goal is simply to discover what we might see of psyche that would have been invisible otherwise.

Then we will attempt to give some shape to the great abstractions of *ethics* and *imagination*. In chapter 2, I survey the use of the terms *imagination* and *fantasy* in the theoretical writing of C. G. Jung, from the 1916 essay "The Transcendent Function" to his late work *Mysterium Coniunctionis*. I pay particular attention to the formal definition of *fantasy* included in *Psychological Types* (Jung, 1971/1960). We will discover that Jung's use of these and related terms lacked superficial stability across his career. Consistent themes—including the reality of imaginal experience, the imagination as context of all psychic experience, the necessary connection of imaginal experience to the unconscious, and the value of engaging the imagination— emerge across these texts. I also consider the theoretical writings of James Hillman and other post-Jungian theorists.

No manual or comprehensive textbook of Jungian hermeneutic method has yet been published. In chapter 3, we explore how Jung and others within the tradition have discussed hermeneutics. We also consider contemporary hermeneutic theory in philosophy, especially in the work of Paul Ricoeur, and place it into conversation with Jung's thought. We discuss the

10 Introduction

hermeneutic approach of Robert Romanyshn, who articulated a method by which to integrate the unconscious of the researcher and the project into the research itself. Finally, I articulate elements of my hermeneutic approach to this topic.

In chapter 4, I examine contemporary psychological and philosophical theories of ethics. I consider at length key texts by C. G. Jung on good and evil, conscience, and ethics, as well as analytical psychologist Erich Neumann's notion of a *new ethic*. Works in the Jungian psychological tradition by Zoja (2007), Guggenbuhl-Craig (1971), Solomon (2000, 2001), and others also are considered. I review contemporary debate between existential-phenomenological and social constructionist conceptions of ethics, reflected in the work of Brinkmann (2006) and Gergen (2006). I introduce philosopher Emmanuel Levinas' ethical theory and explore how it has been appropriated by humanistic and Jungian psychology in the work of Gantt (2000), Harrington (2002), Cohen (2008), and Brooks (2013).

Armed with a clearer understanding of these terms, in chapter 5 I articulate some approaches to the use of the language of ethics to explore the imagination. I discuss the potential developmental value of the assumption of an ethical attitude toward the intrapsychic figures encountered in active imagination and other introspective processes. I articulate some provisional principles of an ethical approach to the imagination and examine the alchemical motif of the king in his sweat-bath (discussed briefly by Jung in *Mysterium Coniunctionis* (1963/1954)) as a potential model for hosting fantasies that evoke ethical conflicts, proposing some practical guidelines for this process in everyday life.

In chapter 6, I apply these ideas to an exploration of Arthur Schnitzler's novella *Dream Story* (2002), along with Stanley Kubrick's film of the novella *Eyes Wide Shut* (1999), which we will use as a model for the exploration of the ethical dimensions of fantasy in everyday life. In chapter 7, we will explore the dynamic interaction of the law (criminal and professional) with the imagination, via an exploration of the notorious case of the Cannibal Cop and a clinical vignette recounted by Jungian analyst Nathan Schwartz-Salant (1989).

Finally, in chapter 8, I draw together the disparate threads of this discussion and attempt to offer a provisional outlook for future research. I reflect on the constructed nature of this discourse and articulate the ways in which it might be useful in contemporary life. I hope to illumine at least part of the shadow of such a project, as it may well create an ethic and a theory that will need at some point to be overthrown.

Notes

1. Avens (1980) argued that the history of Western philosophy and science "largely consists in an aggressive attempt to convert all things, including the psyche of psychology, into controllable objects for a subject" (p. 15).
2. See especially Kearney (1988) for a comprehensive treatment of this topic, which is reviewed in more detail in chapter 2.

Introduction 11

3. See Keener (2009, p. 187), Turner (2008), and Phillips (2005, pp. 102–103) for representative treatments of this passage in Christian exegesis. It is also worth noting the story of the second-century Christian theologian Origen, who castrated himself at the age of 18 to escape intense erotic desire and fantasies, only to find that the fantasies continued.
4. See Ellenberger (1970).
5. Morgan is a composite character who reflects common dynamics among those who suffer ethical conflict around fantasy. No aspect of her story is drawn from a specific person or persons.
6. A further dimension of intrapsychic ethics concerns the effect of one's conduct in fantasy on intrapsychic others, which we explore in more detail later in this work.
7. See Gabbard and Lester (1995) for the classic articulation of the concept of therapeutic boundaries.
8. Although Haule (1996) did not refer directly to alchemy, one can hear that mythology—so important to the development of Jung's thought—embedded in his fantasy of therapy. Haule did not invoke the range of alchemical processes Jung appropriated as an analogue of his psychology. Among the wide range of formulations Jung found in the alchemical literature (seemingly one for each author), he suggested a general pattern: "If the separated condition is assumed at the start, as sometimes happens, then a union of opposites is performed under the likeness of a union of male and female (called the *coniugium, matrimonium, coniunctio, coitus*), followed by the death of the product of the union (*mortificatio, calcinatio, putrefactio*) and a corresponding *nigredo*. From this the washing (ablution, *baptisma*) either leads direct to the whitening (*albedo*), or else the soul (*anima*) released at the "death" is reunited with the dead body and brings about its resurrection" (Jung, 1968/1953, para. 334). Haule's position makes me uneasy; it feels like an overcorrection to fantasies of a sterile therapeutic environment. Haule's vision of therapeutic *coniunctio* needs the mortification and blackening suggested by the full alchemical process.
9. We might use the term *avatar*, were it not for the complex contemporary usage of the word. It commonly describes a character created by an individual in online and offline fantasy gaming. The film *Avatar* (Landau, Cameron, & Cameron, 2009) depicts a future in which technology allows soldiers to take on entirely new bodies on an alien planet while remaining in their original bodies in a state of suspended animation. The parallels to active imagination and dream experience are notable, as is *Avatar*'s status as the all-time highest grossing film as of October 2018 (All time, n.d.).
10. One could, and the discipline usually does, use other concepts—the myth of therapy, the theory of care. By using the word "fantasy" I intend to include the unconscious personal dynamics of the therapist as he or she creates the therapeutic space. We all have fantasies of the experience that cannot be contained by theory and which imply a specificity that does not appear in the profession's guiding myths.
11. A quick note about the use of the terms *analyst* and *therapist* in this work. *Therapist* or *psychotherapist* refers to a class of mental health professionals with training and licensure to practice psychotherapy. This group may include professional counselors, social workers, marriage and family therapists, psychologists, and psychiatrists. *Analyst* or *psychoanalyst* refers to a specific subset of mental health professionals with advanced training and accreditation in psychoanalysis. I do not intend to use the terms interchangeably, but it is worth noting that the work of nonanalyst therapists (such as myself) is frequently influenced by psychoanalytic theory. *Analysand* is used here only when a specific author invokes it.

References

All time box office. (n.d.). In *Box office mojo*. Retrieved March 23, 2014, from http://boxofficemojo.com/alltime/world/

Avens, R. (1980). *Imagination is reality: Western nirvana in Jung, Hillman, Barfield, and Cassirer*. Dallas, TX: Spring.

Bion, W. (1962). *Learning from experience*. New York, NY: Basic Books.

Brinkmann, S. (2006). Questioning constructivism: Toward an ethics of finitude. *Journal of Humanistic Psychology, 46*(1), 92–111. doi: 10.1177/0022167805281231

Brooks, R. (2013). The ethical dimensions of life and analytic work through a Levinasian lens. *International Journal of Jungian Studies, 5*(1), 81–99.

Cohen, B. (2008). The trace of the face of God. *Jung Journal: Culture and Psyche, 2*(2), 30–45. Retrieved from http://dx.doi.org/10.1525/jung.2008.2.2.30

Coleridge, S. (1984). *Biographia literaria, or, biographical sketches of my literary life and opinions*. New York, NY: Leavitt, Lord, & Company. Retrieved from http://www.gutenberg.org/files/6081/6081-h/6081-h.htm#link2HCH0013 (original work published 1814)

Ellenberger, H. (1970). *The discovery of the unconscious: The history and evolution of dynamic psychiatry*. New York, NY: Basic Books.

Ethic. (2014). OED online. Oxford University Press. Retrieved from http://www.oed.com.ezproxy.humanisticpsychology.org:2048/view/Entry/64755?redirectedFrom=ethics

Feldman, B. (2004). A skin for the imaginal. *Journal of Analytical Psychology, 49*(3), 285–293.

Gabbard, G., & Lester, E. (1995). *Boundaries and boundary violations in psychoanalysis*. New York, NY: Basic Books.

Gantt, E. (2000). Levinas, psychotherapy, and the ethics of suffering. *Journal of Humanistic Psychology, 40*(3), 9–28. doi: 10.1177/0022167800403002

Gergen, K. (2006). Social construction as an ethics of infinitude: Reply to Brinkmann. *Journal of Humanistic Psychology, 46*(2), 119–125. doi: 10.1177/0022167805284446

Guggenbuhl-Craig, A. (1971). *Power in the helping professions*. Dallas, TX: Spring.

Harrington, D. (2002). A Levinasian psychology? Perhaps. In E. Gantt & R. Williams (Eds.), *Psychology for the other: Levinas, ethics, and the practice of psychology* (pp. 209–221). Pittsburgh, PA: Duquesne University Press.

Haule, J. (1996). *The love cure: Therapy erotic and sexual*. Woodstock, CT: Spring.

Jung, C. (1963). *Mysterium coniunctionis: An inquiry into the separation and synthesis of psychic opposites in alchemy: Collected works, Vol. 14*. Princeton, NJ: Princeton University Press. (Original work published 1954)

Jung, C. (1968). *Psychology and alchemy: Collected works, Vol. 12*. Princeton, NJ: Princeton University Press. (Original work published 1953)

Jung, C. (1969a). Foreword. In E. Neumann, *Depth psychology and a new ethic* (pp. 11–18). Boston, MA: Shambhala.

Jung, C. (1969b). Foreword to Suzuki's "Introduction to Zen Buddhism." *Psychology and religion: West and east: Collected works, Vol. 11* (pp. 538–556). Princeton, NJ: Princeton University Press. (Original work published 1939)

Jung, C. (1971). *Psychological types: Collected works, Vol. 6*. Princeton, NJ: Princeton University Press. (Original work published 1960)

Kearney, R. (1988). *The wake of imagination*. New York, NY: Routledge.

Keener, C. (2009). *The gospel of Matthew: A socio-rhetorical commentary.* Grand Rapids, MI: Wm. B Eerdmans.

Kubrick, S. [producer and director]. (1999). *Eyes wide shut.* London, UK: Warner Bros.

Murdoch, I. (1986). Ethics and the imagination. *The Irish Theological Quarterly,* *52*(1/2), 81–95.

Metzger, B., & Murphy, R. (Eds.). (1991). *New Oxford annotated bible.* Oxford, UK: Oxford University Press.

Ogden, T. (2004). *Reverie and interpretation: Sensing something human.* Lanham, MD: Rowman and Littlefield.

Phillips, J. (2005). *Exploring the gospel of Matthew: An expository commentary.* Grand Rapids, MI: Kregel.

Scheer, R. (1976, November). Playboy interview: Jimmy Carter. A candid conversation with the democratic candidate for the presidency. *Playboy,* 63–86.

Schnitzler, A. (2002). *Night games and other stories and novellas.* Chicago, IL: Ivan R. Dee.

Schwartz-Salant, N. (1989). *The borderline personality: Vision and healing.* Asheville, NC: Chiron.

Solomon, H. (2000). The ethical self. In E. Christopher & H. Solomon (Eds.), *Jungian thought in the modern world* (pp. 191–214). New York, NY: Free Association Books.

Solomon, H. (2001). Origins of the ethical attitude. *Journal of Analytical Psychology,* *46*(3), 443–454.

Top 10 unfortunate political one-liners. (2013). *Time* (online ed.). Retrieved from http://content.time.com/time/specials/packages/article/0,28804,1859513_1859526_ 1859518,00.html

Turner, D. (2008). *Matthew: Baker exegetical commentary on the New Testament.* Ada, MI: Baker.

Zoja, L. (2007). *Ethics and analysis: Philosophical perspectives and their application in therapy.* College Station, TX: Texas A&M Press.

Chapter 2

Imagining the imagination

Early in my work with clients, I often mention that I use the term *fantasy* in a different sense than they might expect. The word connotes something insubstantial, ephemeral, unreal, indulgent, perhaps sexual, a playground for desire. I tell clients that I intend it to mean any experience in the imagination. We imagine lives that we want to live and experiences we want to have. It is a rehearsal space where we enact future encounters with others, experience memories, and work through our conflicts. It is also the location of real experience or a domain in which we authentically live our lives. I had not reflected much on that small moment when I first found myself doing it; mostly, I wanted to make sure that my clients did not immediately think that all I wanted to know about was their sex lives, thus confirming their worst fears about therapy. Over time, I have realized that it serves as a way to open clients (and our work) to their imaginal lives. It may be the first time that clients have spatialized and legitimized their imaginal experiences. Occasionally, I have wondered to what degree that small clarification is both a therapeutic intervention and the imposition of a fiction. Does it create an imaginal space that previously did not exist as a discrete domain of experience? The act of defining fantasy also can create a new possibility for the imagination or a new way to understand oneself. It can raise a host of questions: Are some imaginal experiences valid and others invalid? How does imaginal experience differ from experience in the realm of "actual fact" (Jung, 1969a/1939, para. 889)? Are there ways of acting in the imagination that we should evaluate in ethical terms? Is imagination an open field in which desire can authentically run without the inhibiting constraints of law and moral custom? Should limits be placed on how therapists engage imagination and fantasy in their work? If so, how? What is a limit in the imagination? If we could constrain the imagination, what might become possible? What might be inhibited?

Before any of these questions, we must wonder: What is the imagination?

For William Blake, imagination is all: "The imagination is not a state: it is the human existence itself" (Blake, 1907, p. 63). But in considering the scope of Western philosophical thought on the imagination, Iris Murdoch (1986) suggested that "we must ask at intervals whether we really need the concept" (p. 94), and Edward Casey (2000) has written that, "Imagination is a word which has come to promise more than it can possibly deliver" (p. 1). *Imagination* has been imagined philosophically and psychologically in scores of ways. Within the tradition of analytical psychology—even within Jung's own corpus—definitions have varied widely, and it is sometimes difficult to understand to what each theorist refers when invoking imagination and fantasy.

I do not mean to dodge the issue, but this may be just the nature of imagination as a category of human experience—resisting a final position, always shifting and presenting a new face. So in this brief exploration of the imagination, we will first of all hold the idea itself lightly, and the terrain we cover will necessarily be limited. The continental philosopher Richard Kearney's work on the history and potential future of the Western idea of the imagination will provide us a contextual ground. Then, we will turn to the tradition of analytical psychology, with primary focus on C. G. Jung, James Hillman, and Henri Corbin. This is well-explored terrain, but worth reconnoitering before we reflect about the imagination in ethical terms.

Western visions of the imagination

Written in 1988, Richard Kearney's rich survey of the history of Western theological and philosophical treatments of the imagination, *The Wake of Imagination,* found the contemporary concept of the imagination deep in crisis—the "wake" of the book's title referred at least in part to the memorial celebration following a death. "We no longer know who exactly produces or controls the images which condition our consciousness," he wrote (p. 3), echoing Baudrillard's concerns. And he framed a tension between a modernist faith in the "authenticity" of the image and the postmodern critique of the possibility of that authenticity.

Kearney provides a useful set of the chief understandings of the concept of imagination:

1. The ability to evoke absent objects which exist elsewhere, without confusing these absent objects with things present here and now.
2. The construction and/or use of material forms and figures such as paintings, statues, photographs, etc. to represent real things in some "unreal" way.
3. The fictional projection of non-existent things as in dreams or literary narratives.
4. The capacity of human consciousness to become fascinated by illusions, confusing what is real with what is unreal. (p. 16)

It is worth noting in a preliminary way that none of these four understandings adequately conveys the terrain explored by depth psychology. The psychological understanding of imagination articulated by Jung (1963/1954,

1966/1929, 1968/1953, 1969a/1939, 1971/1960, 1976/1935, 1977/1943) and Hillman (1975, 1977, 1978, 1979a, 1979b, 1985) and the theological/phenomenological realm articulated by Corbin (1972, 1989) understood imagination primarily as experiential and as real—or, in Corbin's case, more real—than everyday experience. Kearney's (1988) description in items 3 and 4 of experiences that are "fictional" and populated by "illusions" that are "confusing" (p. 16) suggests a suspicious streak within his own understanding of the imaginal. But one can also read this as a philosopher's caution. Throughout his text, Kearney maintained an abiding commitment to the power of the idea of the imagination, and in spite of the powerful and conflictual critical voices within mainstream intellectual traditions whom he summarizes and engages with, he begins the last page of his work on a note of pragmatic hope: "After imagination, is there still not imagination?" (p. 397). However we may critique the concept, we have to accept that the basic human experience it attempts to describe continues. As Samuel Beckett had it, in the opening to his prose poem "Imagination Dead Imagine" (1974), "No trace anywhere of life, you say, pah, no difficulty there, imagination not dead yet, yes, dead, good, imagination dead imagine" (p. 63).

To frame his survey, Kearney categorized three major modes of Western philosophical and theological theorizing of the imagination: the premodern, "mimetic paradigm," which includes a vast range of sources including Greek philosophy and Jewish and Christian theology, the modern, "productive paradigm," which includes transcendental and existentialist philosophical takes on imagination, and the postmodern, "parodic paradigm," which covers continental thought through the end of the 20th century (Kearney, 1988, p. 17).

Kearney's review of the premodern period began with Hebraic models. The Jewish tradition understood imagination to be imitative of the divine creative power and, as such, a source of temptation that should be resisted. The protopsychological notion of mental images first appeared in Platonic models, and it was elaborated and shifted from a metaphysical to a psychological plane in Aristotle.

For the Greeks, the imagination remained primarily imitative of natural phenomena or the creativity of the highest good rather than a productive faculty in its own right. Plato understood imagination as mimesis. We hold a mirror to nature when we imagine and create a form quite inferior to nature itself or to the archetype of nature (a Form or Idea for Plato). What we create is thus three times removed from ultimate reality, an increasingly degraded copy of a copy.[1]

Christian models through the medieval period are similarly suspicious of the temptation that imagination offers to usurp divine power (Kearney, 1988, pp. 130–131). Augustine is an influential example. The fifth-century theologian differentiated between two kinds of imaginative activity: *phantasia* and *phantasma*. *Phantasia* refers to the product of the interaction of the individual with his or her experience, or what we would usually refer to as memory. *Phantasma,* on the other hand, are imaginative creations that are disconnected from experience; they are natural occurrences as we encounter the narratives of others—we imagine what the Other describes to us—but they do not relate to any personal, sensory experience. For Augustine, though, both *phantasia and phantasma* can occlude our vision of the divine. If our eyes are on our images, they cannot be on the truth of the soul. As Djuth (2007) summarizes, Augustine understood our *phantasia* images to be morally neutral, but he also held us responsible for the way we use our memories (p. 83). But *phantasma* are inherently problematic; they are nothing but mere opinion. Augustine understood heretics to be lost in their own images:

> Instead of grounding their beliefs on empirical reality and the memory images derived from it, they speculate or conjure up in their own minds images that have no bearing whatsoever on reality. They then attribute these images to divine entities, such as God and soul, as if they were real. (pp. 83–84)

Augustine's suspicion of the imagination can be heard clearly here. Disconnected from an immediate experience, *phantasma* are the products of speculation or conjuring of the human in isolation both from community and from the divine. To Christianity, imagination has almost always been illusion, fueled by the fallible sensorium (the body), confusing, and dangerous.

Kearney's survey of the premodern West paints a bleak picture of our cultural inheritance, one that brightens only briefly when he turns his eye to modernity. The modern period involves a relocation of the creative power of imagination within the individual human psyche. No longer a mirror reflecting divine light, the imagination "becomes a lamp which projects its own internally generated light onto things" (Kearney, 1988, p. 155). The German idealism of Kant and the neo-Kantians placed imagination as the synthetic power between the sensory realm and the understanding, a "dynamic, creative act" and "transcendental unity" (p. 156) rather than a simple conduit. Following the idealists, Coleridge (1814) envisioned both a mimetic imagination ("fantasy" or "secondary imagination") and a productive imagination along the lines of idealist thought ("imagination"; p. 182): "The primary imagination I hold to be the living power and prime agent of all human perception and as a repetition in the finite mind of the eternal act of creation in the infinite I AM" (Coleridge, 1814, chapter 13, section 2, para. 14). Kearney notes that, by this, Coleridge argued that "we mustn't forget that our creation is the repetition, reactivation, or refiguration of some creative power that both precedes and exceeds us" (Kearney and Kuipers, 2012). To the romantics, creativity and imagining were codetermined; as Casey (2000/1976) summarized it, "to imagine authentically is to be creative; to be

18 Imagining the imagination

genuinely creative is to imagine" (p. 186). The broad transformative power the romantics envisioned for the imagination eventually met, in Kearney's analysis, with the painful truth of history. Imagination could not transform reality and so retreated, in the late-romantic poet William Wordsworth's vision, "to the 'watchtower' of [the] solitary spirit" of the poet (Kearney, 1988, p. 185). This burst of exuberance about the powers of the imagination prefigured Jung's project, and indeed has never really left our cultural horizon, though it has retreated into disreputable corners of the academy and into popular culture.

Existentialist framings of imagination continued this diminution by understanding the creative imagination to be a trap, a "predicament" (Kearney, 1988, p. 196), and the rich interiority of the transcendentalists to be rather, in Kierkegaard's phrase, an "empty contentless I" (Kierkegaard, 1996/1840, p. 128). It is worth noting the full sentence from which this oft-quoted phrase emerges:

> And that does not mean that this empty, contentless *I* steals, as it were, out of this finitude to become volatized and evaporated on its heavenly emigration, but rather that the divine inhabits the finite and finds its way to it (p. 128, original emphasis)

Kierkegaard is here reckoning with the relationship between the metaphysical and the historical, and how the human is positioned between and across them. Kierkegaard's contentless self remains a feeling, acting human; three sentences before, he wrote: "The meaning of the historical is not that it is to be annulled, but that the individual is to be free within it and also happy in it" (p. 127). What matters for our discussion is Kierkegaard's belief that the human is not him- or herself the generator of content.

For Sartre, imagination is unreal and memory refers to the real; imagination is at the same time profoundly negating of the real world and the necessary condition of consciousness—indeed, it is "the whole of consciousness as it realizes its freedom" (Sartre, 2004/1940, p. 270). Because we imagine, we are no longer a "mere thing engulfed in the world" (Kearney, 1988, p. 236) but a separate consciousness that can imagine the real. In an act that is always a fiction, the imagination allows us to make meaning of a meaningless existence: "The imaginary thus represents at each moment the implicit meaning of the real" (Sartre, 2004/1940, p. 272). Brann (1993) offered a pithy summary: for Sartre, freedom is the "ability to posit reality as a whole, and oneself as free from it" (p. 137). Alienation from the real is the definition of human experience. We are insofar as we are not real.

The postmodern imagination snuffs out the humanist vision of imagination altogether, leaving only an inverted mimesis. The image is not the reflection of a divine creator transmitted through a human vessel, nor is it the product of an act of creative invention by an individual subject. In the postmodern imagination, the image transcends the human and imposes itself on subjectivity. It has no author but comes from without and has more reality than the human who receives it. The human is made by the image or by innumerable images that have no external reference points and that reflect each other endlessly. There is no separation between imagination and reality; as suggested by Kearney (1998) in an analysis of Derrida, "We can no longer legitimately ask the question: what is imagination?" (p. 290) because the essence of imagination can nowhere be found or circumscribed. It is everywhere and nowhere at once; no "productive consciousness" (p. 253) originates the images. I think we still have to ask, nonetheless—as does Kearney on the final page of his work. Imagination as a core mode of psychic process may remain mysterious, as does intuition, but it is real nonetheless.

Our reflections to this point make too-quick work of complicated, geographically, linguistically, and culturally constrained networks of thought about the imagination. It helps, however, to orient us as we briefly articulate the analytical psychological understandings of imagination, which are certainly grounded in premodern and modern assumptions and prefigure, and participate in, postmodern discourse about imagination and the human in intriguing ways. As I have noted, what is missing in Kearney's (1988) topography of imagination is a grappling with imagination as *experience*. The tradition of analytical psychology understands at least some aspects of imagination to be a specific psychological event. This event happens in, to, or through the individual in an imaginal geography and across a psychological register that by nature includes the physical body. *Experience* is a trope that merits brief attention; for now, it is worth pointing to Taves (2009), who suggested that the term could be understood at least three ways:

> (1) Specific experiences of something ("I experienced something" or "I had an experience in which" or "the experience was special"); (2) experience as a cumulative abstraction ("my experience suggests" or "in my experience"); and (3) types of experience, some more abstract and some more concrete ("religious experience" or "human experience" or "life experience" or "outdoor experience" or "work experience"). (p. 57)

In the most general terms, I follow Taves' (2009) lead in leaning on the first understanding of experience as well as her further suggestion that it is a rough synonym for consciousness. Experience in this sense is necessarily transitive or an experience *of* something. Even as the imagination may be more process than content, it is never contentless. The issue, suggested by Kierkegaard and underlined by Kripal, is whether we can say anything about the origin of that content with any certainty.

Jung, imagination, and fantasy

Jung's vision of the imagination sits across the complexities of Kearney's premodern, modern, and postmodern imaginations. To Baudrillard's many

20 Imagining the imagination

yearning to be heard, Jungian psychology adds the archetypal chorus and an insistence on an experiential engagement with the Otherness of those many. We often carp about Jung's lack of consistency in articulating his theories; across his *Collected Works,* Jung used a rich and confusing array of terms to refer to the imagination, both as concept and as experience. Chodorow (1997) noted that, just in relation to the narrow category of active imagination, Jung used the terms *picture method, transcendent function, visioning, active fantasy, active phantasying,* and *introspection,* among others. He used the word *fantasy* in positive and pejorative ways, depending on the context, making it sometimes difficult to understand to what experience Jung intended to refer with this term. Jung's complex understanding of the role of imagination in the psychic economy includes value judgments about the ways one might be present in the imaginal space. I use this term, *imaginal space,* as a larger category to include the varying terms used by Jung and post-Jungian writers in this domain. It refers to the space in discourse occupied by these terms as well as a mode of experience. Inevitably, the term also connotes a discrete location of experience. A discussion of the ways this language suggests the visual—and its related traps—appear later in the chapter.

To orient oneself to Jung's ideas requires hermeneutical spadework. In this section, we will examine Jungian and post-Jungian uses of the terms *fantasy, image,* and *imagination.* After a brief survey of key appearances of these terms across his published works, we will focus particular attention on his references to fantasy in *Psychological Types* (1971/1960), which includes an extensive formal definition of the term. We will also consider the writing of James Hillman and others who worked in the tradition of archetypal psychology, which places strong emphasis on Jung's notion that all psychic life is fundamentally imaginal. Is imagination a space in which we act? Or the irreducible bedrock of psychic experience? How we conceptualize the imagination has significant implications for our understanding of ethics.

Fantasy and imagination across Jung's works

In his seminal essay "The Transcendent Function," originally written in 1916 and revised in 1958, Jung suggested that "spontaneous fantasies ... usually have a more composed and coherent character [than dreams] and often contain much that is obviously significant" (Jung, 1969b/1958, para. 155). "Spontaneous fantasies," in this passage, are not further defined. They are implicitly contrasted with dreams, which Jung described as "inferior expressions of unconscious contents" because "the energy-tension in sleep is usually very low" (para. 153). This makes them "easier to understand reductively" than constructively (para. 153). This essay does not provide a more nuanced understanding of what he meant by "fantasies" or what might constitute a fantasy that is not spontaneous. What we understand is that they have a special potential to give us access to the unconscious. Across the texts to come, Jung understood nonsleeping engagement in the imaginal space to enable something more than mere understanding.

In "The Relations between the Ego and the Unconscious," Jung cautioned his readers that "the important thing is not to interpret and understand the fantasies, but primarily to experience them" (Jung, 1977/1943, para. 342), which suggests that to witness and to participate are both options. This is a key element of Jung's understanding of active imagination. Transformation comes from direct engagement with the unconscious rather than from an intellectual puzzling-over the details of the experience. A fantasy in this sense is not like watching a movie; one must enter the frame and affect the action.

Jung (1977/1943) elaborated on the mechanics of this process: "Libido can never be apprehended except in a definite form; that is to say, it is identical with fantasy-images. And we can only release it from the grip of the unconscious by bringing up the corresponding fantasy-images" (para. 345). Later, however, he was careful to qualify this connection of libido and image: "We must on no account mistake the semblance, the fantasy-image as such, for the operative process underlying it. The semblance is not the thing itself, but only its expression" (para. 353). Taken together, these passages suggest a dynamic that, by its nature, we may not be able to precisely articulate. Libido, an "accumulation of value" (para. 344) in the unconscious, is somehow both tied up in images and also distinct from them. Our implicit goal is to loosen that connection, an act that is involuntary and tinged with violence. Libido is gripped by the unconscious and must be released: "The patient's conscious world has become cold, empty, and grey; but his unconscious is activated, powerful, and rich" (para. 345). We might infer that the violence in the system reflects a lack of engagement. From Jung's perspective, a failure to acknowledge and explore the unconscious side of the personality means that the unconscious must seize that attention.

Throughout his works, Jung argued forcefully that our imaginal experiences are just as real as non-imaginal experiences—which does not make them equivalent. He wrote elsewhere that "every psychic process is an image and an imagining" (Jung, 1969a/1939, para. 889), so the distinction between imaginal and nonimaginal experiences is at best a convenient and provisional one: all experience is imaginal in some fashion. In this consideration of Jung's thought, though, I use *imaginal experience* to refer to experiences one locates in an interior space or a "psychic reality" separate from the world to which Jung referred later in the same paragraph as "actual fact" (para. 889).[2]

These distinctions are useful to consider in light of Jung's next statement in "The Relations between the Ego and the Unconscious" (1977/1943). After making a similar distinction between the realities of the unconscious, which appear to us in dreams and fantasies, and the reality of conscious experience, the realm of "actual fact," he wrote, "Both 'realities' are psychic experience, psychic semblances painted on an inscrutably dark back-cloth. To the critical intelligence, nothing is left of absolute reality" (Jung, 1969b/1958, para. 354). (We might hear in this an echo of Sartre.) Our experience is inescapably psychic; we cannot see except through the psyche and cannot comment definitively on what may lie beyond it. He continued,

> Of the essence of things, of absolute being, we know nothing. But we experience various effects: from "outside" by way of the senses, from "inside" by way of fantasy. We would never think of asserting that the colour "green" had an independent existence; similarly we ought never to imagine that a fantasy-experience exists in and for itself, and is therefore to be taken quite literally. It is an expression, an appearance standing for something unknown but real. (para. 355)

Underlying our experience is "absolute being" (Jung, 1977/1943, para. 355), which is inaccessible as such. Jung's Kantian heritage is apparent here; Jung wanted to provide ways other than reason to access the foundation of existence, and his argument is that the fact of our experiencing the world assures us at least that we rest on a foundation or that something saves us from solipsism. What is most important in this passage is the equivalent significance of fantasy in providing this assurance. We observe an aspect of the world and describe it as *green*, which tells us that something external to us has prompted that subjective experience; that the aspect is green tells us nothing fundamental about what we have perceived. Similarly, our fantasies tell us nothing about what has generated them, other than that they have been generated from beyond our subjective experience.

If imaginal experience is just as real as experience in the sensory realm,[3] does imaginal experience have equal value? Could I choose to spend my life primarily or nearly exclusively engaged in imaginal experience without consequence? As a practical matter, we cannot. If I want to sit in a room and actively imagine all the time, I still need nourishment, hydration, exercise, and shelter, all of which require some engagement with the world. Jung was aware of the implications of his ontological argument regarding the imagination. Again in this essay, Jung (1977/1943) wrote that "on no account" was he suggesting "the life of a psychic anchorite" (para. 369). Instead, "fantasies are no substitute for living; they are fruits of the spirit which fall to him who pays his tribute to life" (para. 369). This picture is rendered more complex by observations Jung made nearly 30 years later, in *Mysterium Coniunctionis*: "Since projections involve one in an inadmissible way in externalities, Dorn rightly recommends an almost ascetic attitude to the world, so that the soul may be freed from its involvement in the world of the body" (Jung, 1963/1954, para. 710). The Christian anchorite who found his cave populated by leering demons had direct access to the unconscious; the contemporary city dweller must constantly discern how much of the person he sees before him is actual fact and how much is his own unconscious material. It seems reasonable to wonder whether Jung's age played a role in this shift in tone; the robust public intellectual of 1928 had become less accessible and more introverted by 1954. Perhaps each attitude is appropriate to a different stage of life.

Alongside questions of the reality and value of imaginal experiences, Jung also commented on the question of truth. In what sense can we understand imaginal experience to be true? In a note from his "Commentary on 'The Secret of the Golden Flower'" (Jung, 1967/1938), Jung suggested a distinction between genuineness of imaginal experience and the veracity of its content: "Such [mystical] experiences are genuine, but their genuineness does not prove that all the conclusions or convictions forming their content are necessarily sound. Even in cases of lunacy one comes across perfectly valid psychic experiences" (Jung, 1967/1938, para. 42, n. 20). Just because a god tells one in a vision to slay one's son does not mean that one should. We always retain authority and responsibility for the actions we take, both inside and outside the imaginal space. Another way to understand Jung's articulation of genuineness in imaginal experience is to hear an implicit distinction between experiences that are authentically objective and those that reflect the ego's desires. Autoerotic fantasy would be an obvious example (what do we judge more selfish than a masturbation fantasy?) but even here, the case is not so clear-cut. A sexual experience in the imaginal space that takes into account the reality of the psychic figures encountered there, that allows them their own existence, might represent a more complex or genuine experience. Indeed, the attitude one takes toward imaginal experience seems fundamental to assessments of genuineness and validity.

The question of what is right imagination and what is wrong, what is genuine and false, appears in different terms throughout these texts. Jung moved between passionate defenses of imagination and probing interrogations of its phenomenology. In "The Aims of Psychotherapy" (Jung, 1966/1929), he wrote,

> What we are pleased to call illusion may be for the psyche an extremely important life-factor, something as indispensable as oxygen for the body—a psychic actuality of overwhelming significance. Presumably the psyche does not trouble itself about our categories of reality; for it, everything that works is real. (para. 111)

A few pages earlier, however, he argued, "There are unprofitable, futile, morbid, and unsatisfying fantasies whose sterile nature is immediately recognized by every person endowed by common sense" (Jung 1966/1929, para. 98). Jung's criteria are practical: Does it work? Does it reflect common sense (a phrase that discloses the relativity and locality of Jung's position)? They also remain conceptually elusive. We must make our own decisions about the utility and truth of fantasy; we always must retain a strong ego position in the imaginal space.

Later, in his 1935 Tavistock Lectures (Jung 1976/1935), Jung's language again shifted. In the following passage, Jung assigns pejorative meaning to the term *fantasy*:

> I really prefer the term "imagination" to "fantasy," because there is a difference between the two which the old doctors had in mind when they said that "opus nostrum," our work, ought to be done "per *veram imaginationem et non phantastica*"—by true imagination and not by a fantastical one. In other words, if you take the correct meaning of this definition, fantasy is mere nonsense, a phantasm, a fleeting impression; but imagination is active, purposeful creation. And this is exactly the distinction I make too. (para. 396)

His foundation for this shift is worth investigating. In a note, Jung referred to a passage from *Psychology and Alchemy,* in which he ascribed this distinction between *veram* and *phantastica* to the anonymous author of the *Rosarium Philosophorum* (Jung, 1976/1935, para. 360). The "old doctors" also might refer to the church doctors, especially Bonaventure (and we shouldn't forget Augustine's *phantasma*). Working in the Middle Ages, Bonaventure proposed *imaginatio phantastica* to refer to, in Kearney's (1998) words, "a pervertor of rational judgement and participant in the descent of the mind down the image chain towards evil" (p. 126). For Bonaventure, the imagination performs a mirroring function that can lead to divine truth or to grievous error. Christ is a perfect mirror image of God, who is at once one with God. All other images are imperfect, but they mirror divinity in their ways and can lead to understanding. Bonaventure's thought maps in superficial ways onto the Shi'ite Sufism of Henri Corbin, who understood the *mundus imaginalis* to occupy an intermediate position between the sensory world and the intellect (Corbin, 1972). This echoes Aristotle's position as well (Kearney, 1988, p. 127).

Bonaventure ultimately viewed the imagination as a field of temptation that must be engaged with extreme caution. The prohibitions in the first and second commandments against the creation of idols refer to the mistaken understanding of images as having their own existence or as not ultimately mirroring the divine. Kearney (1988) noted that, in Bonaventure's thought, "The possibility of a divinational role for imagination becomes instead a stern admonition against its diabolic potential" (p. 128). Bonaventure's writings became yet another cudgel with which later Christian thinkers could beat the imagination.

The connection between the author of the *Rosarium* and Bonaventure is not clear. Bonaventure's use of the term, however, helps to illuminate the medieval context of this idea. Jung was wary of the qualitative differences in imaginal experience. Fantasy, for Bonaventure, is doctrinally problematic because it loses its sense of itself as inextricably connected to an underlining divine foundation. Jung also understood fantasy to be ungrounded, although Bonaventure's doctrinal commitments were too confining for him. If true imagination is "active, purposeful creation" (Jung, 1976/1935, para. 396), it echoes Bonaventure's connection of true imagination to divine creativity. It also makes him more human, as suggested by Jung (1966/1929): "The creative activity of imagination frees man from his bondage to the 'nothing but' and raises him to the status of one who plays. As Schiller says, man is completely human only when he is at play" (para. 98). Indeed, although Bonaventure likely would not approve, humans behave most like a true image of the Judeo-Christian God when they are creative, or, indeed, like the Hindu god Brahma or any of innumerable creator gods across traditions.

A formal definition of fantasy

The qualitative judgments *veram* and *phantastica* do not relate to Jung's use of *imagination* or *fantasy* per se. As illustrated by this brief treatment, Jung's conceptual language lacked stability. Indeed, attempts to pin down Jung from a conceptual standpoint are a futile effort; his concepts follow his passion, which he revised throughout his lifetime. The Jung that in 1921 asked, "What great thing ever came into existence that was not first fantasy?" (Jung, 1971/1960, para. 86) in 1935 held that (as mentioned above) "fantasy is mere nonsense, a phantasm, a fleeting impression" (Jung, 1976/1935, para. 396). So this task is intended first as a way to illuminate the complexity of Jung's thought on the matter rather than from a misplaced desire to discover a consistent system. Those who follow him seemingly must coin new terms or make constant disclaimers when using his terms in new ways.

Jung provided a rare formal definition of fantasy in *Psychological Types* (1971/1960). It is worth spending time with that entry and related passages in that volume, although it is important to note that the subcategories he introduced (fantasm vs. imaginative activity, passive vs. active fantasy) do not appear in the rest of "Psychological Types" and must be inferred based on context.

Jung's overarching division between fantasm and imaginative activity (Jung, 1971/1960, para. 711) framed his definition of fantasy. The vast majority of the passage, however, is spent elaborating the concept of *fantasm*, with a paragraph reserved at the end to discuss imaginative activity. Imaginative activity, however, contains fantasm within it: "Imagination is the reproductive or creative activity of the mind in general" (para. 722). It is "identical with the flow of psychic energy" and "the direct expression of psychic life, of psychic energy," whereas fantasy-as-fantasm "is a definite sum of libido that cannot appear in consciousness in any other way than in the form of an image" (para. 722). Fantasy, in this moment of Jung's thought, carried the

26 Imagining the imagination

meaning of the entire field of imagination as well as the specific manifestation or the singular imaginal experience.

Because what we encounter is not the theoretical container but the lived experience, Jung (1971/1960) spent much more time elaborating this idea of the fantasm: "I mean a complex of ideas that is distinguished from other such complexes by the fact that it has no objective referent" (para. 711). He dealt early in the definition with a crucial question: To what degree is a fantasy something that we consciously create? Do I choose to have the fantasies that appear to me or are they the product of unconscious forces? Fantasms may have as much claim upon us as psychological reality or as the alleged actual may exert. Jung stated that it is possible to create a fantasm but that it is only a combination of conscious elements and it can only occur "in so far as psychic energy can be voluntarily directed" (para. 711). Voluntary fantasies have little appeal for Jung; they are "artificial experiment[s] of purely theoretical interest" (para. 711) and seemingly rare. The bulk of our fantasy experiences occur in relationship to the unconscious: "In actual everyday psychological experience, fantasy is either set in motion by an intuitive attitude of expectation, or it is an irruption of *unconscious* contents into consciousness" (para. 711, emphasis in original). In his discussion of medieval Christian attempts to understand the problem of type, Jung underscored this relationship: "Though it undoubtedly includes conscious elements, it is none the less an especial characteristic of fantasy that it is essentially involuntary and, by reason of its strangeness, directly opposed to the conscious contents" (para. 79).

This leaves a picture in the reader's mind that fantasy is something very different from the playground of desire that we typically imagine. Fantasy wells up within us unbidden; we cannot control it but can only resist it or accede willingly. Jung (1971/1960) also referred to fantasy, in a later passage, as "the freest activity of the mind," albeit one that "can never roam into the infinite" (para. 512) because it is tied to the archetypal unconscious (here come those new voices yearning to be heard). The rejection of fantasy, then, is fundamentally a rejection of the unconscious and a refusal to grow and develop. What is unconscious in the individual may be expressed in fantasy. Jung described this in typological terms, as fantasy is an expression "of repressed extraversion in the introvert, and of repressed introversion in the extravert" (para. 93).

Jung (1971/1960) made another important distinction between active and passive fantasy (in the sense of fantasm):

> *Active* fantasies are the product of *intuition* (q.v.), i.e., they are evoked by an *attitude* (q.v.) directed to the perception of unconscious contents, as a result of which the *libido* (q.v.) immediately invests all the elements emerging from the unconscious and, by association with parallel material, brings them into clear focus in visual form. *Passive* fantasies

appear in visual form at the outset, neither preceded nor accompanied by intuitive expectation, the attitude of the subject being wholly passive. (para. 712, emphasis in original)

Passive fantasies irrupt into consciousness because the contents have become charged with the same level of energy as the contents of consciousness. Passive fantasies are often experienced as disruptive or disturbing; by their unconscious nature, they compensate or run counter to the conscious perspective, so their appearance is unexpected and unwanted. Active fantasies, however, are marked by a quality of relationship or an attitude of receptivity on the part of the conscious perspective. We cannot choose to have specific fantasies, Jung seems to have argued, but we can choose for fantasies to emerge by virtue of our willingness to receive them. Our experiences of passive and active fantasies demand different responses. Jung (1971/1960) argued that passive fantasies require criticism because they are by their nature one-sided. Active fantasies, however, demand understanding (para. 714).

Because the bulk of the material that informed Jung's (1971/1960) reflections on psychological type emerged between 1913 and 1917 (p. v), his discussion of how we might achieve understanding of our fantasies (and he considered dreams to be passive fantasies) took place in the context of his relationship with Freud and the psychoanalytic establishment. Jung made an initial distinction between manifest and latent meaning, which mirrors a Freudian understanding of dream interpretation. Manifest meaning relates to the literal, surface experience of the fantasy (the characters, location, colors, sounds, movement, etc.). A Freudian understanding of latent meaning involves relating the elements of the dream to hidden, instinctual causes of the fantasy material. Jung damned this reading with the faint praise that it "suffices for people of a certain temperament, so that no demand for a deeper understanding is made" (para. 716). Jung read dreams and fantasies as reflecting both causative and purposive valences: "Anything psychic is Janus-faced—it looks both backwards and forwards" (para. 718). The elements of a fantasy tell us both about their origins and about where the psyche is headed; each is both symptom and symbol. When we understand fantasy symptomatically, we look for causes and hope for relief from suffering. When we understand it symbolically, we open imaginative horizons and a range of possibilities for future growth.

These do not exhaust the interpretive ways to approach fantasies. In the epilogue, Jung (1971/1960) wrote, "I believe that other equally 'true' explanations of the psychic process can still be put forward, just as many in fact as there are types" (para. 855). Jung's emphasis on the need to reflect on the content of our fantasies, however, underscores the dialogic nature of the experience of fantasy. We always are communicating with the unconscious when we attend to fantasy, whether or not we choose to interpret. The use of the metaphor of dialogue in discussing this relation with the conceptual unconscious suggests a fantasy of relationship, in which the ego communicates with a personified unconscious. This is vividly explicit in Jung's writings, as attested to by the hundreds of pages of dialogues contained in *The Red Book* (2009). It is worth noting that when we imagine ourselves not simply to be interpreting a text but to be engaged with an Other, we might find ourselves exploring questions of the nature of our obligation to that Other. The need for an ethics of relationship with the unconscious begins to arise.

In *Psychological Types,* Jung (1971/1960) used one more overlapping category of fantasy that was not included in the formal definition at the end of the book. In a reflection on Faust, Jung argued for the existence of a traditional opposition of thinking and feeling that needs to be "united in a third and higher principle" (para. 85). This goal is achieved via what Jung termed *creative fantasy.* Elsewhere, Jung (1971/1960) elaborated on this notion:

> Besides the will, which is entirely dependent on its content, man has a further auxiliary in the unconscious, that maternal womb of creative fantasy, which is able at any time to fashion symbols in the natural process of elementary psychic activity, symbols that can serve to determine the mediating will. (para. 182)

Here, creative fantasy seems to refer to the symbol-making function of the psyche. This seems distinct from active or passive fantasy, which relate to the perception or reception of imaginal experience.[4]

Synthesizing Jung's insights

What are we to make of these distinctions? At minimum, Jung's use of the term *fantasy* to refer to all of these seemingly distinct experiences and concepts is confusing. His abandonment of it by the time of the Tavistock Lectures (Jung 1976/1935) 14 years later furthers that confusion. Consciously or unconsciously, Jung's shifting signifiers may reflect a reluctance to reify the imagination. When we talk about imaginal experience, inevitably we speak in metaphors that give shape and form to an experience that is immaterial. The natural traps of language make imagination an orientation in time, a geography, and an interior related in complex ways to an exterior. It is easy to imagine imagination as something that takes place in our minds or bodies, without extension into the realm of "actual fact" (Jung, 1969a/1939, para. 889). The critiques of post-Jungians such as James Hillman (1977, 1978, 1979a) have pointed out these assumptions. When we struggle to reconcile the inconsistencies in Jung's conceptual language, we might understand them as an implicit acknowledgment that the imaginal sands are always shifting or that imagination is something other than intellect or feeling, as he suggested, and that any intellectual discourse about it may well fail to meet it on its own terms. Ultimately, we imagine the imagination; we fantasize fantasy. Indeed, as suggested by Jung's reflections on the introverted types, we imagine the objective world, some of us to a larger degree than others.

As a way to orient oneself in this shapeless expanse, we can sketch some principles present in this text that seem consistent with Jung's larger project. The most important of these is that imaginal experience is as real as any other experience one might have. As suggested by his category of imaginative activity, it is the context of all experience. All experience is at root creative. Another principle is that imaginal experience almost always involves the unconscious. In imaginal experience, the unconscious reveals itself in a process that is fundamentally dialogic, whether in a plain statement of counterposition to the ego or in a mutually created conversation with personified others. A third principle is that imaginal experience becomes increasingly valuable the more we engage it.

Jung (1971/1960) understood imaginal experience to be raw and unrefined; its worth depends entirely on the way we orient ourselves to it and the time we spend with it: "In order to unearth the treasures they contain they must be developed a stage further. But this development is not achieved by a simple analysis of the fantasy material; a synthesis is also needed by means of a constructive method" (para. 93). In a later passage, Jung proposed two new terms for the methods available to work with imaginal experience: the reductive and the synthetic. These seem to parallel his distinctions between causal and purposive introduced earlier, although *synthetic* captures not just the goal of the method but something of its execution. Jung stated, "The former traces everything back to primitive instincts, the latter develops the material into a process for differentiating the personality" (para. 427). When the act of developing imaginal material is done properly, "the libido that was formerly sunk in the unconscious emerges in the form of some positive achievement" (para. 427). Jung did not discuss technique in detail in this text. Done right, we engage in "fantasy activity which is creative and receptive at once" (para. 171). In several places, he referred to this process as play.[5]

It is perhaps worth noting that other writers have looked to play to describe the process of the uncovering and creation of meaning. As we will explore in the next chapter, the philosopher Paul Ricoeur (1981) borrowed Hans-Georg Gadamer's usage of play to describe the essential hermeneutic operation. When we engage a text, as when we engage personal imaginal experience, our very being is open to change. To Ricoeur, both the author and the reader are engaged in existential play. Ricoeur understood the text to be a series of "imaginative variations" on the subjectivity of the author. In his encounter with the text, then, the reader too must undergo an "imaginative variation of his ego" (p. 189). The text opens new, possible ways of being for the reader; we engage with the text in ways that place our subjectivity itself

30 Imagining the imagination

in creative play. It is hard not to hear echoes of Jung's attitude in Ricoeur's thought, though Ricoeur was reluctant to embrace Jung. Jung (1977/1943) understood his work with fantasy to be in a hermeneutic mode, as suggested by the following passage:

> Whence has fantasy acquired its bad reputation? Above all from the circumstance that it cannot be taken literally. Concretely understood, it is worthless. If it is understood semiotically, as Freud understands it, it is interesting from the scientific point of view; but if it is understood hermeneutically, as an authentic symbol, it acts as a signpost, providing the clues we need in order to carry on our lives in harmony with ourselves. (para. 491)

What does it mean to play with our fantasies? Ricoeur (1981) commented, "The child who disguises himself as another expresses his profoundest truth" (p. 187). So do we when we become active participants in fantasy. The many other truths that have yet to be expressed through us gain voice and live in active fantasy; the implicate becomes evident and the possible becomes conscious.

Hillman's revisioning of Jung's imagination

How we imagine imagination was a critical concern of James Hillman and the archetypal school of psychology. Questions of relative rightness or wrongness of imagining seem less important to Hillman; such questions completely misunderstand the nature of imagination. We do not imagine wrongly; we understand imagining to be something that it is not and located in a network of false dualisms. First among them is interior vs. exterior. Instead, imagination is the *a priori* of human psychological life. It *is* human psychological life. Hillman (1975, 1977, 1978, 1979a, 1979b) did not represent a radical revision of Jung but a distillation and a reframing of key elements of Jung's thought. In the following section, I explore the definitions of imagination that emerge from key texts, including three of Hillman's essays published in *Spring* in the 1970s ("An Inquiry into Image" (1977), "Further Notes on Image" (1978), and "Image-Sense" (1979a)), *The Dream and the Underworld* (1979b), *Re-Visioning Psychology* (1975), and others. Core concerns for Hillman included differentiation between symbol and image, how one experiences meaning in the imagination, the confusion of the imaginal with the visual, and the relationship of the image and the archetypal.

It is a decidedly different experience to read Hillman than it is to read Jung. Hillman's tone is critical, sharp-edged, at times playful, iconoclastic. His project of establishing a new school of psychological thought is thrilling and occasionally off-putting in its self-conscious ambition. One is always aware that archetypal psychology is first and foremost Hillmanian psychology, which is more Jungian than perhaps Hillman realized; it is a particular reading of Jung, but Hillman's dazzling intellect tends to obscure the full extent of the debt he owes to Jung, even as he repeatedly invoked him.

In these texts, at least, Hillman did not provide one succinct definition of imagination. He preferred to circumambulate ideas, to tell us what they are not:

> We have considered [imagination] one function among others; whereas it may be essentially different from thinking, willing, believing, etc. Rather than an independent operation or place, it is more likely an operation that works within the others and a piece which is found only through the others—(is it their ground?). So, we can never seem to catch imagination operating on its own and we never can circumscribe its place because it works through, behind, within, upon, below our faculties. An overtone and undersense: is imagination prepositional? (Hillman, 1979a, p. 175)

Later, he invoked Edward Casey's notion that "An image is not what you see but the way you see" and added, "Imagination might here be defined more closely as the subtle sensing of the prepositional relations among events" (p. 176). These are not the most imaginally evocative of definitions. Hillman wanted his readers to understand that imagination is the matrix of all experience and that it is both our experiential geography and orients us within that geography. He frequently invoked Jung's dictum: "Every psychic process is an image and an 'imagining', otherwise no consciousness could exist and the occurrence would lack phenomenality" (Jung, 1969a/1939, para 889). This position is not unique to Jung or Hillman, who agreed with Plotinus' notion that "the soul perceives only this second sense and cannot perceive what you call 'sense data'" (Hillman, 1979a, p. 179). The "second sense" is the image through which we experience sense data or the image that emerges as a result of sensory stimulation.

At the same time, however, Hillman (1979a) understood that this distinction suggests spatial relations he did not intend. All writing about the imagination involves the imagination itself, and we naturally tend to imagine that the imagination is a distinct location within us. He groused that "our habitual minds cannot stick with an imagination within the senses, but must phosphorize it into an epiphanic marvel" (p. 178). What bedevils discourse about the imagination is our need to see in binaries: outer/inner, archetypal/personal, objective/subjective (Hillman, 1977, p. 81). The image exists prior to these and other abstractive distinctions: "Only when we leave the actual image do the two ways divide into sensation and intuition, aesthetics and meanings" (Hillman, 1979a, p. 176).

Hillman wanted to keep imagination from becoming another domain entirely, one which can be devalued and dismissed. Writing in the archetypal

32 Imagining the imagination

psychological tradition, Avens (1980) suggested that this is indeed what has occurred throughout the history of Western philosophy, with the prominent exception of Kant, who was a key influence on Jung. Kearney (1988) echoed this, noting that in the Platonic tradition, imagination has legitimacy only when it acknowledges its imitative nature and subordinate position to reason. The Western theological tradition is likewise deeply suspicious of the sin of imagination; as Kearney incisively noted, "The biblical understanding of imagination is ... indelibly marked by the ethical context of its genesis— the rebellion of Adam and Eve" (p. 40). Standing on the shoulders of such Western romantic writers as Goethe and Coleridge, Jung championed the imagination. Hillman understood Jung to have catalyzed a Copernican revolution that "resuscitated" the images destroyed by the Church councils of Nicea and Constantinople, which "reduced the soul to the rational spirit" (Avens, 1980, p. 32).

Although Hillman was in many ways more conceptually consistent than Jung, his writing reacted against the reifying habits of contemporary readers. In a sense, the entire project of conceptual discourse about the imagination runs counter to Hillman's core values. He seemed to want his discourse to evoke experience rather than understanding, but his at times ostentatious display of his command of the philosophical waterfront only serves to keep the reader's imagination firmly tied to rational expectation. He spoke within a Western philosophical and theological tradition that is thoroughly rational. So in Hillman, the reader experiences a natural tension between icon worship and iconoclasm. He framed evocative definitions that engage the intellectual tradition on its own terms.[6]

I have not encountered a clear differentiation between imagination and fantasy in Hillman, though a closer reading may reveal one. We might use the following passage from *Archetypal Psychology: A Brief Account* (Hillman, 1985) as a succinct treatment of fantasy:

> For archetypal psychology, "fantasy" and "reality" change places and values. First, they are no longer opposed. Second, fantasy is never merely mentally subjective but is always being enacted and embodied. ... Third, whatever is physically or literally "real" is always also a fantasy image. Thus, the world of so-called hard factual reality is always also the display of a specifically shaped fantasy, as if to say, along with Wallace Stevens, the American philosopher-poet of imagination on whom archetypal psychology often draws, there is always "a poem at the heart of things." (Hillman, 1985, p. 23)

The terms may be interchangeable, or they may subtly suggest the conceptual frame (imagination) and specific instance (fantasy). Hillman's way of talking about fantasy certainly echoed his descriptions of imagination and imaging elsewhere: "We perceive images with the imagination, or, better said, we imagine them rather than perceive them, and we cannot perceive with sense perception the depths that are not extended in the sense world" (Hillman, 1979b, p. 55). In this passage, we might notice the way Hillman retained the distinction between sense world and the imagination: we perceive differently with the senses than with the imagination, and the imagination does not perceive but imagines. To imagine is fundamentally a creative act, but we make a fundamental mistake if we imagine that we are willfully creating. The imagination is always imagining beyond our conscious control. Invoking Jung, Hillman (1979b) suggested that images are "the self-perception of instinct" (p. 55).

In keeping with his desire to collapse our expectations of image and imagination, Hillman (1978) directly addressed the ways we equate imagination with the visual. He pointed out our tendency to understand imagination to be a series of pictures, wondering whether "the confusion of images with pictures [is] a residue of sensationist psychology that understands images and even imagination to be left-overs of actual things seen" (p. 158). This makes clinical work difficult because clients believe "they have to see pictures in their minds in order to have an image" (p. 158). Hillman was addressing what he understood to be a central critique of his thought; namely, that it is "mainly visual, hence optically and intellectually distant, hence gutless" (p. 159). Indeed, I found myself feeling uneasy about his thought for this reason, which is an experience I address below. What Hillman also intended, however, was to correct a misimpression of the imagination as two-dimensional. When we imagine, we do so with our entire bodies: "Images hold us; we can be in the grip of an image" (p. 159). He invoked the concept of the subtle body, which has connections to mystical traditions across the globe, to suggest an experience broader than the visual:

> Let's leave it right there: images as instincts, perceived instinctually; the image, a subtle animal; the imagination, a great beast, a subtle body, with ourselves inseparably lodged in its belly; imagination, an animal mundi and an anima mundi, both diaphanous and passionate, unerring in its patterns and in all ways necessary, the necessary angel that makes brute necessity angelic; imagination, a moving heaven of theriomorphic Gods in bestial constellations, stirring without external stimulation within our animal sense as it images its life in our world. (Hillman, 1979a, p. 184)

Our subtle body is our animal body, Hillman (1979a) stated, or "a logos of animals" (p. 184). The use of this notion connects Hillman to a metaphysical shadow, which he again denied: "To speak about 'subtle bodies' and 'second sight' does not mean to posit such things, as things. Metaphorical insight does not require a para-world of its own, over, under, and beyond" (p. 178). This move is representative of the conceptual binds in which Hillman found

34 Imagining the imagination

himself again and again. He wrote much of his text under erasure,[7] because writing by its nature posits: it emerges from the nothingness of the page and stands against it.

Characteristically, this critique of imagination as exclusively visual is complicated by his exploration of the ways in which the image resembles a picture. Hillman (1978) was drawn to the way that a picture is self-contained. "Like a picture, an image too has borders. It sticks to itself, inheres within itself. It doesn't lead somewhere else, as does a story. Thus the mind's activity can find nowhere to go but more deeply into the image" (p. 160). One might object that a picture can indeed tell a story or at least implies a past and a future. Hillman would argue that the implied past and future are imposed by the observation of the subject and that the image itself is contextless. This is itself a challenge to our usual ways of using language; Hillman wrote that "the essential muteness of an image is essential for altering our habitual mind's way of experiencing in language, that is, in stories made up of sentences, strung out in time, based on words, letters, literal" (p. 161). This passage is not explicitly reflexive, but it is perhaps useful in understanding Hillman's attitude toward his own discourse. Is it hermetically sealed, self-contained, and functioning in ways to which we are unaccustomed?

Hillman's interest in ridding us of our tendency to impose narrative reflects his larger case for understanding image as preceding, or as more fundamental than, symbol. This is framed initially as being counter to Jung, but it is more accurate to understand Hillman as taking issue with a particular Jungian analytic orthodoxy. Hillman made his case in the three *Spring* essays on image (1977, 1978, 1979a). To Hillman, the symbol is an abstraction from an image or a container of meaning that relates to other containers of meaning (i.e., other symbols) but does not relate to the original image. Symbolization, he wrote, is "a spontaneous psychological act [that] refers to a curious bunching of significance into compressed form, whether the form be a sensuous image, a concrete object, or an abstract formula" (Hillman, 1977, p. 64). The symbol "condenses a set of conventions that tend toward universality" (p. 64). Whether we apprehend a phenomenon as an image or as a symbol depends on the questions we ask of what appears:

> If we focus on the whenever and the wherever of an image, its generality and conventionality, we are looking at it symbolically. If, on the other hand, we examine the how of a symbol, its particularity and peculiarness, then we are looking at it imagistically. (p. 64)

What Hillman wanted us to do is to avoid lapsing into semiotic formulas: the ocean is the unconscious, an infant is the divine child, and so on. We face a great temptation to abstract and generalize when we encounter images; we want them to fit into neat categories. Hillman, however, draws us again and again to the phenomenon itself. He advised that we keep the symbol

Imagining the imagination   35

dictionary on the shelf and let the experience make its own sense. Meaning is inherent in, or coterminous with, the image.

This line of discourse is dizzyingly intellectual. Hillman wanted us to experience ourselves differently, and his method, at least in these texts, was to play conceptually at high speed and with great technical skill. What seems less clear, however, is to what extent Hillman understood his theorizing to be itself imaginal. Ultimately, this is a fantasy of fantasy that risks much by remaining in the abstract conceptual register. He did battle with the imagined forces of rationality and of psychological materialism, at least superficially, on the enemy's home court. What I miss in Hillman's corpus is a *Red Book* (Jung, 2009) or a *Memories, Dreams, Reflections* (Jung, 2011). Hillman (1979a) referred extensively to the florid vibrancy of imagination, for example: "To recover imagination we must first restore the preposterous sea-monsters and every winged fowl and everything that creepeth" (p. 184). His fantasy, however, was curiously bloodless. Perhaps he was confessional elsewhere. The notable absence of Hillman's humanity from these texts (does he have any skin in the game?) heightens rather than minimizes the subjectivity of his approach. We are trapped in his airy fantasy. On some level, Hillman was likely aware of his emotional remoteness. He protested, "An image does not have to have its emotion literalized. ... There do not have to be big affects or explicit emotional words to make one feel the mood in an image or its emotional weight" (Hillman, 1977, p. 79). Giegerich's (1993) classic critique of Hillman's project—"The birth of the Gods, piety, soul and consciousness, culture itself did not merely arise from the spirit of killing but from actual killings" (p. 8)—rings true for me.

Jung's blood is missing from this brief discussion, but we will discuss it briefly in chapter 5, via a passage from *The Red Book* (2009), which Sonu Shamdasani (2009) referred to as "nothing less than the central book in his oeuvre" (p. 95) and, along with Jung's unpublished *Black Books,* "a private opus that ran parallel to and alongside his public scholarly opus" (p. 91). An encounter with Jung's own vivid imaginal experience will no doubt enrich our understanding of his theoretical conclusions.

Corbin, Bachelard, and Casey

Henri Corbin and the metaphysical Imagination

Before I conclude, I want to make a few brief comments on the scholarship of three figures who influenced and were influenced by Jung and analytical psychology. French Islamicist Henri Corbin, a scholar primarily of Shi'ite Sufism and Ibn 'Arabi, was a contemporary of Jung and the two knew and influenced each other. Along with Jung, Corbin's work was cited by James Hillman as the two core influences on his archetypal psychology. Corbin and Jung used several common terms, including *archetype, active*

36 Imagining the imagination

imagination, and variants of *synchronicity*, albeit in different manners and with different goals.

Rather than offer a new gloss on the traditional concept of imagination, we could say that Corbin articulated a wholly new concept: the Imagination. Our common understanding is only a faint echo of the new frontier Corbin proposed for our exploration. For Corbin, there was nothing new about the Imagination. It has always been present but increasingly obscured in our age by the rational, materialist forces that reduce imagination to a sequence of biochemical processes.

The Imagination is a geography, an organic process, the mechanism that creates symbols, and the location of those acts of creation. Imagination is a realm unto itself. Although Corbin's Islam bears the imprint of the Aristotelian philosophical tradition that entered Islam via such thinkers as Averroes,[8] the Imagination is not simply the middle term between sense and the intellect nor between raw experience and abstract thought. In Corbin's (1969) reading of Ibn 'Arabi, the Imagination is an "intermediate world":

> Between the universe that can be apprehended by pure intellectual perception (the universe of the Cherubic Intelligences) and the universe perceptible to the senses, there is an intermediate world, the world of Idea-Images, of archetypal figures, of subtle substances, of "immaterial matter." This world is as real and objective, as consistent and subsistent as the intelligible and sensible worlds; it is an intermediate universe "where the spiritual takes body and the body becomes spiritual," a world consisting of real matter and real extension, though by comparison to sensible, corruptible matter these are subtle and immaterial. (p. 4)

The first stirring of Imagination is the imagination, which is an insubstantial murmur that errs by failing to maintain connection with the fundamental reality of the phenomenon that engaged it. The Imagination is a domain of existence that coincides with the material world and extends beyond it:

> It is the Imagination that enables us to understand the meaning of death, in the esoteric as well as the physical sense: an awakening, before which you are like someone who merely dreams that he wakes up. It would be difficult to situate the science of the Imagination any higher. (Corbin, 1969, p. 219)

The Imagination is, in Corbin's imagining, more real than the material world. We all have access to it through our dreams, which participate in it fully and which offer the model for understanding Imaginal experience. Imagination reverses what Corbin (1969) called "common knowledge," which

Imagining the imagination   37

involves "a penetration of the sense impressions of the outside world into the interior of the soul" (p. 80). When we Imagine, we "[project] the inner soul upon the outside world" (p. 80). The domain and the action of Imagination is always metaphysical, which presents considerable difficulty for any psychology that appropriates Corbin's model of the Imagination, as does Hillman's. Indeed, Corbin was skeptical about the ways that his thought was used in other intellectual contexts. In a comment that did not directly refer to Hillman but seems intended for him, Corbin warned,

> If this term [the imaginal] is used to apply to anything other than the mundus imaginalis and the imaginal Forms as they are located in the schema of the worlds which necessitate them and legitimize them, there is a great danger that the term will be degraded and its meaning be lost. (1989, p. 105)

Imagination in Corbin's sense, however, is inseparable from a mystical hermeneutics that shares much in common with the psychological hermeneutics of Jung and the analytical psychology tradition.

Ta'wil *and the Imagination*

In *Alone with the Alone* (1969), Corbin briefly retold Ibn 'Arabi's life story and recounted an episode in which Ibn 'Arabi is transfixed by the beauty of the daughter of a shaikh with whom he stayed in Mecca. The 14-year-old girl became, for Ibn 'Arabi, "what Beatrice was to be for Dante; she was and remained for him the earthly manifestation, the theophanic figure, of *Sophia aeterna*" (p. 52, emphasis in original). Corbin's implicit position was that Ibn 'Arabi did not pursue sexual relations with the girl but gave equal weight to her "extraordinary physical beauty" and "great spiritual wisdom" (p. 52) as the crucial factors that constellated Ibn 'Arabi's devotion to her. Matter matters. This theophanic moment, when the divine becomes visible in the sensory, when we see *through,* depends on both the divine and the sensory:

> The problem is similar to that raised by the person of Khidr the prophet, both individual person and, by virtue of his investiture with a theophanic function whose organ is the active Imagination, an archetype. If we fail to grasp this twofold dimension simultaneously, we lose the reality both of the person and of the symbol. (p. 100)

Elsewhere, Corbin (1969) referred to this dual-natured figure as a "person-archetype" (p. 65). The active Imagination invests the sensory, the individual person, with a symbolic significance. The imaginal organ accomplishes this and also is its location. The active Imagination is also a theophanic Imagination because it is the mechanism that makes divinity visible. Further,

38 Imagining the imagination

because the symbolic dimension of the material must be encountered on symbolic terms, it is also the location of the operation of hermeneutics. The experience of the active Imagination must be interpreted, and it is to Corbin's mystical hermeneutics, to his understanding of *ta 'wil*, that we now turn.

Corbin's interpretation of Ibn 'Arabi's mystical vision reflected Corbin's understanding that the singular mystical revelation in Ibn 'Arabi's Sophia is a single case of a comprehensive—though not comprehensively perceptible—theophany. It is a moment when Ibn 'Arabi saw through, and she was the vessel that allowed him to perceive the Imagination. All of creation, however, is a theophany, and we can perceive it via the Imagination. Our task is to interpret our experience—to see it accurately. Corbin (1969) wrote,

> The *ta'wil* is essential symbolic understanding, the transmutation of everything visible into symbols, the intuition of an essence or person in an Image which partakes neither of universal logic nor of sense perception, and which is the only means of signifying what is to be signified. (p. 13)

Corbin's references to "universal logic" and "sense perception" in this passage refers to his fundamental distinction between intellect and sense. The Imagination is between these and is a third dimension of the visible phenomena that appears to each of us. Corbin's suggestion that what is revealed could be a person as well as an essence implies the independent existence of beings in the plane of the Imagination. This existential specificity is amplified by his closing insistence that something specific is meant to be signified and can only be signified in the signifier we encounter. When we see through, we are intended to see another world that is at the same time this world. This idea is not exclusive to Ibn 'Arabi but is fundamental to Shi'ite Islam and is context for Ibn 'Arabi's thought: "The conviction that to everything that is apparent, literal, external, exoteric (*zāhir*) there corresponds something hidden, spiritual, internal, esoteric (*bāṭin*) is the scriptural principle which is at the very foundation of Shi ism as a religious phenomenon" (p. 78).[9]

The loss of the capacity to see imaginally is a "metaphysical tragedy" (Corbin, 1969, pp. 13–14) that results in the collapse of the symbolic realm. Corbin's attribution of metaphysicality to this realm should be unremarkable, as he was exploring the work of a great religious thinker. Given the conversation in which Corbin was clearly engaged with Jung's thought, and especially given the ways in which post-Jungians have appropriated Corbin's ideas within their metapsychologies, it is important to underline Corbin's understanding of the Imagination as a metaphysical field and *ta'wil* as a metaphysical hermeneutics. What exists between intellect and sense is the world of the angels: "[The *ta'wil*] presupposes the angelic world intermediate between the pure Cherubic intelligences and the universe of sensory, historical, and juridical facts" (p. 14). *Ta'wil*, he explained, is "etymologically the 'carrying back' of a thing to its principle, of a symbol to what it symbolizes" (p. 12). That principle is not psychological, nor a causative historical event, but necessarily a transhistorical reality or a metaphysical existent; that is, an Angel:

> This two-dimensional structure of a being seems to depend on the notion of an eternal hexeity (*'ayn thabita*) which is the archetype of each individual being in the sensible world, his latent individuation in the world of Mystery, which Ibn 'Arabi also termed the Spirit, that is, the "Angel," of that being. (p. 210)

All of us are at once human, angelic, sensory, and imaginal. *Ta'wil* is the act of carrying back the sensory to the imaginal. It is important to note that this reflects an implicit metaphysical hierarchy. As noted in an earlier passage, the imaginal is "incorruptible," and the beauty of the beloved is "higher than that which was his" (i.e., that which was strictly sensory; Corbin, 1969, p. 156). This is important because it suggests that the imaginal is more real than the sensory but dependent on the sensory for its existence. Indeed, Corbin (1969) argued that the imaginal dimension of existence to which *ta'wil* returns us is the "true reality" (p. 208). He stated it clearly: "In *ta'wil* one must carry sensible forms back to imaginative forms and then rise to still higher meanings; to proceed in the opposite direction ... is to destroy the virtualities of the imagination" (p. 240).

One of the fundamental metaphysical distinctions made by Corbin (1969) is that between the *creatio ex nihilo* of scholastic theologians (both Islamic and Christian) and the understanding he found in Ibn 'Arabi of creation as an unending revelation of the divine. This is critical to understand, because it means that all of our acts of *ta'wil*, or our entire engagement with Imagination, are one and the same as the creative act of the divinity and reflect the relationship between the divine and creation. Corbin wrote,

> These ideas are strictly related: When you create, it is not you who create, and that is why your creation is true. It is true because each creature has a twofold dimension: the Creator-creature typifies the *coincidentia oppositorum*. From the first this *coincidentia* is present to Creation, because Creation is not *ex nihilo* but a theophany. As such, it is Imagination. The Creative Imagination is theophanic Imagination, and the Creator is one with the imagining Creature because each Creative Imagination is a theophany, a recurrence of the Creation. Psychology is indistinguishable from cosmology; the theophanic Imagination joins them into a psycho-cosmology. (p. 215)

How one could divorce Corbin's theology from his understanding of Imagination is difficult to fathom. Each of us is an appearance of the divine, and each of our creations is one with the creative potency of the divine.

40 Imagining the imagination

Moreover, all of existence is a creative act. The distinctions we make between dreams, visions, and reality are provisional and ultimately collapse when we understand the true symbolic nature of reality and engage in the esoteric hermeneutics of *ta'wil*: "Once it is recognized that everything man sees during his earthly life is of the same order ... as visions in a dream, then all things seen in this world, so elevated to the rank of Active Imaginations, call for a hermeneutics" (Corbin, 1969, p. 242). Indeed, Corbin could not have been clearer about the inextricability of the psychological and the metaphysical: "Our schematization of the imaginative faculty results exclusively from the metaphysical status of the Imagination" (p. 219).

Bachelard and Casey

Before we return to Jung and the tradition of analytical psychology, I want to touch briefly on two more important figures writing outside, but in conversation with, the tradition. The French philosopher Gaston Bachelard (1998) argued that our inherent tendency is to reify images. They are not things but experiences we express; Gaudin (1970) described Bachelard's position as follows: "Images are not primarily visual, auditive, or tactile: they are spoken" (p. xlii). To Bachelard (1998), imagination precedes all experience: "We might go one step further and put the image not only before thought, before narrative, but also before any emotion. ... It is the imagination itself which thinks and which suffers" (p. 14). He was inherently suspicious of psychology's tendency to abstract, to take discrete experiences and then generalize away their uniqueness: "Between concept and image there is no possibility of synthesis. Nor indeed of filiation" (p. 5). Against unnamed psychologists who see imagination as a secondary phenomenon to perception—wherein what we imagine must be constructed of remembered perception and has nothing in it that did not previously appear to us in some material way[10]— Bachelard argued that we should "dream well" rather than "see well" (p. 13). He understood the creative potential of the imagination to emerge from the unconscious.[11] Perhaps like Hillman, Bachelard was suspicious of the ways we co-opt the unreality of the unconscious for conscious purposes: "The notion of symbol is too intellectual" (p. 14).

By valorizing imagination and placing it prior to experience itself, Bachelard (1998) squarely located himself in the romantic tradition; he included the Blake quotation that opens this chapter to justify his assertion that "more than any other power, [the imagination] determines the human psyche" (p. 19). Images are not the central unit of description in the field of imagination, because that would imply that they are discrete phenomena: "If an occasional image does not give rise to a swarm of aberrant images, to an explosion of images, there is no imagination" (p. 19). The function of imagination is not to form images but to deform them or to free the perceiver from the images perceived. Imagination involves a decisive movement away from what presents itself; imagination releases us from the literal and from our own past or our memory. He argued that we engage imagination when we exercise our "desires of otherness, for double meaning, for metaphor" (p. 21). We move into another possible realm, make "a leap toward a new life" (p. 21) using the imagination.

Like Bachelard, the phenomenologist Edward S. Casey wanted to understand imagination separately from perception and other faculties of human experience. His work *Imagining: A Phenomenological Study* (1976) attempted to ground what he saw as overly abstract and airy philosophical reflection on imagination using a rigorous phenomenological experience of imagining. He understood *imagination* to be problematic as a category of philosophical reflection or psychological theorizing, in many of the ways we have discussed; he wrote,

> Imagination as a fixed faculty is indeed dead, eviscerated in the "objective" accounts of many modern thinkers. But imagining is very much alive, its potency as an act manifesting itself in daily feats of fancy as well as in the productions of poets. (p. 3)

Casey's (2000/1976) project attempted to navigate between the wild valorization of imagination that appears in the romantic lineage and the intensely negating critiques of it by such figures as Sartre. Casey acknowledged the likely impossibility of adequately defining imagining, let alone of trying to articulate the extent of its power in determining human psychology. He suggested two basic elements of imagining that seemingly all descriptions of it might accept: it is something easily accessed and almost always happens successfully. He pointed to the inherently problematic nature of describing the experience of imagining, as it occurs outside of the domain of observation; our experiences of images are fleeting, and when we reimagine, or call our images back into awareness, Casey noted that "it is difficult to say whether we are continuing to imagine exactly the *same* object again and again" (p. 7, emphasis in original). Casey intended to articulate imagination from the inside out, so that it could be distinguished from other "mental acts" (p. 9) such as thinking and feeling.

Casey's (2000) conclusion was that imagination functions autonomously and is distinct from (but not subordinate or superordinate to) thinking, feeling, or other "mental acts" (p. 188). He did, however, make the interesting suggestion that imagination's autonomy is from "the robust world of praxis—from the 'life-world' in Husserl's telling term" (p. 189).[12] He took up Jung's understanding of imagination directly in a late section, and he understood it to align well with Husserlian phenomenological method; that is, the endless possibility of images that appear to represent archetypal depth reflect a psychic structure inaccessible as such. He also wondered whether Jung's technique of active imagination "corresponds to everyday imagining

42 Imagining the imagination

as it is depicted in this book" (p. 215), and he wrestled with what it means for imagination to be psychically real when it does not participate in praxis. What Casey meant is that the activity of imagination does not have concrete reality: the figures of our imagination do not have material existence. Aside from extraordinary anecdotes,[13] this seems to make eminent common sense. For Casey, imagination is an activity that can effect psychic change but that cannot by itself effect change in the world; that change must occur as the result of other mental and then physical acts.

Imaginatio veram et phantastica in Jung and Hillman

This brief tour of the theorized imagination does not leave us with answers to the questions that launched this discussion. What is imagination? What is fantasy? Along the way, we have collected other terms: *imaginal space, imaginal experience, image, veram,* and *phantastica.* Each is multivocal, with meaning dependent on context. To impose a new conceptual vocabulary to clarify the situation would inevitably confuse matters, even before the new terms begin to accrue alternate meanings. Our abstractions are images themselves. So we understand that our discourse about the imagination is constructed in this particular cultural moment and through the psyche of this particular researcher, as we reflect on the ways it might be deployed to apply to contemporary life.

Imagination precedes and makes possible all experience. As Jungian analyst Ronald Schenk (1992) argued, "Experience and imagination are inseparable. The world is eternally being made and remade through the imagination, and the totality of imaginative power is what we call 'culture'" (p. 122). Neuroscience is beginning to affirm this. David Eagleman (personal communication, September 13, 2012) related that, as Jung suggested, we are dreaming all of the time, but we cannot perceive it when we are conscious. Llinas and Pare (1996) suggested that our waking experience "may be described as a dreamlike state modulated by sensory input" (p. 4). Imagination is context or the fabric of psychic life. It is also a location that we imagine. Psychic events happen *in* the imagination. When we say this, we set apart imagination as a domain of experience. This experience is always inextricably located in the body. We imagine with our whole being rather than in a mind or in a neurological movie theater where one might passively listen and watch.[14] Imagination is also a discursive space or the territory from which new ideas and experiences emerge into culture.

In its verb form, *to imagine* is action. From a Jungian standpoint, when we say *we imagine,* we are engaged in perhaps a different activity than that suggested by common usage. When we imagine, we open the aperture of awareness. We are not building something but letting it emerge into appearance. The act of imagining involves allowing the unconscious to appear. We might say that the creative acts that we associate with artists—the production of a canvas, a sculpture, a work of fiction—involve two movements. The first is an opening to the activity of the imagination that is constantly working below the threshold of perception and an engagement with it. The second is what emerges from this encounter, which is a product that represents the gaze of the artist. In the same way, the dream text brought by a client to therapy is a product of an opening and a conscious encounter. That text is not the original experience but a new experience that likewise straddles the conscious and unconscious of the dreamer. When we interpret a dream, client and therapist imagine together. Hillman (1978) quoted an Icelandic proverb: "Every dream comes true in the way it is interpreted" (p. 152). Interpretation is itself an act of imagination that has great implications for both client and therapist. Often those interpretations spin forth from whatever complexes have been activated on either side.

Throughout the texts we have considered, fantasy has been used both as a synonym for imagination and as a specific instance of imagination. When I use it with clients, I mean the images that appear in our reverie, their imaginal experiences about a certain issue or incident, or the story they tell to explain some aspect of their lives. Fantasy is an imaginal experience that becomes conscious of itself as imaginal. When we take it seriously—a real experience in which our soul is always at stake—it can be personally and collectively transformative.

How might we value imaginal experience? What is to be critiqued is not the experience itself but our orientation to it and what we make of it. In the most provisional, heuristic way, I will use *imaginatio vera* and *imaginatio phantastica* to refer to two distinct understandings of the imagination that appear across the texts we have discussed.

Under the heading of *imaginatio phantastica*, I include experiences that reflect Jung's descriptors: unprofitable, futile, morbid, unsatisfying, nonsense, phantasms, fleeting impressions. We also might include Coleridge's (1814) understanding of *fancy* (chapter 13, section 2, para. 15). These are all subjective and suggestive. Jung did not give us more structured ways to evaluate experiences. What they seem to share in common is *a failure on the part of the imaginer to take the fantasy as seriously as experiences in actual fact.* Fantasy stops being *phantastica* when we accept the objectivity of the experience: the players and other elements are not simply projections or our own convenient creations but have an independent (if mysterious) existence and communicate a summons to recognize who we are and how we affect the system. Jung (1963/1954) suggested that one can fail at fantasy by engaging it as someone other than who one is, with values other than one's own: "It is, however, possible that if you have a dramatic fantasy you will enter the interior world of images as a fictitious personality and thereby prevent any real participation" (para. 753).[15] I understand Jung here to mean not the necessary, creative play that involves trying on possible, emergent elements of our identity (an idea that resonates with Ricoeur, with whom we will spend more time in the next chapter). He condemned a lack of commitment and a refusal

44 Imagining the imagination

to accord fantasy equal existential significance to other kinds of experience. The five-year-old who crawls on all fours, barks, and growls, is fully engaged in fantasy in the purest sense.

Experiences that reflect *imaginatio vera* have a different ontological status. They are psychically real, but we must include important caveats. The reality of an experience does not imply that the figures we encounter necessarily speak with greater authority. Just as in any encounter with someone in the sensible world, we have to evaluate their contributions with skepticism and measure them against our experience. We can genuinely learn things we did not know in the encounters.

A second caveat is that the imaginal experience is not necessarily privileged. Jung's position was not that of Bonaventure (Kearney, 1988); imagination is not a road to hell or a diminution of experience. Unlike the *mundus imaginalis* of Corbin's Sufi saints, however, an *imaginatio vera* does not represent a step upward in an ontological hierarchy. Naturally, we can identify passages in Jung that render this position problematic. He wrote, "I have no small opinion of fantasy. To me, it is the maternally creative side of the masculine mind. When all is said and done, we can never rise above fantasy" (Jung, 1966/1929, para. 98). This passage does not suggest that *imaginatio vera* is somehow better than sensible experience; instead, all experience is in some way a fantasy. How conscious we remain of the fundamentally imaginal nature of experience determines whether it is *vera* or *phantastica*.

The core requirement of *imaginatio vera* is an attitude. Once we accept that the experiences of the imagination are as real as experiences in the world, we must bring our whole being into the experience. Imaginal experience is not inconsequential. In certain passages, Jung suggested that we bear an ethical responsibility when we engage in imaginal experience: "Right action comes from right thinking. ... There is no cure and no improving of the world that does not begin with the individual himself" (Jung, 1977/1943, para. 373). Jung's understanding of the way imaginal experience carries an ethical responsibility is perhaps best expressed by the tale of the rainmaker, which he frequently referenced. To make the rain fall (i.e., to change an imbalance in the world), the rainmaker first restores balance within himself. Our ethical responsibility then has two dimensions: to the objective Others we encounter within and to the objective Others we encounter without. From Jung's vantage, the first ethical question is whether we have the courage to accept the reality of imaginal experience and the interpenetration of imaginal experience with our encounter with the world.

Ethics among the Bigs and Littles

When we accept the reality of imaginal experience and engage in an active imagining, we are at existential play. As Ricoeur (1981) suggested, an imaginative variation of the ego becomes possible. Imagination is where identity becomes malleable. Imagination is the playground where we try on new futures and the crucible in which our soul is melted and reshaped.

One of the shadows of this discourse that connects play and imagination, however, is the sentimentalization of childhood. As we conclude, it is worth a brief detour from theory into clinical experience. In my therapeutic work, I have encountered communities of adults who pretend to be children. These enactments occur online and during in-person contact. The role playing can involve one's taking on the accouterments of childhood (pacifiers, diapers, bedding decorated with cartoon characters) and the speech and mannerisms of children. Individuals seek these experiences for different reasons, but one crucial desire is for an experience of nurturing, play, and comfort provided by other adults who are drawn to the communities to have experiences as loving parents. The yearning for a lost or never-experienced fantasy relationship with a parent is heartbreaking. I would not presume to say that it might not have healing power. The communities exist, however, as subsets of online fetish communities, and the individuals' experiences in these contexts invariably involve boundary-setting and boundary violation. Sexual desire is present, both from predatory parents (or *Bigs*) and desirous children (or *Littles*). Participants police themselves, sending those who desire sexual satisfaction to different spaces in the forum related to incest fantasies or to private chat spaces, which simply reinforces the active shadow market for this taboo sexual experience in the so-called safe space of the public chat room. For the adult who seeks a child experience in this space, the move into a private chat room can involve a seemingly pragmatic tradeoff: you (i.e., the parent) get to have your sexual fantasy experience, and I (i.e., the child) will provide it for you in exchange for nonsexual experiences. This situation mimics the worst incestuous encounters from childhood and is justified by the thin veneer of adult choice and responsibility.

The unconscious is present in this situation. An archetypal urge to experience parental love no doubt drives the impulse. It is not so-called *active* fantasy, in Jung's sense: the encounters take place between material Others rather than visionary Others, but that is also not quite true. The parent encountered by the child is real in the sense that one understands another human to be typing the lines that bring the parent into the fantasy. How that Big looks, feels, smells, and sounds, however, are products of the Little's unconscious. The experience occurs in the psyches of the Little and the Big, and the room exists only as a mutually agreed-upon imaginal space. As in an active fantasy, the Little understands the parent to be an objective Other who is subject to mutual influence. The Big who insists on sexual gratification in that imaginal space commits "incest" but I think also commits incest. The vulnerable human being who enters the shared space looking for the experience of a child no doubt is in a similar place of psychic vulnerability as that of a child who faces an incestuous parent. It could just as likely reinforce old wounds as heal them.

This kind of example underlines the conceptual difficulties we face when trying to separate imagination from praxis, in Casey's (2000) formulation. A shared imaginal space is created by this context, in which real psychic damage can occur. These two people usually do not meet in the life-world. The lines of text appear in that world, however, and those messages from the unconscious (whether the unconscious of the Other or an intersubjective unconscious field) can damage the reader in psychic and material ways.

Jung (1964/1958) wrote,

> We are still so uneducated that we actually need laws from without, and a task-master or Father above, to show us what is good and the right thing to do. And because we are still such barbarians, any trust in the laws of human nature seems to us a dangerous and unethical naturalism. Why is this? Because under the barbarian's thin veneer of culture the wild beast lurks in readiness, amply justifying his fear. But the beast is not tamed by locking it up in a cage. There is no morality without freedom. When the barbarian lets loose the beast within him, that is not freedom but bondage. Barbarism must first be vanquished before freedom can be won. This happens, in principle, when the basic root and driving force of morality are felt by the individual as constituents of his own nature and not as external restrictions. How else is man to attain this realization but through the conflict of opposites? (para. 357)

The situation of clients traumatized in these encounters troubles me. We could imagine that the behavior is some variant of Freud's repetition compulsion; these clients are drawn to situations that recreate an original trauma. The barbarians grow bolder where the thin veneer of culture slips, as it certainly does online. Jung's solution to this problem—that we should develop an internal moral compass not by internalizing laws but by repeatedly holding the tension of opposites—is elegant and also requires education and psychological resources unavailable to most of us. We continue to need laws from without as we develop a new ethic within.

As we turn in chapter 4 to a discussion of ethics through depth psychological and postmodern philosophical lenses, I suggest, following Jung, that my nascent fantasy of an ethic of the imagination takes a different form than our rational laws to cage the barbarian. Clearly, a strong ego is necessary, both to avoid traumatization and to avoid traumatizing Others. We might say that a pure experience of active imagination involves no material Others, however disembodied, such that their presence is suggested only by lines of text on a flickering screen. Even without material Others, there are Others to harm. If we imagine the intrapsychic Others of these experiences to be purely intrapsychic, violence or violation inflicts intrapsychic harm. The imaginal space can be a playground of desire, but enactments still have consequences that are felt in the experience of nightmares, crippling psychopathology, violence met by violence.

Notes

1. See Auerbach (1953) for a discussion of the history of mimesis in Western thought.
2. We see how this interior/exterior distinction is challenged by Hillman and others in a later section.
3. This distinction is provisional; the relationship between imaginal and sensory realms is more complex and blurry than can be explored in this chapter. Imaginal experience also always involves sensory experience, but that experience is internal in a physical sense. When dreaming, eyes move, muscles tense, the heart speeds up; we feel all of these experiences in a physical way as well as in a metaphorical, emotional way. I further explore the relationship between image and sense in the section on Hillman's thought below. The choice between imaginal and sensory domains of experience is a false one or at least only heuristic.
4. It is worth noting that Jung considered the archetypes to be autonomous fantasies; that is, formative processes of chaos and/or desire that have a teleological intent and occur without conscious attention, intention, or reflection.
5. Guerra (2013) elaborated on the notion of play in this context, defining it as "allowing the emergence of imaginal material into conscious awareness" (para. 2). Her thought makes play an ethical imperative for therapists, who must encourage their clients to allow this material, however problematic or frightening, to come into awareness.
6. This is a conundrum present in this study that I do not attempt to resolve.
7. Writing *sous rature*, or under erasure, is a technique devised by Martin Heidegger and used extensively by Jacques Derrida and other postmodern thinkers. It refers to the act of writing a concept and then crossing it out but allowing it to remain in the text (e.g., God). The technique is used to denote concepts that are "inadequate yet necessary" (Sarap, 1993, p. 33). The notion is also used metaphorically to describe discourse that is inadequate and necessary, which is how I intend it here. Hillman did not strike through his text.
8. See Wohlman (2009, p. 119, n. 78) and Bashier (2012) on the influence of Averroes on Ibn 'Arabi.
9. This formulation shares much in common with the symbolist movement, which was active in France in the last third of the 19th century. A good example is Baudelaire's "Correspondences": "Man walks through woods of symbols, dark and dense,/which gaze at him with fond, familiar eyes" (Baudelaire, 1958, para. 26).
10. This position is reflected in Thomas Hobbes' understanding of imagination and memory as decaying sense (Thomas Hobbes, 2013, sec. 2.1, para. 2).
11. Gaudin (1970) related that Bachelard remarked that he regretted having encountered Jung's work "too late" (p. xxxviii, n. 11).
12. Buckley (1992) offered this definition: "The most general definition of the life-world is that it is the world of everyday experience, the concrete world, the 'real' world" (p. 93).
13. Jeffrey Kripal (2011) reported many stories of imaginal experiences materializing in uncanny and often disturbing ways. See, for instance, the extraordinary account of comic-book author Doug Moench, who wrote a scene in which a hooded gunman held the hero's wife hostage, only to walk across the house to find his wife held hostage by a hooded gunman (p. 3).
14. Schwartz-Salant (1989) referenced the notion of the subtle body as a way of discussing the somatic nature of imaginal experience as well as the way that the unconscious of analyst and analysand interact in therapy. I discuss how Schwartz-Salant described this as playing out in practice in chapter 7.

48 Imagining the imagination

15. This notion of a fictitious personality presents conceptual difficulty when viewed through a social constructionist lens, which understands all personalities to be fictive. How does one distinguish between a fictitious and a real personality? Jung seemed to refer to a choice to behave in ways other than one might normally behave or in a manner that is somehow inauthentic. One might imagine, however, that a fictitious personality might express an unrealized truth about the total person. In a sense, all complexes are fictive; that is, constructs, things made within the psyche.

References

Auerbach, E. (1953). *Mimesis: The representation of reality in Western literature.* Princeton, NJ: Princeton University Press.

Avens, R. (1980). *Imagination is reality: Western nirvana in Jung, Hillman, Barfield, and Cassirer.* Dallas, TX: Spring.

Bachelard, G. (1998). *On poetic imagination and reverie.* Woodstock, CT: Spring.

Bashier, S. (2012). *Ibn al-'Arabi's Barzakh: The concept of the limit and the relationship between God and the world.* Albany, NY: SUNY Press.

Baudelaire, C. (1958). Correspondances (J. LeClerq, Trans.). Retrieved from http://fleursdumal.org/poem/103

Beckett, S. (1974). *First love and other shorts.* New York: Grove Press, Inc.

Blake, W. (1907). *The prophetic books of William Blake: Milton.* London: A. H. Bullen.

Brann, E. (1993). *The world of the imagination: Sum and substance.* Lanham, MD: Rowman & Littlefield.

Buckley, R. (1992). *Husserl, Heidegger, and the crisis of philosophical responsibility.* Dordrecht, The Netherlands: Kluwer Academic.

Casey, E. (2000). *Imagining: A phenomenological study* (2nd ed.). Bloomington, IN: Indiana University Press. (Original work published 1976)

Chodorow, J. (Ed.). (1997). *Jung on active imagination.* Princeton, NJ: Princeton University Press.

Coleridge, S. (1814). *Biographia literaria, or, biographical sketches of my literary life and opinions.* New York, NY: Leavitt, Lord, & Company. Retrieved from http://www.gutenberg.org/files/6081/6081-h/6081-h.htm#link2HCH0013

Corbin, H. (1969). *Alone with the alone: Creative imagination in the Sufism of Ibn 'Arabi.* Princeton, NJ: Princeton University Press.

Corbin, H. (1972). Mundus Imaginalis, or the imaginary and the imaginal. In W. Sells (Ed.), (2000), *Working with images: The theoretical base of archetypal psychology* (pp. 70–89). Woodstock, CT: Spring.

Corbin, H. (1989). *Spiritual body and celestial earth.* Princeton, NJ: Princeton University Press.

Djuth, M. (2007). Veiled and unveiled beauty: The role of imagination in Augustine's esthetics. *Theological studies, 68,* 77–91. Retrieved July 8, 2018 from http://cdn.theologicalstudies.net/68/68.1/68.1.4.pdf

Gaudin, C. (1970). Introduction. In G. Bachelard (Ed.), *On poetic imagination and reverie* (pp. xxx–lix). Woodstock, CT: Spring.

Giegerich, W. (1993). Killings. *Spring, 54,* 1–18.

Guerra, A. (2013). Keeping imagination in play: Some thoughts on the microethics of our professional rules of conduct. *The C. G. Jung Page.* Retrieved from http://cgjungpage.org/learn/articles/analytical-psychology/941-keeping-play-in-imagination-some-thoughts-on-the-microethics-of-our-professional-rules-of-conduct

Hillman, J. (1975). *Re-visioning psychology.* New York, NY: Harper & Row.

Hillman, J. (1977). An inquiry into image. *Spring, 44,* 62–88.

Hillman, J. (1978). Further notes on images. *Spring, 45,* 152–182.

Hillman, J. (1979a). Image-sense. *Spring, 46,* 130–143.

Hillman, J. (1979b). *The dream and the underworld.* New York, NY: Harper & Row.

Hillman, J. (1985). *Archetypal psychology: A brief account.* Dallas, TX: Spring.

Jung, C. (n.d.) *The black books.* Unpublished manuscript.

Jung, C. (1963). *Mysterium coniunctionis: An inquiry into the separation and synthesis of psychic opposites in alchemy: Collected works, Vol. 14.* Princeton, NJ: Princeton University Press. (Original work published 1954)

Jung, C. (1964). A psychological view of conscience. *Civilization in transition: Collected works, Vol. 10* (pp. 437–454). Princeton, NJ: Princeton University Press. (Original work published 1958)

Jung, C. (1966). The aims of psychotherapy. *The practice of psychotherapy: Collected works, Vol. 16* (2nd ed.; pp. 36–51). Princeton, NJ: Princeton University Press. (Original work published 1929)

Jung, C. (1967). Commentary on "The secret of the golden flower." *Alchemical studies: Collected works, Vol. 13* (pp. 1–55). Princeton, NJ: Princeton University Press. (Original work published 1938)

Jung, C. (1968). *Psychology and alchemy: Collected works, Vol. 12.* Princeton, NJ: Princeton University Press. (Original work published 1953)

Jung, C. (1969a). Foreward to Suzuki's "Introduction to Zen Buddhism." *Psychology and religion: West and east: Collected works, Vol. 11* (pp. 538–556). Princeton, NJ: Princeton University Press. (Original work published 1939)

Jung, C. (1969b). The transcendent function. *The structure and dynamics of the psyche: Collected works, Vol. 8* (pp. 67–90). Princeton, NJ: Princeton University Press. (Original work published 1958)

Jung, C. (1971). *Psychological types: Collected works, Vol. 6.* Princeton, NJ: Princeton University Press. (Original work published 1960)

Jung, C. (1976). The Tavistock lectures. *The symbolic life: Collected works, Vol. 18,* (2nd ed.; pp. 5–184). Princeton, NJ: Princeton University Press. (Original work published 1935)

Jung, C. (1977). *Two essays on analytical psychology: Collected works, Vol. 7.* Princeton, NJ: Princeton University Press. (Original work published 1943)

Jung, C. (2009). *The red book: Liber novus.* New York, NY: W.W. Norton.

Jung, C. (2011). *Memories, dreams, reflections* (Aniela Jaffe, Ed.). New York, NY: Random House.

Kearney, R. (1988). *The wake of imagination.* New York, NY: Routledge.

Kearney, R. (1998). *Poetics of imagining: Modern to post-modern.* New York, NY: Fordham University Press.

Kearney, R., & Kuipers, R. (2012). Evil, ethics, and the imagination: Part 1. *The other journal: An intersection of theology & culture.* The Seattle School of Theology and Psychology. Retrieved July 2, 2018 from https://theotherjournal.com/2012/03/06/evil-ethics-and-the-imagination-an-interview-with-richard-kearney-part-i/

50   Imagining the imagination

Kierkegaard, S. (1996). *Papers and journals: A selection.* New York: Penguin. (Extract originally published 1840)

Kripal, J. (2011). *Mutants and mystics: Science fiction, superhero comics, and the paranormal.* Chicago, IL: University of Chicago Press.

Llinas, R., & Pare, D. (1996). The brain as a closed system modulated by the senses. In R. Llinas and P. Churchland (Eds.), *The mind-brain continuum: Sensory processes* (pp. 1–18). Cambridge, MA: MIT Press.

Murdoch, I. (1986). Ethics and the imagination. *The Irish Theological Quarterly, 52*(1/2), 81–95.

Ricoeur, P. (1981). *Hermeneutics and the human sciences* (J. Thompson, Trans.). New York, NY: Cambridge University Press.

Sarap, M. (1993). *An introduction to post-structuralism and postmodernism.* Harlow, Essex, UK: Pearson Education.

Sartre, J. (2004). *The imaginary: A phenomenological psychology of the imagination.* New York, NY: Routledge. (Original work published 1940)

Schenk, R. (1992). *The soul of beauty: A psychological investigation of appearance.* Cranbury, NJ: Associated University Presses.

Schwartz-Salant, N. (1989). *The borderline personality: Vision and healing.* Asheville, NC: Chiron.

Shamdasani, S. (2009). Introduction. In C. Jung, *The red book: Liber novus* (pp. 1–95). New York, NY: W.W. Norton.

Taves, A. (2009). *Religious experience reconsidered: A building-block approach to the study of religion and other special things.* Princeton, NJ: Princeton University Press.

Thomas Hobbes. (2013). *Stanford encyclopedia of philosophy.* Stanford, CA: Stanford University. Retrieved from http://plato.stanford.edu/entries/hobbes/

Wohlman, A. (2009). *Al-Ghazali, Averroes, and the interpretation of the Qur'an: Common sense and philosophy in Islam.* New York, NY: Routledge.

Chapter 3

What do we make of fantasy?

The ways in which we have been reflecting on imagination are fantasies, too. The digital world of the Bigs and Littles exists in my imagination, a fantasy created in encounters with a client that is at once of a piece with her imaginal experiences and also distinct from them. The Bigs of her online chats (and real-world encounters) are predatory monsters when they emerge in my imagination, shaped by my clinical training and my biases, fears, and desires. She had experiences in time, which she related in a later moment to me, ongoing experiences affected by temporal distance and her capacity to reflect. Those moments of expression in my office were imaginal experiences in time for me, too, a shared fantasy affected in this moment of writing by a dynamic history of conscious and unconscious reflection in the years since it occurred. Far from a copy of a copy, the fantasy continues to grow and change.

We make reality through fantasy, and fantasy makes reality through us.

We use the word *interpret* to express a cluster of attitudes toward, and actions related to, imaginal experience. Depth psychological texts often deploy an etymological move, looking past contemporary definitions to different meanings found in translations of the linguistic roots of key ideas. It's a useful way to open up our sense of imaginal possibility, though sometimes it is framed as somehow giving us access to a deeper or more significant level of meaning (I'm dubious about that). But the etymological roots of our word *interpret* are worth discussing. Linguists bring "inter-" into English via a proto-Indo-European root "enter-" meaning "between" or "among," and "-pret" via another PIE root, "per," meaning "to traffic in, sell" (Interpret, 2018). Written language emerged in societies well after the development of highly articulated economic and political systems (Bringhurst, 1983);[1] as Tom Cheetham (2015) noted, the original uses of written language "were in the service of management and control" (p. 54). Cheetham makes a larger point about the double nature of language; it takes effort to achieve and maintain an awareness that we are controlled by our language, and that we can use language not only to manage and control, but also to manifest new ways of being. The emergence of the terms "gay" and "transgender"

52 What do we make of fantasy?

to describe affirmative identities in the late 19th and 20th centuries—and the profound social movements that coincided with the adoption of these terms[2]—testify to the power of language to manifest social change.

The act of reflecting on imagination is itself imaginal experience. Having a reflective, reflexive imaginal experience (that we might call interpretation) may lead to what we call understanding. If it does, that understanding is at least in part dependent on the words we have available to channel the fullness of our (extra-linguistic) experience. Think for a moment about that label "predatory monsters" from the first paragraph of the chapter. By its nature, it limits the phenomena, values them, evokes a web of associative images, expresses a primal affective reaction, and tends to foreclose other experiences. That foreclosure is likely valuable, in that it allows judgment and action to emerge quickly. But it also happens unconsciously and creates shadows. When we interpret, we are *being with* fantasy in specific ways. So it is useful to explore interpretation as we approach the ethical dimension of the imagination.

A brief account of Western hermeneutics

Although the history of the use of the term *hermeneutic* extends back to ancient Greece, the first systematized approach to interpretation appears with Philo of Alexandria, in his work with Old Testament texts (Ramberg & Gjesdal, 2005).[3] The Western history of hermeneutics is inextricably bound with the desire to understand religious texts; Ramberg and Gjesdal (2005) cited Origen, Augustine, and Thomas Aquinas as key influences on contemporary hermeneutic theorists. The work of the 19th-century theologian Friedrich Schleiermacher "mark[ed] the beginning of hermeneutics in the modern sense of a scientific methodology" (Bohman, 1995, p. 323). Schleiermacher coined the term *hermeneutic circle*, which Bohman described:

> The circularity of interpretation concerns the relation of parts to the whole: the interpretation of each part is dependent on the interpretation of the whole. But interpretation is circular in a stronger sense: if every interpretation is itself based on interpretation, then the circle of interpretation, even if it is not vicious, cannot be escaped. (pp. 323–324)

Although the modern history of hermeneutics begins with the religious thinker Schleiermacher, it grows quickly outside of the theological frame with the thought of the late 19th-century theorist Wilhelm Dilthey. One of Dilthey's projects was to articulate a method for the human sciences that would be distinct from that of the natural sciences (Ramberg & Gjesdal, 2005). Ricoeur (1981) described Dilthey's discrimination between these two perspectives:

> For Dilthey, "explanation" referred to the model of intelligibility borrowed from the natural sciences and applied to the historical

disciplines by positivist schools; "interpretation," on the other hand, was a derivative form of understanding, which Dilthey regarded as the fundamental attitude of the human sciences. (p. 145)

Ricoeur (1981) further suggested that, in the century since Dilthey's work, both of these categories of methodological encounter with research material have been challenged. Explanation has lost its foundation in the methods of the natural sciences, and interpretation has become divorced from the way Dilthey constructed understanding in psychological terms. Interpretation, for Dilthey, required understanding the person behind the text, the ostensible author, which, for Ricoeur, led into the psychological and to the past, rather than to the new world made possible by the text: "The text must be unfolded, no longer towards its author, but towards its immanent sense and towards the world which it opens up and discloses" (p. 53). This statement reflects Ricoeur's distinction between interpretation behind and in front of the text, which I take up in detail below. It also parallels Jung's suggestion (in the epigraph) of causal and purposive approaches to fantasy.

For the next generation of theorists of hermeneutics, the emphasis shifts from the epistemological to the ontology that underlies such conceptual systems as Dilthey's.

Heidegger, Gadamer, and the ontological turn

The "turn to ontology" (Ramberg & Gjesdal, 2005, section 3, para. 6) began with the publication of Martin Heidegger's *Being and Time* (1927). Before we conceptualize our world, measure, analyze, and hypothesize it, we experience it. The world makes sense to us before we theorize it. Thus, whatever we encounter in the world cannot be separated from our experience of it prior to our conceptualization of it. As Tan, Wilson, and Olver (2009) suggested, "Heidegger asserted [in *Being and Time*] that nothing can be encountered without reference to a person's background and preunderstanding and that we cannot have a life in the world except through acts of interpretation" (p. 4). Heidegger's hermeneutic circle reflects the ways in which our preunderstanding both influences our reading of a text and is influenced by it; that is, how our very being is changed by the encounter.

Heidegger's student, Hans-Georg Gadamer (2004), understood this ongoing process, the co-creation of both reader and textual interpretation in the encounter between reader and text, as reflecting what he referred to as the "fusion of horizons" (Tan, Wilson, & Olver, 2009, p. 4), which Ramberg and Gjesdal (2005) defined as the "co-determination of text and reader":

As important as the interplay between the parts and the whole of a text is the way in which our reading contributes to its effective history, adding to the complexity and depth of its meaning. The meaning of the text is not something we can grasp once and for all. (para. 44)

The historical horizon of the text—its context, tradition, and inherent and accumulated authority—exists in the hermeneutic moment with the existence and experience of the interpreter. Gadamer did not articulate specific methods or a concise theory of hermeneutics, suggesting rather that one learn "by following the example of others" (Ramberg & Gjesdal, 2005, para. 40).

Ricoeur and interpretation in front of the text

In various texts throughout his career, Paul Ricoeur developed a theory of interpretation that was influenced by the thought of Dilthey, Heidegger, Gadamer, and others. As I have already suggested, Ricoeur was concerned that interpretation understood as glance backward to the author does not adequately serve the full potential and power of the text. Ricoeur was most famously associated with his concept of the *hermeneutics of suspicion*, which looks to the larger cultural patterns and the deeper structures and movements of power that undergird and contextualize authorial intent: "Hermeneutics seems to me to be animated by this double motivation: willingness to suspect, willingness to listen; vow of rigor, vow of obedience. In our time we have not finished doing away with *idols* and we have barely begun to listen to *symbols*" (Ricoeur, 1970, p. 27, emphasis in original). Ricoeur stated, "Symbols give rise to thought" (p. 38); they are, in Doran's (1994) understanding of Ricoeur, "exploratory rather than etiological or explanatory" (p. 116). Key to understanding Ricoeur's thought are his concepts of *the text, distanciation, assimilation, interpretation behind the text*, and *interpretation in front of the text*, which I summarize briefly below.

The text The text is "any discourse fixed by writing" (Ricoeur, 1981, p. 145). Ricoeur was keen to establish the differences between speech and writing, as well as the relative newness of writing in human history. Although it may seem that the reader of a text is like the interlocutor of a speaker, the relations are quite different and crucial in understanding the nature of interpretation. An interlocutor engages in dialogue, but a reader cannot address the author directly.

> The emancipation of the text from the oral situation entails a veritable upheaval in the relations between language and the world, as well as in the relation between language and the various subjectivities concerned (that of the author and that of the reader). (p. 147)

The author of a text is "already dead" and his text is "posthumous" (p. 147). The methods of interpretation of a text serve as the separate, parallel relation to the methods of interview and living discourse with a speaker.

Distanciation This understanding of the text reveals it to be distanced from the author in several key ways: (1) The initial fixation in writing separates the discourse from its creator; (2) Because of this separation, the text reflects the "eclipse of the author's intention," which makes it open to "unlimited reading and interpretation";[4] (3) The text is "emancipated" from its original context and becomes available for interpretation in many new contexts, across history, geography, politics, and philosophy; and (4) Although speech requires a direct, immediate transaction between the speaker and the interlocutor, the text does not depend on a single communicative moment (Geanellos, 1999, p. 113). One of the core points Ricoeur made in this articulation of distanciation is the necessary freedom of the reader to read the text in ways other than as a search for the author or for the text's historical moment; as he stated, "From the moment that the text escapes from its author and from his situation, it also escapes from its original audience. Hence it can procure new readers for itself" (Ricoeur, 1981, p. 192).

Appropriation using play If the fact of distanciation loosens the text from its imagined tethers in a specific moment, it must then be approached in particular ways by its audiences. "For whom does one write?" Ricoeur asked; "For anyone who can read" (p. 182). Ricoeur articulated two great, contrasting movements in interpretation theory. *Historicism* involves the attempt to interpret a text in its historical context, as a document written by an historically-determined author to a particular audience at a specific moment in time. Ricoeur took seriously the second movement, anti-historicism, which understands a text to be "a kind of atemporal object which has, as it were, broken its moorings with all historical development" (p. 185). In particular, Ricoeur embraced the anti-historicist position on the general objectivity of meanings. The reader must make an existential response to this objective meaning in the act of appropriation, which Ricoeur explained is a translation of the German word *aneignen,* which means "to make 'one's own' what was initially 'alien'" (p. 185). The entire task of hermeneutics, then, is "to struggle against cultural distance and historical alienation. Interpretation brings together, equalizes, renders contemporary and similar" (p. 185).

Play is the method of appropriation. Ricoeur's inventive use of this term, which he borrowed from Gadamer, allowed him to avoid the trap of self-seriousness and to address the larger problem of subjectivity in interpretation. Play, for Ricoeur, implies that one gets lost in the process, forgets oneself in such a way that the meaning of the text can emerge: "Play shatters the seriousness of a utilitarian preoccupation where the self-presence of the subject is too secure. In play, subjectivity forgets itself; in seriousness, subjectivity is regained" (p. 186). Playfulness itself, however, has its own seriousness; Ricoeur read Gadamer to understand play as both "heuristic fiction" and revealing of "true being": "Everyday reality is abolished and yet everyone becomes himself. Thus the child who disguises himself as another expresses his profoundest truth" (p. 187). Ricoeur understood both the author and the reader to play in crucial ways. As the text is a series of "imaginative variations" on the subjectivity of the author, the reader too must undergo an "imaginative variation of his ego" (p. 189) in the process of reading. The text opens new, possible ways of being for the reader; Ricoeur's interpretation requires an existential engagement with the text that places the reader's subjectivity itself at creative play.

Ricoeur invoked Freud to underscore this need to make present and malleable the subjectivity of the reader. Ricoeur did not invoke the unconscious by name in the 1981 essay "Appropriation"; indeed, in *Freud and Philosophy* (Ricoeur, 1970), he had no interest in arguing for the conceptual veracity of Freud's metapsychology. The unconscious is implied, however, in Freud's interpretive assumptions, which Ricoeur found valuable, famously suggesting that Freud's position was that "the subject is not master in his own house" (Ricoeur, 1981, p. 191). Ricoeur was concerned that interpretation include an awareness of the ways in which the "narcissism of the reader" (p. 191) can intrude on the text. We must be aware of the fact of our unconsciousness in the interpretive process, though we cannot presume to know how we are unconscious. Here be shadows, things missed, feelings avoided.

Subjectivity and the hermeneutics of suspicion

What to do with our subjectivity is a central theme of Ricoeur's work. We must understand that we cannot have access to the author's original intention nor the original audience's understanding of the text. Our subjective interpretation is not the revelation of a truth hidden behind the text. Ricoeur grouped Freud with Nietzsche and Marx as practitioners of an interpretation of suspicion. Further behind the text than the author's intention or the original audience's hearing of a text are foundations of which the author and audience are themselves unaware. To Ricoeur, these three writers shared "the decision to look upon the whole of consciousness primarily as 'false' consciousness" (Ricoeur, 1970, p. 33). Each develops methods of decoding the texts to uncover the falseness in consciousness. In Freud, for example, this appears in the distinction between the manifest and latent contents of dream symbolism. From Ricoeur's vantage, Freud was not simply interested in destroying consciousness. This move to uncover the covered meaning— and the illusion of a Cartesian certainty of consciousness—is a hermeneutics performed in the service of the expansion of consciousness.

Ricoeur (1970) characterized Freud, Marx, and Nietzsche as offering "the most radically contrary stance to the phenomenology of the sacred and to any hermeneutics understood as the recollection of meaning and as the reminiscence of being" (p. 35).

What do we make of fantasy? 57

At issue in this controversy is the fate of what I shall call, for the sake of brevity, the mytho-poetic core of imagination. Over against illusion and the fable-making function, demystifying hermeneutics sets up the rude discipline of necessity. It is the lesson of Spinoza: one first finds himself a slave, he understands his slavery, he rediscovers himself free within understood necessity. The Ethics is the first model of the ascesis that must be undergone by the libido, the will to power, the imperialism of the dominant class. But, in return, does not this discipline of the real, this ascesis of the necessary lack the grace of imagination, the upsurge of the possible? And does not this grace of imagination have something to do with the Word as Revelation? (pp. 34–35)

Once this illusion is defeated,[5] one is left with an absence that cries out to be filled. Peter Homans' *The Ability to Mourn* (1989) suggested the ways Freud intended psychoanalysis to provide a mechanism to experience this absence of broad religious influence in culture and the personal loss of the religious symbols that mediated meaning for an individual psyche. The problem, then, is what is to follow the absence. Ricoeur's (1970) final questions in this passage evoke the instability of this absence. The "mytho-poetic core of imagination" (p. 34) seems to exist prior to the absence and is destined to fill it again. Writing in the *Journal of Analytical Psychology,* Hewison (1995) noted that Ricoeur distinguished between "demystifying" and "demythologizing" (p. 388). Freud's banishment of illusions represents a demystification or a smashing of idols so that their hidden truth (for Freud, a symbolic act of patricide hidden in historical memory) can be revealed. Demythologization, on the other hand, "assumes that things have not been hidden but rather that they have been compacted into one another and that what is required is the explication and re-living of the mythical in all its original variety" (p. 388). As Ricoeur (1970) stated, "Freud deliberately turns his back on the demythologizing interpretations which, from Schelling to Bultmann, deprive myths of any etiological function so as to restore to them their mytho-poetic function capable of leading to a reflection or a speculation" (p. 537). The demystifying act of the hermeneutics of suspicion ignores or refuses to acknowledge the mytho-poetic core, destroying the calcified, reified forms of illusion without recognizing that, upon their destruction, imagination begins to flow again, into new forms. Kearney (1998) captured this succinctly: "The best response to the post-modern news that *'l'imagination est mort'* is: *'Vive l'imagination!'"* (p. 236).

Interpretation in front of the text

Ricoeur's (1970) famous formulation of the hermeneutics of suspicion appears in his mid-career work, *Freud and Philosophy.* In later work, he articulated what the Jungian analyst Alan Jones (2002) referred to as a "hermeneutics of hope" (p. 45). One can interpret in front of the text, Ricoeur argued, and hermeneutics should involve both a backward and a forward movement. Interpretation in front of the text means "to be dispossessed of one's self by the text, to become exposed to the trajectory of its possibilities, and finally to appropriate a new self" (Jones, 2002, p. 51). Ricoeur stated, "To understand oneself in front of a text is quite the contrary of projecting oneself and one's own beliefs and prejudices; it is to let the work and its world enlarge the horizon of the understanding which I have of myself" (Ricoeur, 1981, p. 178). Embedded in this conceptualization of interpretation is an awareness of one's own beliefs and prejudices. Readers who intend to read in front of the text must be aware of their own subjectivity. Although Ricoeur did not advocate analysis per se as a valuable means by which to acquire this awareness, he stated early in *Freud and Philosophy* (1970) that his interest in psychoanalysis was "justified neither by the competence of an analyst nor by the experience of being analyzed" (p. 3). His interest in psychoanalysis as a critique of subjectivity suggests that personal analytic work is a valid path, perhaps one of many, to the starting state from which a forward interpretive move is possible.

A Jungian analytic hermeneutics

Whereas Ricoeur articulated his hermeneutic method in clear, meticulous prose, Jung's hermeneutics evolved over time and must be derived indirectly from its application; we cannot find a concise, systematic articulation of his psychological hermeneutic method, as Smythe and Baydala (2012) have noted. The analytic literature includes several treatments of hermeneutics in light of Jung's thought. In this brief survey, we examine some of the references to hermeneutics to be found in Jung's *Collected Works.* Then, we turn our attention to the critical overview of Jungian hermeneutics provided by Smythe and Baydala (2012).

References to hermeneutics in Jung

Jung never articulated his interpretive method in an exacting, easily reproducible way (Smythe & Baydala, 2012). Twelve of the 17 references to hermeneutics in the *Collected Works* refer directly to Christian hermeneutics: "To understand the phoenix myth it is important to know that in Christian hermeneutics the phoenix made an allegory of Christ" (Jung, 1963/1954, para. 474); "Our civilization has long since forgotten how to think symbolically, and even the theologian has no further use for the hermeneutics of the Church Fathers" (Jung, 1967/1952, para. 683); and so on. Throughout these references to religious hermeneutics, Jung was uniformly critical of the ways in which the symbolic richness of traditional scriptural interpretation has been lost or ignored. Ten of the references to hermeneutics occur in Jung's three texts on alchemy, including one brief reference to an "alchemical hermeneutics" (Jung, 1963/1954, para. 366), which he did not elaborate.

What he meant by *thinking symbolically* is suggested by this passage from *Psychological Types*:

> A fantasy needs to be understood both causally and purposively. Causally interpreted, it seems like a *symptom* of a physiological state, the outcome of antecedent events. Purposively interpreted, it seems like a symbol, seeking to characterize a definite goal with the help of the material at hand, or trace out a line of future psychological development. (1971/1960, para. 720)

Although there was no explicit articulation of hermeneutic method in Jung's writing, he clearly understood his work to be in the hermeneutic mode. Early in his career, in 1916, Jung used the term to differentiate himself from Freud:

> Whence has fantasy acquired its bad reputation? Above all from the circumstance that it cannot be taken literally. Concretely understood, it is worthless. If it is understood semiotically, as Freud understands it, it is interesting from the scientific point of view; but if it is understood hermeneutically, as an authentic symbol, it acts as a signpost, providing the clues we need in order to carry on our lives in harmony with ourselves. (Jung, 1977/1943, para. 491)

Jung (1977/1943) further articulated his theory of the symbol as "something that is still entirely unknown or still in the process of formation" (para. 492). He understood the violence worked by a semiotic interpretation on the appearance of the symbol, suggesting that "to attribute hermeneutic significance to it is consistent with its value and meaning" (para. 492). He then outlined his understanding of the "essence" of hermeneutics, suggesting that it

> consists in adding further analogies to the one already supplied by the symbol: in the first place subjective analogies produced at random by the patient, then objective analogies provided by the analyst out of his general knowledge. This procedure widens and enriches the initial symbol, and the final outcome is an infinitely complex and variegated picture the elements of which can be reduced to their respective *tertia comparationis*. Certain lines of psychological development then stand out that are at once individual and collective. There is no science on earth by which these lines could be proved "right"; on the contrary, rationalism could very easily prove that they are wrong. Their validity is proved by their intense value for life. (para. 493)

In this passage, Jung roughly outlined the analytic method that would evolve throughout his career but would remain remarkably true to this early formulation. Most remarkable is his rejection of the myth of rationality as the only path to the truth. What is important for the individual life may have no relation to rational truth, but the analyst (and, by extension, the textual scholar working in an analytic mode) must understand that another order of truth can emerge from interpretation. The criterion of *value for life* could be read as vague, subjective, and fraught with illusion, but we can also understand it as unmediated, comprehensive, and unrestricted to the narrow range of phenomena that can be observed, measured, and quantified. Jung's ambivalent relationship with scientific authority—as both suitor and heretic—haunted his project.[6] Smythe and Baydala (2012) suggested that this ambivalence is reflected in his interpretive method: "His methodological formulations continued to cling to a natural science framework that was inconsistent with his actual hermeneutic practices" (p. 63).

Indeed, Jung took up this subject directly in the late work *Mysterium Coniunctionis* (Jung, 1963/1954), in another passage that refers to hermeneutics. In the midst of a reflection on psychological interpretations of religious experience, Jung referred to the result of his amplificatory method as

> a kind of amalgamation of ideas of—so it would seem—the most varied provenance, and this sometimes leads to parallels and comparisons which to an uncritical mind unacquainted with the epistemological method may seem like a devaluation or a false interpretation. (para. 457)

He suggested that early Christian hermeneutics, and textual criticism in general, can certainly be viewed as "dubious" from an empirical vantage (para. 457). He then reflected that "a rapprochement between empirical science and religious experience would in my opinion be fruitful for both. Harm can result only if one side or the other remains unconscious of the limitations" (para. 457).

Jung referred directly to the relationship of his interpretive work to the tradition of hermeneutics. In "Principles of Practical Psychotherapy," originally delivered in 1935, Jung referred to his way of working with patients as a "dialectical method" that involves "adopting [an] attitude that shuns all methods" (Jung, 1966/1935, para. 6). In this passage, Jung clearly was in conversation with the Freudian psychoanalytic tradition, as he referred to the importance of "the *multiple significance of symbolic contents*" (para. 9, emphasis in original) and distinguished between "analytical-reductive" interpretation and "synthetic-hermeneutic" (para. 9), with the latter reflecting his approach. He used the example of "the so-called infantile fixation on the parental imago" (para. 9) as a way to differentiate these approaches:

> The analytical-reductive view asserts that interest ("libido") streams back regressively to infantile reminiscences and there "fixates"—if indeed it has ever freed itself from them. The synthetic or anagogic view, on the contrary, asserts that certain parts of the personality which are

capable of development are in an infantile state, as though still in the womb. Both interpretations can be shown to be correct. We might almost say that they amount virtually to the same thing. But it makes an enormous difference in practice whether we interpret something regressively or progressively. It is no easy matter to decide aright in a given case. (para. 9)

This distinction refers to another core theme in Jung's work: the teleological unfolding of the personality across its development. Jung's greater point, however, was that no theoretical position is privileged. Sitting across from a client, the therapist must abandon the semiotic calculation of treatment protocols (this symptom equals this cause, this therapeutic intervention, and this outcome) and the power inequities of the analytic encounter, in which the therapist is the all-powerful, antiseptically objective healer and the client is the powerless, wounded subject. It is significant that Jung's embrace of hermeneutics to describe his interpretive method occurred in the context of a larger argument for the uncovering of the interpreter's subjectivity. Subjectivity is woven into the method; the analyst/interpreter must bring his own analogies into the room as part of the amplification process. Later critical commentators put the objectivity of these analogies very much in question. Jung's selection of analogies was by no means systematic; they were guided by his intuition and, some have argued, their convenience: "Jung revolves the 'hermeneutical circle' as if it were a wheel of fortune; if you win, you win (another telling parallel!) and if you lose (you fail to find a parallel), you can always try again" (Pietikäinen, 1999, as cited in Smythe & Baydala, 2012, p. 66). Despite the valid objections of Pietikäinen and others, Jung's amplification method can often unfold meanings that may be foreign to both object and subjects.

The archetypal background of experience

Jung distinguished between "archetypal expressions" (i.e., what we see, hear, or otherwise register in material ways) and the "archetype as such" (i.e., the empty form that cannot be explored or perceived except through its mediated expressions (p. 64)). The archetype-as-such is "a background not previously suspected, a true matrix of all conscious phenomena, a preconsciousness and a postconsciousness, a superconsciousness and a subconsciousness" (Jung, 1969/1954, para. 356). Smythe and Baydala (2012) linked this understanding of the archetypal as background to the contemporary philosophical hermeneutic concept of pre-understanding, which we have already encountered in the summary of Heidegger. By its nature, we cannot explore, examine, articulate, or delineate the archetypal background; it is "both the basis for and an essential limitation on [the] articulation of meaning" (p. 65). The archetypal background is a limitation on meaning in that the kind of semiotic meaning of Freudian inquiry is not possible; the archetypal background can express, but it cannot denote in the one-to-one relationship of manifest to latent: "By virtue of their non-conceptual structure, archetypes lack the most basic logical properties of well-defined concepts" (p. 67). Archetypes produce a myriad of potential meanings rather than a single meaning.

One can sense from even this limited treatment that Jung understood the truth to be uncovered as of a different order than that which we are accustomed to calling *objective* or imagining as univocal. Indeed, Hewison (1995) suggested that Jung attempted "to radicalize our relationship to our own subjectivity" (p. 400). Jung's ultimate allegiance was to the "value for life" (Jung, 1977/1943, para. 493) and for his interpretive method of creating mosaics of analogies, in which the truth might make its appearance. The interpretive practice of Jungian psychology depends on a dialogic process (Beebe, 1992; Smythe & Baydala, 2012). Jungian analyst Priscilla Murr suggested that the truth of a clinical interpretation depends on an experience of the interpretation *clicking* for both the analyst and the client (P. Murr, personal communication, October 8, 2011). The Jungian technique of active imagination involves an imaginal dialogue between the ego and an imaginally or inwardly experienced Other; von Franz (1993, as cited in Smythe & Baydala, 2012) described the final stage of active imagination as involving a collaborative partnership between ego and imaginal Other with "ethical decisions" and "moral confrontations" (p. 71). The truth is the product of a mutual process of coming to understand and respecting the needs and perspectives of the Other. Smythe and Baydala only sketched the way that this might be applied to textual hermeneutics, suggesting that the dialogue also can take place "with entire cultural traditions," with the marker of truth analogous to the shared click (i.e., a "mutual fit" between archetypal expressions and the specific contexts, personal and cultural, in which they emerge; p. 71).

The post-Jungian theorist Robert Romanyshyn (2007) articulated a hermeneutic method that places Jung's radicalized subjectivity at its heart. Once we have taken the position that bracketing one's experience—in a way perhaps analogous to a Husserlian phenomenological *epoché*—is impossible, we can begin to imagine the work as a dialogue between researcher and research rather than a revelation of objective truth. Romanyshyn's method involves a repurposing of active imagination to articulate the levels of the researcher's engagement with the work. Research itself emerges from an archetypal background; it speaks through individual researchers and in conversation with their personal and cultural contexts. In psychological language, "a topic chooses a researcher through his or her complexes as much as, and perhaps even more than, he or she consciously chooses it" (p. 135). Romanyshyn's method is a systematic engagement with those complexes and with the imagined Others that populate the research, from the spouses, parents, and friends of the researcher; to the theorists and prominent historical figures who have contributed to the field; to the ancestors; and even to the animal world. He theorized research as taking place within a "transference field" (p. 135) wherein the researcher's unconscious and the theorized unconscious of the work (i.e., the subject of research that has a cultural and historical context and is larger than its particular expression in a single researcher's productivity) mutually influence each other. Rather than a hermeneutic circle, he suggested a "hermeneutic spiral," which "follows the arc of the hermeneutic circle, but in such a way that the engagement of the two takes into account the unconscious aspects of the researcher and the work" (p. 222). Although Romanyshyn engaged with the tradition of philosophical hermeneutics, he argued that his method is distinct from a philosophical approach; his goal was to "[make] philosophical hermeneutics more psychologically aware" (p. 222).

Interpretation and the unconscious

It is clear from these brief treatments that the subjectivity of the researcher—in particular, the theorized unconscious—is a fundamental concern in contemporary hermeneutic discourse. The unconscious keeps us from believing we stand on any kind of firm, objective ground.

Romanyshyn (2007) argued that "it is [the] pre-existent reality of the unconscious, its sui generis character, which ... poses for the philosopher Paul Ricoeur the most significant challenge to the language of philosophical speculation and the work of hermeneutic interpretation" (p. 324). Romanyshyn commented extensively on Ricoeur's engagement with the conceptual unconscious in his mid-career writing, particularly his landmark work *Freud and Philosophy* (1970). Romanyshyn read Ricoeur as understanding the unconscious in Freudian terms. Indeed, Ricoeur commented directly on his unease with a Jungian unconscious:

> As Kant has taught us, a limit is not an external boundary but rather a function of the internal validity of a theory. Psychoanalysis is limited by the very thing which justifies it, namely, its decision to know, in cultural phenomena, only that which falls under an economics of desire and resistances. I must say that it is this firmness and rigor which makes me prefer Freud to Jung. With Freud, I know where I am and where I am going; with Jung, everything (the psyche, the soul, the archetypes, the sacred) is in danger of becoming confused. (Ricoeur, 1974, pp. 207–208)

Freud limited the field of inquiry and made his approach systematic; Jung left it open to remain true to the breadth and depth of the unconscious. One implication of Ricoeur's position is that Freud's unconscious is simply easier to address philosophically because of its "firmness and rigor"

64 What do we make of fantasy?

(Ricoeur, 1974, p. 208). The Jungian unconscious, in Romanyshyn's view, includes the Freudian unconscious. Ricoeur's failure to engage Jung's more comprehensive view of the unconscious means that he was unable to perceive or address "that region where image is not just the ideational representation of the instinct in consciousness, but co-equal with instinct on a continuum that marks the range of soul" (Romanyshyn, 2007, p. 256). Ricoeur's reading traps the unconscious as the subject of "psychology as a natural science," rather than of a "science of the soul" (p. 256).

Romanyshyn (2007) outlined three ways in which Jung's understanding of the unconscious pose problems for Ricoeur's position. First, the Jungian understanding of the unconscious as "a sui generis reality and not just the outcome of the conflict between instinct and culture" (p. 324) means that it is not simply hidden from consciousness but has a consciousness of its own: that is, a true Otherness. Ricoeur (1970) could not accept this: "'Against this naïve realism,' he says, 'we must continually emphasize that the unconscious does not think'" (p. 256). The second problem follows from this radical Otherness. In Ricoeur's (1970) view, the unconscious of one person becomes real as it is witnessed by the consciousness of another. Romanyshyn (2007) objected that, although this may be true from the perspective of a consciousness encountering the unconscious in a particular moment, it places an unnecessary limitation on the Otherness of the unconscious. The unconscious does not reside between consciousnesses; instead, "it is composed of two witnessing consciousnesses in the presence of the unconscious as a sui generis epiphany that belongs neither to the one nor the other" (p. 258). Romanyshyn's third objection is again closely linked to the previous two. Ricoeur's (1970) statement that the being of the unconscious "'is not absolute but only relative to hermeneutics as method and dialogue'" (p. 258) makes the unconscious dependent on the hermeneutic methods that render it visible.

It is worth noting that Romanyshyn (2007) drew upon a relatively narrow range of Ricoeur's writing on hermeneutics and the unconscious, particularly *Freud and Philosophy* (1970) and the essays published variously but collected in *The Conflict of Interpretations* (1974). Casting our net more widely, we can find themes in Ricoeur's writings that are more consonant with a Jungian hermeneutics.

A significant opening for comparison between Jung's hermeneutics and Ricoeur's appears in Ricoeur's distinction between interpretation behind vs. interpretation in front of the text. A hermeneutics of suspicion that understands meaning to be hidden behind the text (i.e., behind consciousness) is not enough. Meaning is not simply contained in a web of historical and cultural context or in an economics of desire and resistances. It is created in the "critical moment" when the "literal reference" (Jones, 2002, p. 51) of any text is held in abeyance. One then can choose to interpret behind or to look in front of the text, where one releases a metaphorical reference from the surplus of meanings contained in the words and grammar of the text. To go behind the text is an act of suspicion; to interpret in front of the text is to be dispossessed of one's self by the text, to become exposed to the trajectory of its possibilities, and finally to appropriate a new self. (Jones, 2002, p. 51)

When the literal reference of the text is released, the metaphoric can speak in tongues its implications for the life of the reader. We are in the realm of "the nonliteral real of the imagination" where one can "play at imagining the possibilities of a new being" (p. 54). Jones found in this movement a natural opening to the Jungian unconscious. Ricoeur described metaphor as "that strategy of discourse by which language divests itself of its functions of direct description ... to reach the mythic level where its function of discovery is set free" (Ricoeur, 1978, as cited in Jones, 2002, p. 51). Language itself has agency in this passage; Jones suggested that Ricoeur was "reaching to describe the agency of the transpersonal but nontransparent subject of the collective unconscious" (p. 51). This understanding of language as itself reflecting an agency apart from the consciousness that created it appears elsewhere in Ricoeur. A text, in Ricoeur's (1981) understanding, is different from spoken discourse in that it is unmoored from the specific context of its enunciation. This unmooring or release from particular reference does not mean that it lacks any reference: "The task of reading, qua interpretation, will be precisely to fulfill the reference. The suspense which defers the reference merely leaves the text, as it were, 'in the air,' outside or without a world" (Ricoeur, 1981, p. 148). Once it becomes unmoored from its reference, however, it creates imaginary worlds in the reader: "This imaginary world is itself a creation of literature" (p. 149). One wonders whether a mature Ricoeur might not have found much to enrich his own thought had he engaged deeply with Jung's understanding of the unconscious. Even a younger Ricoeur acknowledged that Jung operated within the hermeneutic tradition that restores "the myth as symbol" after it dissolves "the myth as explanation," engaging in "criticism that is no longer reductive but restorative. That is the purpose which animated Schelling, Schleiermacher, Dilthey, and today, in various ways, Leenhardt, van der Leeuw, Eliade, Jung, Bultmann" (Ricoeur, 1967, p. 350).

What all these thinkers share—implicitly in Jung, explicitly in Ricoeur, Romanyshyn, and Jones—is an understanding of the interpretive process as play, which is fundamentally an immersion in the imaginary. I refer again to Ricoeur's (1981) articulation of play as both heuristic fiction and revealing of true being: "Everyday reality is abolished and yet everyone becomes himself. Thus the child who disguises himself as another expresses his profoundest truth" (p. 187). We are released from our self-consciousness—our ego—in play, which allows the unconscious to speak through us. Jones (2002) stated that to work in front of a text allows us to "play at imagining the possibilities of a new being" (p. 54). Romanyshyn's (2007) method involves the creation of "a ritual space of play" in which "the researcher steps out of his or her ego position in relation to the work and steps with it into an imaginal landscape, which is neither the world of nocturnal dreaming, nor the world of focused daytime wakefulness" (p. 137). A related, significant consonance between Jung and Ricoeur is the multivocality of the symbol. Ricoeur's understanding of the symbol as "exploratory" (Doran, 1994, p. 116) rather than leading backward toward causes suggests Jung's teleological reaching for the meaning that offers the greatest "value for life" (Jung, 1977/1943, para. 493).

We should not understand Ricoeur to have been engaged in the same hermeneutic project as Jung, nor should we minimize Romanyshyn's (2007) objections to Ricoeur's understanding of the unconscious. These perspectives, however, are mutually enriching. Romanyshyn's alchemical hermeneutics described a way to acknowledge and deeply explore the subjectivity of the researcher in his or her research, which is of paramount importance to Ricoeur. Jung's metapsychology is itself a heuristic fiction or an exploration of the self that appears in the imaginal play of interpretation. To engage the imagination with a Jungian hermeneutic that understands its chief truth criterion as value for life stays true to Ricoeur's defense of the transformative potential of an encounter with texts understood to be freed from literal reference. Ricoeur's (1970) yearning for the "grace of imagination, the upsurge of the possible" (p. 35) suggests that he too intuited the objective Other at work within him, the consciousness of the unconscious, and the deep encounter with meaning that emerges from an elsewhere that transcends conceptual understanding.

Many other hermeneutics abound, of course, and here we have simply put brief summaries of two traditions in conversation with each other. Although they might seem strange bedfellows, it is worth noting the social constructionist strand in contemporary psychology as we conclude this chapter. Kenneth Gergen (2009) asserted that "the investigator is always making interpretations, which is to say, constructing what the data mean" (p. 64). When we work with the imagination, we are in some ways interpreting interpretations. We make meanings that have no greater or lesser value than other meanings except insofar as they are more or less useful. Gergen suggested that "as we describe and explain, so do we fashion our future" (p. 11). This sentiment is remarkably resonant with Ricoeur's (1981) notion of interpretation in front of the text, which might "let the work and its world enlarge the horizon of the understanding which I have of myself" (p. 178).

As we head next into a consideration of ethical theory, I will conclude by drawing some basic assumptions from this discussion:

1. When we approach fantasy, there is no single, semiotic meaning to be uncovered, following Ramberg and Gjesdal's (2005) understanding of Gadamer ("the meaning of the text is not something we can grasp

once and for all" (para. 44)) and Jung's belief that his hermeneutic method results in "an infinitely complex and variegated picture" (Jung, 1968/1953, para. 493) that cannot be reduced.

2. Interpretation is play. This follows Ricoeur (1981), who understood interpretation as a series of "imaginative variations" (p. 189) on the subjectivities of both the author and the reader. Romanyshyn (2007) and Jung (1971/1960) also relied on the notion of creative play; following Schiller (1845), Jung (1971/1960) suggested that "the creative mind plays with the object it loves," motivated by "the play instinct acting from inner necessity" (para. 197).

3. Interpretation is a dialogic process. In Jung's (1966/1935) vision of clinical interpretation, this took place between analyst and patient; the analyst is not the ultimate arbiter of truth. Meaning is always contextual, situational, open-ended, and unfolding.

4. The validity of interpretations is "proved by their intense value for life" (Jung, 1977/1943, para. 493).

Notes

1. I'm indebted to Tom Cheetham's scholarship for introducing me to Bringhurst's work.
2. See Morris (2017) for a succinct history.
3. *Hermeneutics* is derived from the Greek god Hermes, messenger of the gods, the god of in-betweens; his Roman counterpart was Mercurius, whose wing-footed image was adopted by Western Union telegraph. We will explore the Hermes myth in more detail in chapter 5.
4. This reflects the notion of the intentional fallacy in literary theory, in which the attempt to establish meaning via the intention of the author is critiqued. See Wimsatt (1954, pp. 3–20) for a description of this idea and its usage.
5. To do this, Ricoeur invoked *The Future of an Illusion* (Freud, 1961), which is Freud's critique of religion.
6. See Shamdasani (2003).

References

Beebe, J. (1992). *Integrity in depth.* College Station, TX: Texas A&M Press.

Bohman, J. (1995). Hermeneutics. In R. Audi (Ed.), *The Cambridge dictionary of philosophy* (pp. 323–324). New York, NY: Cambridge University Press.

Bringhurst, R. (2011). *The solid form of language: An essay on writing and imagination.* Kentville, Nova Scotia, Canada: Gaspereau Press.

Cheetham, T. (2015). *Imaginal love: The meanings of imagination in Henry Corbin and James Hillman.* Thompson, CT: Spring Publications.

Doran, R. (1994). *Subject and psyche.* Milwaukee, WI: Marquette University Press.

Freud, S. (1961). *The future of an illusion.* New York, NY: W.W. Norton.

Gadamer, H. (2004). *Truth and method.* New York: Bloomsbury Academic.

Geanellos, R. (1999). Hermeneutic interviewing: An example of its development and use as research method. *Contemporary Nurse, 8*(2), 39–45. doi: 10.5172/conu.1999.8.2.39

68 What do we make of fantasy?

Gergen, K. (2009). *An invitation to social construction.* Thousand Oaks, CA: Sage.

Heidegger, M. (2008). *Being and time.* New York, NY: Harper Perennial. (Original work published 1927)

Hewison, D. (1995). Case history, case story: An enquiry into the hermeneutics of C. G. Jung. *Journal of Analytical Psychology, 40*(3), 383–404.

Homans, P. (1989). *The ability to mourn: Disillusionment and the social origins of psychoanalysis.* Chicago, IL: University of Chicago Press.

Interpret. (2018). The Online Etymological Dictionary. Retrieved Aug. 12, 2018 from https://www.etymonline.com/word/interpret

Jones, A. (2002). Teleology and the hermeneutics of hope: Jungian interpretation in the light of Paul Ricoeur. *Journal of Jungian Theory and Practice, 4*(2), 45–55. Retrieved from http://www.junginstitute.org/pdf_files/JungV4N2p45-56.pdf

Jung, C. (1963). *Mysterium coniunctionis: An inquiry into the separation and synthesis of psychic opposites in alchemy: Collected works, Vol. 14.* Princeton, NJ: Princeton University Press. (Original work published 1954)

Jung, C. (1966). Principles of practical psychotherapy. *The practice of psychotherapy: Collected works, Vol. 16* (2nd ed.; pp. 3–19). Princeton, NJ: Princeton University Press. (Original work published 1935)

Jung, C. (1967). *Symbols of transformation: Collected works, Vol. 5.* Princeton, NJ: Princeton University Press. (Original work published 1952)

Jung, C. (1968). *Psychology and alchemy: Collected works, Vol. 12.* Princeton, NJ: Princeton University Press. (Original work published 1953)

Jung, C. (1969). On the nature of the psyche. *The structure and dynamics of the psyche: Collected works, Vol. 8* (pp. 159–233). Princeton, NJ: Princeton University Press. (Original work published 1954)

Jung, C. (1971). *Psychological types: Collected works, Vol. 6.* Princeton, NJ: Princeton University Press. (Original work published 1960)

Jung, C. (1977). *Two essays on analytical psychology: Collected works, Vol. 7.* Princeton, NJ: Princeton University Press. (Original work published 1943)

Kearney, R. (1998). *Poetics of imagining: Modern to post-modern.* New York, NY: Fordham University Press.

Morris, B. (2017). History of lesbian, gay, bisexual, and transgender social movements. Retrieved Sept. 2, 2018 from http://www.apa.org/pi/lgbt/resources/history.aspx

Pietikäinen, P. (1999). *C. G. Jung and the psychology of symbolic forms.* Helsinki: Finnish Academy of Science and Letters.

Ramberg, B., & Gjesdal, K. (2005). Hermeneutics. *Stanford encyclopedia of philosophy.* Retrieved from http://plato.stanford.edu/entries/hermeneutics/

Ricoeur, P. (1967). *The symbolism of evil.* Boston, MA: Beacon Press.

Ricoeur, P. (1970). *Freud and philosophy: An essay on interpretation.* New Haven, CT: Yale University Press.

Ricoeur, P. (1974). *The conflict of interpretations: Essays in hermeneutics.* Evanston, IL: Northwestern University Press.

Ricoeur, P. (1981). *Hermeneutics and the human sciences* (J. Thompson, Trans.). New York, NY: Cambridge University Press.

Romanyshyn, R. (2007). *The wounded researcher: Research with soul in mind.* New Orleans, LA: Spring Journal.

Schiller, F. (1845). *The aesthetic letters, essays, and the philosophical letters of Schiller.* Boston, MA: Little Brown.

Shamdasani, S. (2003). *Jung and the making of modern psychology: The dream of a science.* London: Routledge.

Smythe, W., & Baydala, A. (2012). The hermeneutic background of C. G. Jung. *Journal of Analytical Psychology, 57*(1), 57–75. doi: 10.1111/j.I468–5922.2011.01951.x

Tan, H., Wilson, A., & Olver, A. (2009). Ricoeur's theory of interpretation: An instrument for data interpretation in hermeneutic phenomenology. *International Journal of Qualitative Methods, 8*(4), 1–15.

Wimsatt, W. (1954). *The verbal icon: Studies in the meaning of poetry.* Lexington, KY: University Press of Kentucky.

Chapter 4

Imagining ethics

All ethics are local. My father's mother spent many months in a Pennsylvania psychiatric hospital in the 1960s. When I knew her a decade later, she smelled of cigarettes and bacon, with a smoky laugh and a sharp tongue for the adults. She was at the center of the kitchen at all times, while my grandfather, a caring, deeply introverted man, usually sat in his rocking chair near the window, listening. I knew nothing of her hospitalization until I was an adult, and the details my father could supply were sketchy, as it happened after he had left for the army. She became catatonic and was eventually treated with electroconvulsive therapy. She had suffered bouts of paralyzing religious scrupulosity throughout her life, and apparently this time was the worst. Nothing she could do was good enough to avoid eternal damnation.

This is all I know about this passage in my grandmother's life, which occurred in social and historical contexts I can only tentatively link to her story. Her scrupulosity was Catholic, a religious heritage that extends back through her lineage to Ireland, where the family lived prior to the Great Famine of 1845–1855. Reflecting on the context of his Irish Catholic parents, the essayist Peter Quinn (2007) wrote that Irish Americans carry "a deeply ingrained belief in original sin and a tribal history which until recently always seemed to end in disappointment and tragedy" (p. 76). As a teen and young adult, my grandmother lived through the Great Depression, perhaps deepening an ancestral imprint of lack and despair, a fervent desire to keep a dangerous, ever-present chaos at bay. Framing her difficulties as pathological allowed the family to be released for a time from their intrusion on family life, and by the few accounts I have heard, treatment was successful. But her mental health issues were a scandal that was almost never discussed in my family, perhaps because it might lead to difficult questions about how the potential remains foundational in the family. My father struggled with unreasonable standards and lived with an undiagnosed obsessive-compulsive disorder that I only became aware of at the end of his life, when it was revealed by his dementia. My mother never talked about it, though she had been its witness and sometimes its victim for nearly 40 years.

My grandmother struggled on a daily basis with fundamental existential questions. Can I trust this life? Can I minimize suffering? How do I make sense of death and disaster, of my immense fear? One of her answers was to reach for a symbolic language and a moral code that gave her a sense of place, stability, and right action. Her orienting fantasy was that she could control her fate—and allay her existential anxiety—through constant, vigilant evaluation of her thoughts, intentions, and desires. Rules could keep her safe.

My grandmother's questions are likely familiar to many of us. Our answers vary, but it is impossible to avoid encountering ethical codes that present themselves as guides, whether voluntary or enforced. We make decisions about whether to accept collective ethical codes or reject them. The rejection of a code does not mean we are unethical but discloses distinctive elements of one's own ethic. We may be unaware of the complex desires and values that steer us through life; indeed, we likely are unaware to some degree. Life poses fundamental existential questions to each of us, and our attempts to answer them are shaped by these ethics, which emerge from our individual, particular existential circumstances—family, religion, community, culture, education, language. As William Blake told us, "One Law for the Lion & Ox is Oppression" (Blake, 1994/1794, loc. 236).

In this chapter, I explore the unique contributions made by analytical and humanistic psychologies, as well as Levinasian philosophy, to a contemporary conversation about ethics. A survey of Jungian psychoanalytic writing on ethics and conscience is followed by a brief consideration of current conversations about ethics among humanistic psychologists, as well as a sketch of the continental ethical philosophy of Emmanuel Levinas and his influence on humanistic and analytic psychological thinking about ethics. I then consider how these diverse conversations might influence the articulation of an ethics that might address the complexities of imaginal experience.

Ethics in the Jungian analytic tradition

Jung on good, evil, and conscience

Ethical action involves a choice between a perceived set of options. Ethics evaluates; it values and discriminates. To act ethically involves one's understanding the untaken paths as lesser, more problematic, and with greater potential hazard for creating suffering. Ethical choice is often artificially framed as a binary: right, wrong; good, evil; pleasure, displeasure. In the OED (2014) definition of *ethic*, the list of historical citations that justified its definition of *ethic* as "a scheme of moral science" includes the following quotation from British philosopher W. K. Clifford (1886):

> By Morals or Ethic I mean the doctrine of a special kind of pleasure or displeasure which is felt by the human mind in contemplating certain courses of conduct, whereby they are felt to be right or wrong, and of a special desire to do the right things and avoid the wrong ones. (p. 287)

72 Imagining ethics

In conventional understandings of ethics, there are rights things and wrong things, pleasurable and unpleasurable, and we are to accept these binary oppositions as in some way reflecting reality and then discern adequately which is which.

In his late-career essay, "Good and Evil in Analytical Psychology" (1964b/1960), Jung offered a concise summation of his position on the psychological dynamics at work in discussions of the binary of good and evil. The metaphysical status of evil is bracketed, though as usual in Jung, one can see his metaphysics peeking through the concept of the archetypal. In the essay, Jung engaged in a dance between absolute and relative understandings of these ideas. Good and evil are principles that transcend the individual. He wrote,

> When we speak of good and evil we are speaking concretely of something whose deepest qualities are in reality unknown to us. Whether it is experienced as evil and sinful depends, furthermore, on our subjective judgment, as also does the extent and gravity of the sin. (para. 860)

What appears evil to one person may not appear evil to another. Customs and mores vary across cultures. These issues of subjectivity and cultural relativity, however, sit atop the objectivity of the ideas, which extend forever outside of our awareness. Jung (1964b/1960) pointed to the Genesis story, in which Adam and Eve were tempted to discover the knowledge of good and evil, which would make them like gods. For Jung, this meant that "Only the Gods know, not us. This is profoundly true in psychology" (para. 862). So Jung posited an evil that cannot be known as such. Any appearance of this principal evil must be a common evil for us to perceive it. His position was not a pure relativism, but he put any metaphysical extension out of reach.[1]

Jung (1964b/1960) wrote, "Evil is terribly real, for each and every individual. ... If you regard the principle of evil as a reality you can just as well call it the devil" (para. 879). By invoking the devil, Jung put us into relationship with a supraordinate imaginal being. He captured the feeling that our will is opposed by something greater. The devil disempowers us; he is beyond our capacities to overcome. Jung mixed his terms (i.e., evil is archetypal, a principle, the devil), but all of these serve to underline our subjection to larger forces. He wrote, "Principles, when reduced to their ultimates, are simply aspects of God. ... Good and evil are principles of our ethical judgment, but, reduced to their ontological roots, they are 'beginnings,' aspects of God, names for God" (para. 864). These good and evil principles that extend beyond us and are greater than we are influence the individual and impinge on any theoretical freedom we might imagine for ourselves. Proulx (1994) argued that "Jung's central image for human beings is one of complete determinism" (p. 114). The unconscious undercuts arguments for free choice. It acts through us; the God of the unconscious may have derived from Jung's grappling with his Christian upbringing, but it bears little resemblance to the God of contemporary Christian fantasy, a "loving and caring father" (p. 115). Instead, Jung's unconscious looks "like some blind force that uses individuals and nations to further its own aims, and dumps them when they are no longer useful" (p. 115). Good and evil as archetypal principles are two sides of an amoral whole, an energy that forces itself upon us without concern for our well-being. Hollis (2007) suggested that, "From the standpoint of a divinity, or from the perspective of nature, there is no good, no evil. The cancer eating us, the shark pursuing us, the grim specter of our approaching annihilation is not 'evil.' It simply is" (p. 167). Yet Jung retained a belief in the teleological goodness that could manifest when one engages honestly with our human dilemmas. Proulx (1994) commented that "Jung remained, all his life, faithful to the insight he had as a young boy: that God would see to it that whatever he asked of one would somehow always turn out right" (p. 117). This belief is apparent in "Good and Evil in Archetypal Psychology": "Often we cannot say in such situations how the problem of good and evil will work out. We have to put our trust in the higher powers" (Jung, 1964b/1960, para. 883).[2]

I return to Proulx's (1994) characterization of Jung's God-image; she did not simply argue that he was a determinist. For me, it is worth pausing for a moment in the fantasy that my forebears' struggles, and my own, are driven by forces well outside my control. Control, in fact, is exactly the wrong response to the upwellings of intense feeling that impel me to behave in unbalanced ways (i.e., good and evil). My grandmother's scrupulosity was good in intention and evil in effect. Jung made a developmental argument that retains the absolute status of evil while underscoring the relative nature of our experience of it:

> Because I take an empirical attitude it does not mean that I relativize good and evil as such. I see very clearly: this is evil, but the paradox is just that for this particular person in this particular situation at this particular stage of development it may be good. Contrariwise, good at the wrong moment in the wrong place may be the worst thing possible. (para. 866)

Jung presented a harrowing example of his commitment to this idea in *The Red Book* (2009). His first visionary encounter with his soul occurred when he came upon the mutilated corpse of a young girl. A severe woman identified herself as the girl's soul and admonished him to cut out her liver and eat a piece. He resisted, but eventually he capitulated to her imploring argument that it was the only way to redeem the girl's death. Jung later described the act as having been done by evil through him (p. 323). The act was beyond his capacities, so evil accomplished it for him. When he was done, the woman identified herself as his own soul. What went unstated was the cause of the girl's horrific death. It is not hard to identify Jung's tortured relationship to the feminine as context[3] or as an unconscious evil likewise expressed throughout the first half of his life. It was a developmentally necessary evil to eat the liver or an act of incorporation of both the essence of his soul and his own destructive unconsciousness. Jung (1964b/1960) stated, "To confront a person with his shadow is to show him his own light" (para. 872). I will return to Jung's imaginal encounter with the young girl in chapter 5, as the story reflects dynamics of imaginal experience that challenge our traditional understandings of ethics.

We might imagine that conscience is the field in which that confrontation takes place, but Jung's understanding was more complex. In "A Psychological View of Conscience" (Jung, 1964a/1958), he posited that the locus of conscience is unconscious: "If conscience is a kind of knowledge, then it is not the empirical subject who is the knower, but rather an unconscious personality who, to all appearances, behaves like a conscious subject" (para. 829). Conscience is "a complex phenomenon consisting on the one hand in an elementary act of the will, or in an impulse to act for which no conscious reason can be given, and on the other hand in a judgment grounded on rational feeling" (para. 825). Conscience rights imbalance. This does not make it an agent of good but a corrective to the excesses of the ego. The ego, in Jung's view, is boundless in its capacity for self-aggrandizement. The conscience is a function of the larger psyche, which arises when the "acquisitive greed of the ego" (para. 829) must be checked. Moreover, the conscience is a feeling, not an intellectual conclusion. Conscience is a compelling experience that comes unbidden.

Why must conscience be unconscious? If it were conscious, we would have more luck reshaping our psyches to fit our models. Augustine would not have just accepted responsibility for his dreams but would have had the capacity to assert control over them. Jung (1964a/1958) stated that we cannot control the psyche: "It is nature, and though nature can, by skill, knowledge, and patience, be modified at a few points, it cannot be changed into something artificial without profound injury to our humanity" (para. 831).

Jung (1964a/1958) maintained that morality is a universal dimension of human psychic functioning, whereas a moral code is a specific cultural product or a set of mores that both reflects the unconscious and is separate from it. Moral codes appear in conscious discourse as "a late concomitant of moral behavior, congealed into precepts" (para. 837), and because each one bears the appearance of the cultural unconscious that birthed it, it "evokes the impression that the moral code also controls the unconscious" (para. 833). When the priorities of conscience mirror those of the moral code, conscience appears identical with collective morality, but it is unquestionably distinct. When we experience what Jung called a "conflict of duty" (para.

837), conscience pops into relief. It is "a psychic reaction which one can call moral because it always appears when the conscious mind leaves the path of custom, of the mores, or suddenly recollects it" (para. 855). Jung used the dramatic example of a person caught between the moral prohibition against lying and the urgent need to lie to keep someone from grievous harm. Religiously conservative parents who experience a conflict between moral prohibitions against homosexuality and the discovery that one of their children is gay face a similar choice. Whatever they do, the old way of being is betrayed: if they affirm traditional values, they betray their identity as good parents along with the child; if they affirm the child's experience, then they believe themselves to be undermining fundamental structures of personal and collective meaning.

The ethical begins in a conflict between irreconcilable opposites. Conscience may evoke the conflict, but it does not necessarily resolve it. Conscience is a "reaction to a real or supposed deviation from the moral code, and it is for the most part identical with the primitive fear of anything unusual, not customary, and hence 'immoral'" (Jung, 1964a/1958, para. 855). A so-called *attack of conscience* is just that: an involuntary imposition. To react to conscience by conforming one's behavior to the moral code may alleviate the uncomfortable experience, but it does not reflect any kind of developmental achievement. The father who shuns his lesbian daughter because he is afraid of divine punishment remains unconscious, if not also a coward. Yet he could shun his daughter in an action that responds to the urging of conscience. By the same token, however, conscience can speak against a prevailing moral code. Proulx (1994) suggested that such a moral reaction "takes hold of someone and causes him/her to spurt out that 'this is wrong'" (p. 108). Experiences of conscience are no more or less than irruptions from the unconscious. If every psychic process is imaginal, then so is this irruption. The ethical speaks in the imaginal register.

When conscience speaks in opposition to a moral code, the individual is caught in a dilemma. The most direct way out of the dilemma is to choose one or the other path and accept the harm that comes with the choice by "suppressing one of the opposites" (Jung, 1964a/1958, para. 856). Conscience becomes ethical when it stays in the dilemma and becomes conscious of its irreconcilability. Somewhat misleadingly, Proulx (1994) suggested that what Jung (1964a/1958) called *ethical* is "a judgment that someone makes after an elaborate consideration of all possibilities" (Proulx, 1994, p. 108), which implies a coolly intellectual process. Later, however, she noted that an experience of the ethical conscience is numinous: "A person is asked by what appears to be the Voice of God to do something which goes against the moral code" (p. 112). Ultimately, an ethical reaction to a dilemma involves one's suffering the conflict rather than succumbing to an amputation that avoids a direct confrontation with our ambivalence. Jung (1964a/1958) stated, "If one is sufficiently conscientious the conflict is endured to the end,

76 Imagining ethics

and a creative solution emerges" (para. 856). Only from this suffering can a solution emerge that "is in accord with the deepest foundations of the personality as well as with its wholeness; it embraces conscious and unconscious and therefore transcends the ego" (para. 856). Ethical conscience, Jung believed, is the only genuine conscience because, as noted by Proulx (1994), "something new and essential" (p. 114) is happening when we suffer the conflict of the opposites. That new something is what emerges via the transcendent function.

We are ethical when we consciously suffer the unmade, impossible choice. It runs counter to our inclination on many levels. We want to avoid suffering, appear decisive, and respect collective values. We want to stay within the herd, because our leaving places our safety at hazard. When we are ethical, we hold rather than divide. We are fertilized by these opposites in the womb of the psyche, and the solution must grow within us before it can be birthed in pain and blood.

By invoking the transcendent function, Jung placed the exercise of ethical conscience at the center of his developmental model and his understanding of psychopathology. In his foreword to Neumann's *Depth Psychology and a New Ethic* (1969/1949), Jung wrote, "The chief causes of a neurosis are conflicts of conscience and difficult moral problems that require an answer" (Jung, 1969a/1949, p. 11). In "A Psychological Approach to the Dogma of the Trinity" (Jung, 1969b/1948), Jung wrote, "Individuation is an exceedingly difficult task: it always involves a conflict of duties, whose solution requires us to understand that our 'counter-will' is also an aspect of God's will" (para. 292). Each developmental transition we face involves a reconciliation of the foundations of meaning that have structured one's life with the contrary movement of psyche that threatens to destroy those foundations. Caught between stagnation and annihilation, the ethical, developmental choice is a nonchoice: that is, not to do nothing but to act by inaction, to bear the counterintuitive and countercultural burden of an uncertain stillness.

Jung and Neumann on ethics

Jung's only direct statement on ethics appeared as the foreword to Israeli analyst Erich Neumann's work *Depth Psychology and a New Ethic* (1969/1949). The psychological trope of the unconscious—which, it should be noted, is central to depth psychological models of the psyche but not necessarily to contemporary cognitive-behaviorism or other theories—upends fantasies of self-discipline and control that go hand-in-glove with traditional ethical theory. Jung's position was a pragmatic acknowledgment that there is little the psychotherapist can do to change the moral disposition of a client: "Having learnt by long and often painful experience the relative ineffectiveness of trying to inculcate moral precepts, he has to abandon all admonitions and exhortations that begin with 'ought' and 'must'" (1969a/1949, p. 11).

Indeed, Jung (1969a/1949) stated openly that the implications of his thought render ethical codes the product of an earlier era that we have left behind: "The formulation of ethical rules is not only difficult but actually impossible because one can hardly think of a single rule that would not have to be reversed under certain conditions" (p. 13). Ethical codes are not artificial creations of the conscious mind imposed from without, as from a "crabbed grandfather," in Jung's (1969a/1949, p. 15) wryly funny phrase; they too reflect unconscious, archetypal dynamics. Their archetypal and thus collective nature, however, does not make them universally applicable to all situations and in all contexts.

We remain on the cusp of the era of a new ethic, and Jung (1969a/1949) invoked one of the shadows of his psychology; that is, an elitism that maintains a quasilegitimacy for the old ethical codes as guides for those unable to move into the new era of idiosyncratic personal responsibility for one's ethical vision. He wrote that the new ethic is the provenance only of "those uncommon individuals who, driven by unavoidable conflicts of duty, endeavour to bring the conscious and the unconscious into responsible relationship" (p. 15). It is far more common for individuals to choose artificially between conflicting options, and those who choose against existing moral codes suffer guilt and a range of social consequences.

The new ethic involves a discernment process that varies for each individual. The principal concern is the dethronement of ego from the center of the psyche, a monarch in a "totalitarian" regime (Jung, 1969a/1949, p. 18). The new ethic means one must allow the unconscious room for expression in the solution to the conflict. What Jung did not suggest, although it seems implicit in his metaphor, is the establishment of a democracy of psyche. The move is from a partial ego position to a whole psychic position. Jung seems to have been trapped by his reliance on binary oppositions, which are perhaps inextricably embedded in his theory: "Life is a continual balancing of opposites, like every other energic process. The abolition of opposites would be equivalent to death" (p. 15). The act of perception necessarily involves differentiation; each position always implies others. The question remains: are ethical conflicts always either/or? Do we impose binaries because multiplicity might seem overwhelming? Jung's larger theoretical point—that any urge toward a particular course of action masks other urges or other courses of action that must be considered and included consciously for an authentic solution to emerge—remains valid if we shift our metaphor from simple opposition to a broader competition. Indeed, Jung suggested that one's recognizing and attempting to integrate the unconscious in ethical reflection creates a situation that "is so complicated, delicate, and difficult" that our old attempts to advise along proscribed lines—to say "you ought"—is impossible (p. 15). Oppositions, however emotionally intense, are not complicated.

In the text that follows Jung's foreword, Neumann (1969/1949) pointed out that such oppositions, and the conflict between them, provide the foundation of the old, superseded ethic (p. 45). Neumann's volume is likely the most influential text on ethics in the Jungian analytic tradition; it has been cited by many post-Jungian ethical theorists (Becker, 2004; Proulx, 1994; Robinson, 2005; Stein, 1993, Zoja, 2007). Written in Israel during and just after World War II, Neumann's project was driven by the urgent need to interrogate the Western ethical tradition in light of its utter failure to prevent the Holocaust: "Have problems of ethics or even of a 'new' ethic any relevance at all in an age dominated by a dance of death, to which National Socialism in Germany was little more than a prelude?" (p. 19).

Neumann's (1969/1949) thought reflects the ideas articulated by Jung in his preface. Neumann was principally concerned with the psychic amputations that invariably happen when an individual tries to conform to a collective set of values. What we exclude with the use of the mechanisms of repression and suppression creates a tension that is unleashed on the individual and the collective alike. We cannot avoid acknowledging our most uncomfortable desires. Time and again in the Jungian theoretical tradition, writers have argued that the Jungian developmental process is at the same time a necessary ethical process.[4] The consequences of failure are dire: "The further progress of mankind will in fact depend, to no small degree, on whether it proves possible to prevent the occurrence of this splitting process in the psyche" (p. 58).

Neumann's (1969/1949) old ethic derived from Greek and Judeo-Christian sources: "A codified and transmittable value which governs human conduct in a 'universal' manner" (p. 33). He laid the blame for the mass conflict of the first half of the 20th century on the conflicts created by this old ethic within binaries. It is a "partial" ethic (p. 74); in a noteworthy passage, Neumann suggested that a classic example of the old ethic is Augustine's oft-referenced argument that he is not responsible for what he does in dreams. For Neumann, this was exactly the problem; we must "take into consideration [and] evaluate the tendencies and effects of the unconscious" (p. 74).[5]

Neumann (1969/1949) developed Jung's idea of conscience[6] by discriminating between conscience (i.e., the introjected moral code of the collective) from what he termed *the Voice*. The Voice is typically heard by the founders of religions, who perceive it has having come from God (p. 62). It speaks against the collective ethical code or supersedes it. The Voice brings about the institution of a new ethic, but the natural process of human development ensures that this ethic will one day become old and need to be superseded again. Neumann termed "the psychological law of the relativity of ethical revelations" (p. 67) that process by which a new ethic is given to the inner circle of its founder, wherefrom it is passed down to the community and becomes an introjected, artificial conscience. For those who did not experience the revelation directly, the problems of conscience assert themselves: "All those forces which run counter to the revelation are suppressed or repressed" (p. 67). It becomes an old ethic.

The process of leaving behind all old ethics, then, is not collective but necessarily personal and manifests in a so-called personal crisis when one discovers that one's personality includes an *other side* that is hostile and alien to the ego: "The old idealized image of the ego has to go, and its place is shaken by a perilous insight into the ambiguity and many-sidedness of one's own nature" (p. 79). Neumann navigated the same delicate position regarding the relative nature of evil as Jung; Neumann noted that "'my' evil may not be an evil at all in my neighbor's eyes" (p. 80) and that this problem is the foundation of the crisis of conscience that each individual faces. Each of us is evil in a particular way and must accept this. If we do not, violence is the result. This process is experienced as profound ego deflation or a shift away from the spiritual heights of traditional religion to the ground of lived reality.

Neumann (1969/1949) seemed to answer the earlier-voiced objection to Jung's reliance on binaries. In the ethical, developmental process, we are trying to build a new personality, the stability of which "will be proportionate to the strength of the tension between the combined opposites and the number of the polar forces which enter into the new combination" (p. 101). It is unclear whether Neumann meant the assimilation of multiple binaries or an understanding of psychic conflict as being between multiple poles simultaneously, but his identification of "the tension between the opposites" as "the distinguishing mark of the old ethic" (p. 99) suggests a model that transcends Jung's dualisms. It is important to note the teleological character of Jung's thought and of many who have written in his tradition. What one moves toward is a mythic wholeness, wherein the disparate elements of the psyche are brought together in a harmonious unity. Neumann stated, "In this wholeness, the inherent contrast between the two systems of the conscious mind and the unconscious does not fall apart into a condition of splitness" (p. 102). Neither advocates for a true democracy of the psyche; the shadow of this fantasy of psychic wholeness is the way it lends itself to idealizations. What happens if we cannot integrate the whole? How do we distinguish this new univocality from the seeming univocality of the old, ego-centered psyche? Indeed, could this fantasy of wholeness not be quickly reimagined by the ego as an imperial ego consciousness, marshalling the disparate players in the psyche to its own agenda? This is not an old critique; the archetypal school of analytic psychology (see especially Hillman (1975)) noted that this way of understanding the psyche seems to reinforce a monotheistic religious sensibility: we seek wholeness from intrapsychic connection to a Godlike Self. It is worth simply noting objections and keeping the myth of psychic wholeness in mind, as, read simplistically and unconsciously, it can inflate unreasonable expectations and mask the undramatic but necessary work of bringing the unconscious into relationship with consciousness.

80 Imagining ethics

Except for Guggenbuhl-Craig (1971), considered below, Neumann is one of the few ethical theorists I have encountered who directly addressed the ethical status of fantasy:

> Responsibility for the totality of the personality, which is demanded by the total ethic, is not confined to external reality but also covers the inner reality of dreams, fantasies, thoughts, etc. This reality of the psyche obliges us to recognise that a fantasy can have effects just as serious as those of an act—a truth which has long been taught in the Far East. ... Individuals and groups—and nations, too, and movements in history— are conditioned by the power of inner psychic realities which often enough appear in the first place as fantasies in the mind of an individual. This influence of the inner world is to be found at work in such diverse spheres as politics and religion, technology and art. War and destruction are repeatedly let loose to devastate the world at the behest of men driven by fantasies of power; at the same time, the inner images of creative artists become the cultural possession of the whole human race. (p. 107)

In this passage, fantasy itself does not have an ethical valence. Fantasies themselves are not good or bad. What matters is how they enter the collective sphere. Neumann (1969/1949) argued that our ethical responsibility is to understand the external consequences of our inner lives. This implicit dualism between inner and outer has pragmatic value; we distinguish between what we think and how we act. It is, however, also artificially clean; the fist that hits a face in actuality also hits it in fantasy. The punch always reflects the psychic experience of the person who throws it. Neumann did not prescribe how we should work with such fantasies. What is important is that we recognize the implications of our actions. The fantasy has psychic reality, and the impulse that would have destructive consequences if enacted must somehow be realized: "To realize it and to live it from within is by no means the same as simply to abreact it. The multiplicity and complexity of this situation makes any kind of theoretical proscription for ethical conduct completely impossible" (p. 107).

Ethics in analytical psychology after Jung and Neumann

To complete this brief overview of ethical theory in the tradition of analytical psychology, we consider the notion of the ethical attitude as developed by Solomon (2000, 2001) and Solomon and Twyman (2003), and elaborated and critiqued by Allphin (2005) and Sebek (2002); Luigi Zoja's (2007) articulation of the gray zone; and Guggenbuhl-Craig's (1971) reflections on the role of fantasy in the analytic relationship.

Solomon (2000, 2001) suggested that an ethical attitude is a critical dimension of the process of human development. Relying on the psychoanalytic thought of D. W. Winnicott and Melanie Klein, as well as the postmodern philosophical thought of Baumann and Levinas (to whom we turn in a later section), Solomon (2001) argued that an ethical attitude is "an active and energetic way of being, without necessarily acting, or indeed without enacting, something" (p. 443). Its development is made possible by the infant's experience of unconditioned acceptance. When, via the symbolic and literal breast, the infant experiences the Other as available without expecting the infant to respond or imposing its needs on the infant or when the mother "manage[s] internally, through her own capacity for containment ... her inevitable negative, shadow responses towards her infant" (Solomon, 2000, p. 204), the infant receives what is needed to begin to move beyond "a narcissistic mode of relating" (p. 204). This initial, preverbal experience of another's taking full and open responsibility for oneself, rather than the postverbal acquisition of an external moral code, makes one's own responsibility for others possible. Ethical development thus depends on the quality of the earliest experiences with parents. For those whose early childhood experiences were marked by empathic failures, neglect, or trauma, the development of an ethical attitude is fundamentally impaired.

So an essential task of analytically informed therapeutic work is to provide symbolic ways for the individual to have those fundamental experiences of being cared for unconditionally. Therapists' ethical attitudes—their capacity to mimic the caring parents' containment of their own needs while accepting the experience of the client, however withholding or aggressive—is not simply a means by which to reduce harm but integral to the developmental process of the client. As suggested by Solomon and Twyman (2003), "The analyst's capacity to forgo the gratification that retaliation or other libidinal enactments might bring allows the reality of the subjective Otherness of the patient to be recognised and protected. This attitude is in essence ethical" (p. 5).

Sebek (2002) and Allphin (2005) both argued that Solomon (2001) and Solomon and Twyman (2003) placed too much emphasis on early developmental experiences in shaping one's ethical perspective: "People who are understanding, attuned, and helpful to others—for example, many therapists—were not infrequently treated terribly as children. It does not always follow that good early care is the main basis for developing an ethical attitude" (Allphin, 2005, p. 455). Allphin made an interesting distinction between the ethical attitude and the analytic attitude, in which the ethical attitude emerges when one faces a dilemma; this dilemma is usually one that involves a conflict with an external authority, such as professional codes of ethics. Citing Beebe's (1992) notion of a *dialetic of integrity*, Allphin (2005) noted that the experience of the ethical attitude is marked by an uncomfortable inner dialogue, an "endless self questioning" (p. 459) that does not have an easy resolution.

82 Imagining ethics

Jung's distinctive contribution to theory regarding the development of the ethical attitude, in Solomon's (2001) and Solomon and Twyman's (2003) views, is the concept of the shadow and the teleological movement in the development of psyche. The core developmental task of bringing what is potential in the individual into actuality is always already an ethical task, as what is potential is so often threatening to the current ego position. The shadow, which contains "what is treacherous and subversive—what is unethical—in the self, and hides it" (Solomon, 2001, p. 199), must be examined and integrated for development to progress. Jung's myth of the teleological movement toward wholeness demands this exceedingly difficult work of recognizing our own destructive, unethical capacities and understanding them as fundamentally and necessarily ours.

Zoja's (2007) elegant reflections on psychotherapeutic ethics examine the archetypal underpinnings of our ethical discourse. He argued that an archetypal "universal longing for justice" (p. 8) precedes and extends beyond the common understanding of ethics as a set of mutually agreed-upon rules. The Greeks, he suggested, believed that ethics and aesthetics are inextricably tied in the concept of excellence. This loss of emphasis on beauty is part of a wider cultural shift away from the contemplation and encouragement of beauty in community and toward an entertainment that increasingly occurs in isolation, on flat screens that continue to multiply exponentially. Our ethics cannot be understood outside of their cultural context; "this comprehensive fact about our common life plays a role in the diffusion of senseless unethical behavior" (p. 16). Like the other theorists we have considered, Zoja understood psychotherapeutic ethics to inform the whole of ethics rather than simply that of the consulting room. The unique contribution of a depth psychological perspective on ethics is its notion of the shadow or the ways in which each of us must be responsible not only for our intended actions but also for what is unexamined within us and what others suffer that we do not intend.

Zoja's (2007) core trope is the gray zone. Like Neumann (1969/1949), Zoja was concerned with the urgent need to revise ethics radically following the Holocaust. We are always already compromised; we cannot live according to a standard of perfection, and we participate powerlessly in institutional evils. Acknowledgment of our powerlessness does not, however, rob us of our responsibility. Zoja's example of the "prototypical gray" (p. 54) person is a figure from the life of author and Holocaust survivor Primo Levi, a manager in a concentration camp factory who was "incapable of criticizing the rules he was carrying out" and also "incapable ... of ignoring the suffering of the camp victims and enduring his corresponding guilt feelings" (p. 54). The man's position suggests the inevitable complexity and imperfection of any ethical inquiry. The man could exist only in the gray zone. The task of analytical psychology is "the deepening of consciousness" (p. 55) so that we might "ease our inner contradictions" (p. 56). The gray zone is "the ethical

Imagining ethics 83

territory par excellence" where "we will never be able to claim that we have found the final truth, yet we shall always find ourselves standing in the landscape that is most apt for ethical elaboration" (p. 66).

Although he did not explicitly invoke professional ethics, Guggenbuhl-Craig's (1971) reflections on the role of power in therapeutic work includes incisive commentary on the ways that the fantasies of helping professionals can have profound implications for those in their care. He differentiated "creative fantasies" (p. 45) from countertransferential projections, which relate primarily or exclusively to the psychic experience of the professional and say little, in Guggenbühl-Craig's view, about the client. A creative fantasy, however, is a reflection of the relationship between client and analyst, and the analyst's creative fantasy about a client involves "circling around his potential" (p. 45). Analysts' positive fantasies about their client can contain important suggestions about the future development of the client, as discussed in chapter 1 in reflections on the relationship between Ramona and Mason. Like a parent whose fantasies about her child's future may emerge out of the parent's true perception of the child's strengths and desires, the analyst's fantasies can be important incubators for the new lives their clients cannot imagine for themselves. Guggenbul-Craig underscored the ongoing fantasy process as neither inherently good or problematic but as always needing reflection and review. The therapist is just as likely as the parent to be dazzled by one potential future to the exclusion of all others. The ethical imperative is to understand that fantasy is always happening (we are always imagining each other and acting on the basis of those fantasies) and to examine how our fantasies influence our work.

Social constructionism and the universalizing impulse

Can contemporary ethics rest on an irreducible foundation in human nature? Is there a way to articulate transcultural and transhistorical ethical principles, or are ethical potentials, like ethical codes, always bound by language and locality? The shade of relativism hangs over contemporary discourse on ethics. Although the impact on ethical discourse of existential-phenomenological and social constructionist psychological theories deserves a more substantial treatment, the dialogue between Brinkmann (2006) and Gergen (2006) offers a window on humanistic psychological conversations about the possibility of articulating a worthy foundation for ethical theory.

Writing in the existential-phenomenological tradition, Brinkmann (2006) articulated a succinct summary of social constructionist theory and its implications for ethics. Four constructionist notions form the backbone of his summary: "a) flexible identities and identity-morphing, b) the denial of the tragic, c) the decline of the referentials, and d) a general aesthetization

84 Imagining ethics

of life" (p. 94). Each of these ideas is described in turn and linked with a movement in contemporary consumer culture that Brinkmann found objectionable. Brinkmann's vision of social construction is a theory that renders all discourse open to revision in a creative, forward-looking exploration of possibility without grounding in an irreducible facticity. All concepts are provisional; all perspectives are valid locally. Some cultures worship cows; others eat them. What emerges from social constructionist thought is an "ethics of infinitude" that "promotes limitless possibilities, incessant change, persistent instability, and fleeting preferences" (p. 94). Brinkmann argued forcefully that the universal reality of mortality and interdependency precede any constructed experience and as such make possible "solidarity, compassion, and care of the other person" (p. 95), which are the essential elements of ethics.

The crux of Brinkmann's (2006) critique of Gergen (2006) and social constructionism is a seemingly unbridgeable divide. Brinkmann suggested,

> By questioning all givennness, social constructionism becomes unable to understand the ethical dimensions of human life. … If the social constructionist project is antifoundational, I would say that the existential-phenomenological project is not so much foundational as it is anti-antifoundational. (p. 106)

Either one takes the position that human experience includes irreducibly common features, or one does not. Gergen, for his part, agreed that the social constructionist position means that "all attempts to generate ethical foundations may be inimical to human life" (p. 119). After agreeing with much of Brinkmann's characterization of his thought, Gergen related that he found Brinkmann "a careful and caring expositor of these texts" (p. 123). Gergen argued that Brinkmann's desire to articulate "yet another foundation for good behavior" (p. 124) forced him into a false dichotomy: "Declarations such as his, of essential, undeniable, unconstructed realities serve as the rhetorical grounds for virtually all moral codes. … Yet all declarations of this sort create an exterior, that which is evil, reprehensible, and loathsome" (p. 124).

Stasis and finality are the enemies of social constructionist discourse. Its ethics, in Gergen's (2006) vision, lies precisely in its refusal to accept any articulation of ethics as complete. We must always consider what is rejected in our vision, as we can never see the whole. This shares resonances with the Jungian perspective articulated thus far. The crux of a Jungian ethics is shadow integration, which is the process by which we give space for the unconscious to become conscious. That unconscious is theoretically inexhaustible; we can never know everything about our own motivations, let alone about those of the others we encounter ethically. The perspectives that, from a social constructionist frame, lie outside of current discourse are likewise inexhaustible. The dynamic Jungian psyche never comes to a position of final equilibrium but is a movement toward equilibrium. This leans toward essentialism, as does archetypal theory; Jung's reading of myths across culture and era is squarely essentialist and ethically problematic.[7] Jung sat on the border of modernity and postmodernity, but it is useful to notice that a Jungian ethics, at least as has been articulated in this brief treatment, reflects the same dynamism as the Jungian psyche and can remain nimble and responsive to what continues to emerge afresh into psyche, culture, and discourse.

Levinas and postmodern philosophical ethics

What do we lose when we accept social constructionism's refusal to ground ethics in a theorized essential truth about human nature? What happens when all ethics are truly local and provisional? Gergen (2006) used charged imagery to attack Brinkmann's (2006) notion that awareness of mortality is a universal condition for the development of ethics: a conceptually meaningless death might as easily lead the Columbine High School shooters to their horrific conclusions as it would toward an awareness of our shared suffering and uncertainty. Both imply that the other's position can lead toward a dangerous disengagement with the Other: Brinkmann on the grounds that social constructionism denies the shared dimension of our experience and Gergen on the grounds that any foundational assertion blinds us to the infinite possibility of the human and the singularity of the Other before us.

Both perspectives reflect an attempt to orient us or to allay the profound anxiety that elicits and answers the questions above. However Gergen (2006) might have praised Brinkmann for the use of social constructionist inquiry to analyze itself, Gergen remained committed to the frame. Social constructionism cannot, it seems, be taken apart in such a way that exposes its local and provisional nature and to the hope it inspired in him: "So long as the dialogue among differences is sustained, ethics will always be in the making" (p. 124). Each of these perspectives has a personal, psychological role to play for the theorist.

Brinkmann (2006), along with some of the theorists discussed so far (Solomon, 2001; Zoja, 2007), and other Jungian theorists such as Hillman (1999), Cohen (2008), and Brooks (2013), have referenced the philosophical thought of Emmanuel Levinas as an important contemporary discursive partner outside of the realm of depth psychology. Levinas' work (1985, 1989/1984, 2008) resists superficial treatment. Perhaps the most important ethical theorist in the continental tradition, Levinas holds particular appeal for psychotherapists because he placed responsibility for the Other prior even to ontology. Before we are, we relate, or we come into being as the result of an encounter with a specific Other, a Face, in Levinas' conceptual language. As argued by Gantt (2000), the therapist bears a "fundamental

86 Imagining ethics

responsibility … to suffer-with and suffer-for the client" (p. 12). So do we all, Levinas would have argued.

Like Neumann, Zoja, and many ethical theorists in the 20th century, Levinas' thought was inextricably related to the Holocaust and the phenomena of manmade mass death.[8] He was affected by the Holocaust on a profoundly personal level. His immediate family went into hiding, members of his extended family died in camps, and Levinas himself was interned in a prisoner of war camp for five years (Morgan, 2011). Heidegger, who notoriously served actively in the National Socialist party, influenced Levinas indelibly, leading him to mount a fundamental challenge to Heidegger's ontology (Morgan, 2011). The meaning of the Holocaust lies in its utter ruination of theodicy; no defense of the divine is allowable when confronted by such meaningless death (Morgan, 2011).

What Levinas (1989/1984) proposed is difficult to accept. Our responsibility for each other does not arise out of a moral good articulated in community and internalized as in a Freudian superego. This responsibility precedes thought, consciousness, and being and indeed is "otherwise than being," a phrase that serves as the title of a late work (Levinas, 2008). As he put it,

> Responsibility for the Other, for the naked face of the first individual to come along. A responsibility that goes beyond what I may or may not have done to the Other or whatever acts I may or may not have committed, as if I were devoted to the other man before being devoted to myself. Or more exactly, as if I had to answer for the other's death even before *being*. A guiltless responsibility, whereby I am none the less open to an accusation of which no alibi, spatial or temporal, could clear me. … A responsibility stemming from a time before my freedom— before my (*moi*) beginning, before any present. (1989/1984, pp. 83–84, emphasis in original)

Levinas (1985, 1989/1984, 2008) admitted no escape into an original self, a privileged interiority from which one can choose one's engagements. The paradoxicality of a "guiltless responsibility" that is yet unavoidable suggests the radicality of Levinas' vision. It would be easy to understand Levinas to intend that our being is always a being-for-the-other or that our responsibility is never to ourselves. Morgan (2011) pointed out that failure seems certain in Levinas' ethics and that one must be "a sinner all the time" (p. 12). Cohen (1985) summarized Levinas' position: "Ethical priority, according to Levinas, occurs as the moral height of the other person over being, essence, identity, manifestation, principles, in brief, over me" (p. 10). This relationship is asymmetrical. The Other's responsibility to me, as *her* Other, is not accessible to me: "It is precisely insofar as the relationship between the other and me is not reciprocal that I am subjection to the Other; and I am 'subject' essentially in this sense. It is I who support all" (Levinas, 1985, p. 98).

Levinas wrestled with an ethical reality present in the clinical encounter, whether we clinicians consider it consciously or not. How does the person sitting across from me relate to what I perceive of them? How can I remain aware that the images I form of them in my mind are *separate* from them, do not begin to encompass them in their fullness? In the early essay "Is Ontology Fundamental?" he wrote:

> By relating to beings in the openness of being, understanding finds a meaning for them in terms of being. In this sense, understanding does not invoke them, but only names them. And thus, with regard to beings, understanding carries out an act of violence and of negation. A partial negation, which is violence. And this partialness can be described by the fact that, without disappearing, beings are in my power. The partial negation which is violence denies the independence of beings: they are mine. Possession is the mode by which a being, while existing, is partially denied. (1998a/1951, p. 7)

When we sit across from other human beings and experience—and express—understanding, we foreclose some portion of them that escapes us (perhaps the whole of them), and we put what they have expressed under our control.

Recently, I resumed work with a client who had been absent from my practice for several years. As she re-presented herself, I noted the intensity of her speech and the anxious rush of her need to express. A clinical voice within me began to label: *racing thoughts, flight of ideas, mania*. I wondered whether I'd missed diagnosing her with bipolar disorder when we last worked together, and how her psychiatrist had diagnosed her. I was worried for her, and also worried for myself: Could I manage her treatment? Had I failed her all those years I was working with her?

Not long afterwards, I started a course of training in trauma-informed care. The trainer suggested the use of the Adverse Childhood Experiences questionnaire, among other instruments, and proposed that we race to psychiatric diagnosis too quickly. This is a perspective that normally I share; diagnosis is a form of understanding in the Levinasian sense, one that obscures as often as it reveals or clarifies. In my rush to contain my own anxiety, though, I knew I had leapt to a preliminary diagnosis. We often miss trauma, the trainer told us, because we race to capture clients' behavior in our diagnostic framework. My "bipolar" client might be better understood—and more accurately diagnosed—in relation to her traumatic history. In session, I administered the ACE questionnaire. The results were shocking to both of us: out of ten questions assessing potentially traumatic childhood events, she affirmed all of them. An ACE score of 10. Through the use of that instrument, the client was able to recall events that had been outside of her accessible memory, that she could not have understood as

88 Imagining ethics

psychologically damaging until framed that way in the consulting room. The intensity of her self-blame, the constant agonized stream of worry about her failure to fix her own "craziness," began to ease, at least temporarily. The trauma trainer repeated a mantra, which I gave to my client: *It is not what's wrong with you. It's what was done to you.*[9]

But there is that word "understood" lurking in this new therapeutic narrative. What do I "understand" about her? "Trauma" can foreclose other experiences of her. It can lead the two of us to think of her as a "victim," a "survivor." In Levinas' sense, I possess her in a way that violates her as a person. She infinitely escapes an understanding that believes itself to be complete, and when I "treat" her with my knowledge of her, I run the significant risk of blinding myself and harming her.

This is not to say that the treatment is not helpful. It is rather to say that, to practice psychotherapy—attention to the soul—entails a constant risk that we will reduce the Other and deny the radicality of their difference. A partial negation, in Levinas' language. Our capacity to remain aware of our work as fictive, of our experience of the Other as forever, necessarily provisional, is a profound ethical task. A task that is never completed, an obligation never exhausted. Again, Levinas:

> It is like an animal fleeing in a straight line across the snow before the sound of the hunters, thus leaving the very traces that will lead to its death. Thus we are responsible beyond our intentions. It is impossible for the attention directing the act to avoid inadvertent action. We get caught up in things; things turn against us. That is to say that our consciousness, and our mastery of reality through consciousness, do not exhaust our relationship with reality, in which we are present with all the density of our being. (1998a/1951, p. 3)

Harrington (2002) asked a fundamental question regarding how psychology might approach Levinas' thought: "Does Levinas describe an 'is' or preach an 'ought'?" (p. 218). Because for Levinas ethics is prior to thought and speech, can we talk sensibly about how it might influence the thinking and speaking of psychotherapy? To Harrington, what Levinas prescribed is a challenge to those who devise and practice psychotherapies to release the radical alterity of our clients from our systems: "to consciously allow people to evade our conceptual taxonomies" (p. 221). Levinas provided not a *how* or a *what* but a *why* for psychology.

Indeed, Levinas was specifically critical of psychoanalytic approaches to the human, the conceptual taxonomies that we constantly risk reifying:

> The non-philosophical end result of psychoanalysis consists in a predilection for some fundamental, but elementary, fables—the libido, sadism, or masochism, the Oedipus complex, repression of the origin,

aggressivity—which incomprehensibly, would alone be unequivocal, alone in not translating (or masking or symbolizing) a reality more profound than themselves: the end terms of psychological intelligibility. The fact of their having been collected from among the debris of the most diverse civilizations and called myths adds nothing to their worth as clarifying ideas, and at most evinces a return to the mythologies, which is even more amazing since forty centuries of monotheism have had no other goal than to liberate humanity from their obsessive grip. Still, the petrifying effect of myths must be distinguished from the comfort they are thought to offer the intelligence. (1998b/1954, p. 31)

Levinas' reading of psychoanalysis here is loaded and lacking in nuance, but his point is, as ever, that our race to understand obscures our relating with the Other. We hear in this passage his disdain for myth, which analytical psychology treats with reverence as a window onto the unconscious. Myths are, of course, non-philosophical, speaking the language of something pre-philosophical, even extra-philosophical: image and the soul. The power of the core Levinasian trope of the *face-to-face,* for instance, lies in its quality as an image.

Levinas' resistance to psychoanalysis in the passage does not mean that his thought cannot influence the practice and ethical theory of psychotherapy. Gantt (2000) used Levinas' work to criticize a psychotherapy that mimics the medical model. A therapy influenced by Levinas would prioritize over all clinical techniques the experience of "suffering-with" a client: "a supremely concerned moment of un-concern in which we abandon the vain justifications of our professional self-indulgences and, in their stead, offer up ourselves in ethical response to the plea of the suffering other we find before us" (p. 22). This suffering-with is not then the master technique, justified by its outcomes, but instead a fundamental obligation to respond to suffering. It is worth noting that Gantt's discourse has the form of *ought,* in Harrington's sense; we do not necessarily experience ourselves as existentially compelled to respond to suffering without the prompting of Gantt's appropriated Levinas.

Along with Zoja (2007), who suggested that Jung, like Levinas, placed ethical reflection at the center of human experience, other writers in the Jungian tradition have been influenced by Levinas' thought. Cohen (2008) tended to appropriate Levinas as an *ought*: "We must never forget the basic responsibility to the Other, never forget to be hospitable to the stranger, the widow, the orphan" (p. 37). Curiously without citation, she suggested that "Levinas says the self *must* first be nurtured in order to then nurture the Other" (p. 38, emphasis in original), which is a psychotherapeutic truism that cries out for textual support. Levinas can be deployed therapeutically, Cohen argued, when working with self-absorbed clients who need reminding of the fundamental intersubjectivity of their existence. She also made unsubstantiated connections between Levinasian and Jungian theory, suggesting that Levinas understood ethics to be "instinctual and archetypal" (p. 39).

Brooks (2013) took a different approach, using Levinasian theory to critique vividly Jungian epistemological assumptions and the ethical implications of the failure to adjust theory accordingly. She characterized analytical psychology as "both belonging and not belonging to the era of modernity in which it was born or to the post-modernity in which we find ourselves now" (p. 82). Brooks was particularly concerned with the totalizing tendency in Jung's thought, which plays out in an archetypal theory that can be used to impose meanings on the clinical other. Although analytic dream interpretation begins with the collection of personal associations to the dream, thus staying close to the experience of the other, the client would often then be "held hostage to Jung's analytical sovereignty" (p. 82) when he chose to make archetypal interpretations. Brooks recounted a poignant and difficult clinical encounter with the radical suffering of a client, to which the only ethical response could be silent witnessing. Like Gantt (2000), Brooks (2013) was drawn to the fundamental importance of the response to the Other's suffering. When we impose our own stories, desires, and therapeutic goals on others, we fail in our ethical responsibility to their Otherness: "What the Levinasian sensibility has to offer us, in my reading of him, has more to do with bearing the affect of enigmatic primal trauma without attempting to concretize it through interpretation" (p. 94).

Toward an ethics of the imagination

How are all ethics local? My grandmother's scrupulosity emerged in multiple contexts. One of these was a biological inheritance that may or may not be literal context for my own inquiry but certainly motivates it symbolically. It may be that medical science will sooner or later provide a detailed mapping of that context and a discursive explanation of it, one that might allay some anxiety or provide some sense of control of one's fate. My suspicion is that it will remain one explanation among others, however, and that the yearning for a structuring, or at least reassuring, narrative for the encounter with existential anxiety will continue.

Our choices make us who we are. This cliché loses its banality in the particularity of an individual life—at least when considered by the one living it. When I was 21, I traveled by Greyhound bus from Houston to Connecticut to intern with a radical Catholic priest and liberation theologian for part of the summer. Overnight, my future narrowed to a choice between righteous renunciation and a consumerist comfort that required permanent moral blinders. An impossible choice. A wife always eventually appeared in my fantasies of a missionary life in Central America. I saw myself both as destined for moral failure—at least according to the standard of the Catholic priesthood—and as authentically responding to the call of another life. I stayed with my girlfriend in Houston, who has now become my wife and mother of our child. My choice remains a nonchoice. It frames my life, a tension of opposites. When I read Flannery O'Conner's *Wise Blood*, I instantly recognized Hazel Mote's Jesus, who moved "from tree to tree in the back of his mind, a wild ragged figure motioning him to turn around and come off into the dark" (O'Conner, 2007). Hazel could not avoid him, however he tried. That Jesus chased my father, too, though I could not see it until the last weeks of his life.

Jung's psychology reckons with the shade of his father's Christianity. His response to an orienting myth that had ossified into cold abstraction was to plunge into his own visionary depths and to relocate the heart of the religious impulse in experience. Many wild, ragged figures populate Jung's *The Red Book* (2009). Jung's solution to the ethical dilemmas we face—to hold the tension of opposites—reflects a hard-won humility before impossible choice. In his vision, we cannot avoid suffering our contradictions.

Further, we cannot avoid our inherent intersubjectivity. Levinas' (1985, 1989/1984, 2008) radical location of ethical commitment prior to existence reflects the simplest truth of our origins. We came into existence as a result of relationship: the union of biological father and mother, sperm and egg. We are always already related. We cannot escape our obligation to the Other, nor can we fulfill our commitment to Otherness. It necessarily transcends the old ethics and demands a new, highly personal and endlessly revised ethical attitude. The request that the Other makes of us is mute and outside of the tidy ethical rules that shelter us from suffering as often as they compel us to act. Levinas' student, the postmodern theorist Zygmunt Bauman (1993), wrote that this request,

> unlike the comfortably precise order, is abominably vague, confused and confusing, indeed barely audible. It forces the moral self to be her own interpreter, and—as with all interpreters—remain forever unsure of the correctness of interpretation. However radical the interpretation, one can never be fully convinced that it matched the radicality of the demand. I have done this, but could I not do more? There is no convention, no rule to draw the boundary of my duty, to offer peace of mind in exchange for my consent never to trespass. (p. 80)

As we turn to an articulation of an ethical approach to imaginal experience, we understand that our ethical obligations, by their nature, can never be fulfilled and that no code or procedure can ensure our salvation. We see this clearly in the context of typical psychological discourse about ethics or the profession's concern with the behavior of its practitioners. Zoja (2007) pointed to the paradoxicality inherent in ethics investigations among psychoanalysts. The analytic attitude of uncovering and accepting what is hidden is contradicted by the need to come to a judgment: "Both parties involved in such a procedure evidently believe in analytical values and in Neumann's new ethics, otherwise one would not have become an analyst and the other would not have entered analysis" (p. 72). To reach a decision, however, "they are compelled, to a very large extent, to betray their shared belief" (p. 72). This is the meaning of applied ethical discernment: a conflict of ideals, negotiated settlements, disappointment and dis-illusion. It is precisely in this limitation that our need for the ethical imagination is disclosed.

Notes

1. Dostoyevsky's *Notes from the Underground* (1992/1864) critiqued the Socratic notion that one will do the good if one only knows it; this is a fantasy that cannot help but drive liberal education. Dostoyevsky viewed history as a theatre of conscious human choices of what is convenient and evil over what is inconvenient and good.
2. It is worth noting, however, that the notion of God for Jung did not necessarily mean the Yahweh of the Old Testament nor the good Father of the New. Jung included an image of the Gnostic god Abraxas in a mandala drawn in 1916. Abraxas appears significantly in Jung's Seven Sermons of the Dead, published in *Memories, Dreams, Reflections* (2011): "Hard to know is the deity of Abraxas. Its power is the greatest, because man perceiveth it not. From the sun he draweth the *summum bonum*; from the devil the *infimum malum*; but from Abraxas LIFE, altogether indefinite, the mother of good and evil" (p. 412). Abraxas is the god beneath the poles of good and evil.
3. Ulanov (2013) suggested that Jung's "neglected feminine" (p. 34) is apparent in this passage.
4. A good example is Becker (2004).
5. The tendency to understand the ego as wholly in control of action is deeply rooted in Christian theology. In Romans, Paul argued that we do not do the good out of akrasia (i.e., the dilatory nature of the will). The autonomous unconscious and its tendency to impose agendas upon us that we would not consciously choose is nowhere to be found.
6. It is worth noting that Jung would not publish his essay on conscience for nearly a decade following Neumann's (1969/1949) original publication of this work. Gerhard Adler's preface noted that it was the first of Neumann's works to be published, in German, and it was controversial in Germany.
7. Zoja (2007) forcefully critiqued this tendency of Jungian writers as "recapitulat[ing] the practices of colonialism: using our privileged position, we Westerners 'rape' … some culturally rich but economically poor society, and (ab)use its mythology for our own interest" (p. 91).
8. See Wyschogrod (1985) for a review of the philosophical roots of these events and their impact on subsequent theory.
9. I am grateful to the Houston Galveston Trauma Institute (Rosalie Hyde, Naomi Rosborough, and Jean Goodwin) for their excellent training and for this insight, which they attribute to John Briere.

References

Allphin C. (2005). An ethical attitude in the analytic relationship. *Journal of Analytical Psychology, 50*(4), 451–468.
Bauman, Z. (1993). *Postmodern ethics.* Malden, MA: Blackwell.

Imagining ethics   93

Becker, C. (2004). *The heart of the matter: Individuation as an ethical process.* Wilmette, IL: Chiron.

Beebe, J. (1992). *Integrity in depth.* College Station, TX: Texas A&M Press.

Blake, W. (1994). *The marriage of heaven and hell: A facsimile in full color* (Dover Fine Art, History of Art). Dover Publications. Kindle Edition. (Original work published 1794)

Brinkmann, S. (2006). Questioning constructivism: Toward an ethics of finitude. *Journal of Humanistic Psychology, 46*(1), 92–111. doi: 10.1177/0022167805281231

Brooks, R. (2013). The ethical dimensions of life and analytic work through a Levinasian lens. *International Journal of Jungian Studies, 5*(1), 81–99.

Clifford, W. (1886). On the scientific basis of morals. *Lectures and essays, by the late William Kingdon Clifford* (2nd ed.; pp. 287–299). London, UK: Macmillan.

Cohen, B. (2008). The trace of the face of God: Emmanuel Levinas and depth psychology. *Jung Journal: Culture and Psyche, 2*(2), 30–45). Retrieved from http://dx.doi.org/10.1525/jung.2008.2.2.30

Cohen, R. (1985). Translator's note. In E. Levinas (Ed.), *Ethics and infinity: Conversations with Philippe Nemo* (pp. 1–15). Pittsburgh, PA: Duquesne University Press.

Dostoyevsky, F. (1992). *Notes from the underground* (Constance Garnett, Trans.). New York, NY: Dover. (Original work published 1864)

Ethic. (2014). OED online. Oxford University Press. Retrieved from http://www.oed.com.ezproxy.humanisticpsychology.org:2048/view/Entry/64755?redirectedFrom=ethics

Gantt, E. (2000). Levinas, psychotherapy, and the ethics of suffering. *Journal of Humanistic Psychology, 40*(3), 9–28. doi: 10.1177/0022167800403002

Gergen, K. (2006). Social construction as an ethics of infinitude: Reply to Brinkmann. *Journal of Humanistic Psychology, 46*(2), 119–125. doi: 10.1177/0022167805284446

Guggenbuhl-Craig, A. (1971). *Power in the helping professions.* Dallas, TX: Spring.

Harrington, D. (2002). A Levinasian psychology? Perhaps. In E. Gantt & R. Williams (Eds.), *Psychology for the other: Levinas, ethics, and the practice of psychology* (pp. 209–221). Pittsburgh, PA: Duquesne University Press.

Hillman, J. (1975). *Re-visioning psychology.* New York, NY: Harper & Row.

Hillman, J. (1999). *The force of character.* New York, NY: Random House.

Hollis, J. (2007). *Why good people do bad things: Understanding our darker selves.* New York, NY: Gotham.

Jung, C. (1964a). A psychological view of conscience. *Civilization in transition: Collected works, Vol. 10* (pp. 437–454). Princeton, NJ: Princeton University Press. (Original work published 1958)

Jung, C. (1964b). Good and evil in analytical psychology. *Civilization in transition: Collected works, Vol. 10* (pp. 456–465). Princeton, NJ: Princeton University Press. (Original work published 1960)

Jung, C. (1969a). Foreword. In E. Neumann, *Depth psychology and a new ethic* (pp. 11–18). Boston, MA: Shambhala. (Original work published 1949)

Jung, C. (1969b). A psychological approach to the dogma of the Trinity. *Psychology and religion: West and east: Collected works, Vol. 11* (2nd ed.; pp. 107–199). Princeton, NJ: Princeton University Press. (Original work published 1948)

Jung, C. (2009). *The red book: Liber novus.* New York, NY: W.W. Norton.

Jung, C. (2011). *Memories, dreams, reflections* (Aniela Jaffe, Ed.). New York, NY: Random House.

Levinas, E. (1985). *Ethics and infinity: Conversations with Philippe Nero* (R. Cohen, Trans.). Pittsburgh, PA: Duquesne University Press.

Levinas, E. (1989). Ethics as first philosophy. In S. Hand (Ed.), *The Levinas reader.* Malden, MA: Blackwell. (Original work published 1984)

Levinas, E. (1998a). Is ontology fundamental? *Entre nous: Thinking-of-the-other.* New York, NY: Columbia University Press. (Original work published 1951)

Levinas, E. (1998b). The I and the totality. *Entre nous: Thinking-of-the-other.* New York: Columbia University Press. (Original work published 1954).

Levinas, E. (2008). *Otherwise than being or beyond essence* (A. Lingis, Trans.). Pittsburgh, PA: Duquesne University Press.

Morgan, M. (2011). *The Cambridge introduction to Emmanuel Levinas.* New York, NY: Cambridge University Press.

Neumann, E. (1969). *Depth psychology and a new ethic.* Boston, NA: Shambhala. (Original work published 1949)

O'Conner, F. (2007). *Wise blood.* New York, NY: Farrar, Straus and Giroux.

Proulx, C. (1994). On Jung's theory of ethics. *Journal of Analytical Psychology, 39*(1), 101–119.

Quinn, P. (2007). *Looking for Jimmy: A search for Irish America.* Woodstock, NY: Overlook Press.

Robinson, D. (2005). *Conscience and Jung's moral vision: From id to thou.* Mahwah, NJ: Paulist Press.

Sebek, M. (2002). Some critical notes on Solomon's paper, "The ethical attitude: A bridge between psychoanalysis and analytical psychology." *Journal of Analytical Psychology, 47*(2), 195–201.

Solomon, H. (2000). The ethical self. In E. Christopher & H. Solomon (Eds.), *Jungian thought in the modern world* (pp. 191–214). New York, NY: Free Association Books.

Solomon, H. (2001). Origins of the ethical attitude. *Journal of Analytical Psychology, 46*(3), 443–454.

Solomon, H., & Twyman, M. (2003). Introduction: The ethical attitude in analytic practice. In H. Solomon & M. Twyman (Eds.), *The ethical attitude in analytic practice* (pp. 443–452). London, UK: Free Association Books.

Stein, M. (1993). *Solar conscience, lunar conscience.* Wilmette, IL: Chiron.

Ulanov, A. (2013). *Madness and creativity.* College Station, TX: Texas A&M Press.

Wyschogrod, E. (1985). *Spirit in ashes: Hegel, Heidegger, and man-made mass death.* New Haven, CT: Yale University Press.

Zoja, L. (2007). *Ethics and analysis: Philosophical perspectives and their application in therapy.* College Station, TX: Texas A&M Press.

Chapter 5

Eating the liver, killing the tortoise

The ethical and the imaginal

Bauman's (1993) assertion that we are all interpreters of our moral obligations suggests that, in a postmodern, post-Jung, and post-Neumann world, interpretation is the foundation of ethical action. The ethical actor discerns, with limited clarity, the best way to respond to the call of the Other and revises that interpretation, discovers that it is insufficient or even wrong, discards it, and starts again. So as we begin this reflection on how ethical discourse might be useful in approaching imaginal experience, a Jungian or depth psychological hermeneutic seems an imperfect but valuable tool in our ongoing discernment process. Our goal resonates with Paul Ricoeur's observation that "[t]he challenge is to bring conflicts to the level of discourse and not let them degenerate to the level of violence" (Ricoeur, 1999, p. 12).

Killing the tortoise

The classist Carl Kerenyi (1951) retold the origin story of the Greek god Hermes, son of Zeus and the nymph Maia and symbolic father of hermeneutics. In the first moments after his birth, Hermes encountered a tortoise outside of his cave. Overjoyed, Hermes brought him into the cave, telling him, "It is better to be indoors, outdoors it is dangerous. Even in thy life thou art a protection against harmful magic. When thou diest, thou shall beautifully sing!" (p. 163). He killed the tortoise, freed the shell, and used it to create the first lyre. Kerenyi wrote, "His words and his actions were as swift as thought" (p. 163). After playing songs that celebrated his conception and birth, "his thoughts were elsewhere" and he left the cave in search of food (p. 163).

Many interpretations of this story are possible, and I am committing an act of violence against the text by removing it from the context of Kerenyi's (1951) retelling and the larger context of Greek myth. Given that interpretation rests at the heart of the ethical attitude, however, this story reflects to me a dynamic that it will be useful to keep in our awareness as we move forward:

This is the first hermeneutic act, and already we have blood on our hands.

Hermes saw through the tortoise's presence to its possibility. His first encounter with creation was joyful; he saw in the tortoise something other than a tortoise, something more: "Whence, tortoise, didst thou take so delightful a toy, the protecting shell on thy back, thou who dwellest in the mountains?" (Kerenyi, 1951, pp. 162–163). He was transfixed, however, by only a part of the whole. The tortoise cannot become a lyre; only his shell can. The shell is essential protection for the tortoise but a plaything for Hermes. So Hermes killed the tortoise to free the shell, thus ending a life to create something completely different: a tool for a specific purpose. The tortoise cannot appreciate the beauty of Hermes' songs; his tortoise-ness was not transformed but destroyed in the act of creation.[1]

The cautionary parallels to the act of interpretation are clear. Ricoeur's (1981) understanding of the distanciation of the text from its author notwithstanding,[2] we hear within the Hermes story the danger of inflicting violence on a text, of making it something it is not. No doubt, I have committed this crime scores of times across this book. Hermes did not encounter a dead tortoise; it was quite attached to its shell.

So it is with the act of interpreting our intrapsychic encounters. This point resonates with Hillman's (1977, 1978, 1979) position regarding the image and the symbol. Interpretation always entails an ethical obligation to respect the Otherness of the interpreted, and that Otherness always eludes us. We cannot interpret without killing the tortoise or without taking it from its context and incorporating it into our personal project. The tortoise becomes something other than it was when we laid claim to it. The tortoise cannot be both a tortoise and a lyre. It is the profound dialectic of life that something is always being killed to enable life to continue, even at the cellular level.

Eating the liver

The story of Hermes and the tortoise suggests that the act of interpretation always occurs in an ethical gray zone, to recall Zoja's (2007) notion. Moral perfection is always already unattainable; our simple engagement in the complexity and ambiguity of the world precludes it. This is true of our experiences in dreams and active imagination. Because we are both part of the system and the system itself, we are responsible for the violence and injustice we encounter. In every moment, that responsibility exists on a continuum between Levinas' "guiltless responsibility" (Levinas, 1989/1984, p. 84) and a more personal relationship to the conditions we encounter.

Although we cannot help but be influenced by ethical and legal codes we accumulate in the concrete world of praxis, our experiences in the imagination seem distinct in that they are not governed by those codes in material ways. We encounter the odd, deformed, revolting, and repellent in active imagination and dreams, and the choices we are given can directly

Eating the liver, killing the tortoise 97

contradict conventional morality. The ethics we assume in the material world do not necessarily apply in imaginal experience.

As a way to explore the ethics of intrapsychic imaginal experience, I consider a passage from Jung's *The Red Book* (2009) at some length. Although *The Red Book* represents Jung's later creative elaboration on visionary experiences originally recorded in the unpublished *Black Books* (Jung, n.d.), the experiences recorded in *The Red Book* (2009) offer remarkable insight into Jung's psyche as he began to formulate his understanding of the imagination. In the second section of the book, "Liber Secundus," Jung recounted, "The vision that I did not want to see, the horror that I did not want to live" (Jung, 2009, p. 320). He found himself walking through a "dreary and unsightly valley" where he was "seized by disgust and horror" (p. 320). As he walked, he encountered

> a marionette with a broken head … before me amidst the stones—a few steps further, a small apron—and then behind the bush, the body of a small girl—covered with terrible wounds—smeared with blood. One foot is clad with a stocking and shoe, the other is naked and gorily crushed—the head—where is the head? The head is a mash of blood with hair and whitish pieces of bone, surrounded by stones smeared with brain and blood. My gaze is captivated by this awful sight—a shrouded figure, like that of a woman, is standing calmly next to the child; her face is covered by an impenetrable veil. (p. 320)

Recall for a moment Ricoeur's (1999) suggestion that we need to bring conflict into discourse, which he referred to as the "ethics of discourse" (p. 12). If we can bring conflict into awareness, we can keep it from becoming violent. His comment appeared in the context of a discussion about intransigent political and religious conflicts, such as those that emerge from the clash of Islamic and Western cultures, but he could as easily have been talking about intrapsychic conflict. Indeed, this clash begins as an intrapsychic conflict, which spills into the concrete, material register. In Jung's experience, the conflict enters discourse as violence. This passage depicts a crime already committed by an unknown assailant. Jung did not kill the girl, but he was responsible for her death and its redemption. He entered into a dialogue with the mysterious shrouded woman near the body:

> She asks me:
>
> S: "What then do you say?"
> I: "What should I say? This is beyond words."
> S: "Do you understand this?"
> I: "I refuse to understand such things. I can't speak about them without being enraged."

S: "Why become enraged? You might as well rage every day of your life, for these and similar things happen every day."

I: "But most of the time we don't see them."

S: "So knowing that they happen is not enough to enrage you?"

I: "If I merely have knowledge of something, it is easier and simpler. The horror is less real if all I have is knowledge." (Jung, 2009, pp. 320–321)

The woman challenged Jung to bring his intrapsychic experience into discourse, and he objected that it is not possible. The image (i.e., the experience itself) cannot be re-presented in words. When we enter the situation, the violence and its consequences have already occurred because they cannot enter discourse. The violence happened because a conflict below the level of conscious awareness has not been made conscious. It has, however, become apparent in the inner world in the body of the girl. The cost of inattention to his inner world was this girl's death.[3]

The woman's second challenge elicited a different response. Understanding is perhaps possible, but Jung's rage kept him from that work and from *standing under* the experience. Jungian analyst R. Schenk (personal communication, February 27, 2014) suggested this gloss on the term *understand* that reflects an encounter with alterity:

Psychological understanding of the "other" ... requires a "standing under," a sacrifice of assumptions, preconceptions, systems of comprehending, rational priorities, even of subjective identity, in order to encounter the "other" of the image, the *prima materia*, and to address it on its terms (the opus) by "seeing through" to its core elements, i.e., its "soul" (the "goal" of the work).

Jung's affective response functioned as a defense against his assuming responsibility for the crime by going under its appearance to what it might force him to accept about himself. The unknown assailant is Other and a screen for his projections of anger and revulsion. As she pushed him to accept responsibility for the security afforded him by his rage, Jung admitted something uncomfortably familiar to all of us: he knew this happens, all of the time, and used his experiential distance from it to avoid taking responsibility for it.

In an introductory journalism class in my freshman year of college, when I intended to become a reporter, the professor wrote the following equation on the board:

One death in Houston = news
10 deaths in New York = news
100 deaths in Paris = news
1000 deaths in Kinshasa = news

Eating the liver, killing the tortoise   99

I was appalled, and, full of naïve self-righteousness, I changed my major. The equation, however, expresses a fundamental psychological truth. According to a study published in the British medical journal *The Lancet* (Burnham, Lafta, Doocy, & Roberts, 2006), more than 600,000 violent deaths directly attributable to the American invasion occurred in Iraq between 2003 and 2006. As an American citizen, taxpayer, and voter during the American invasion, I bear responsibility for all those lost lives. I've known this number since it was reported in the media here. I am not, however, paralyzed with horror and guilt. It is easier and simpler if I know about horrific violence than if I have been forced to confront it directly.

Jung (2009) continued,

> S: "Step nearer and you will see that the body of the child has been cut open; take out the liver."
> I: "I will not touch this corpse. If someone witnessed this, they would think that I'm the murderer."
> S: "You are cowardly; take out the liver."
> I: "Why should I do this? This is absurd."
> S: "I want you to remove the liver. You must do it."
> I: "Who are you to give me such an order?"
> S: "I am the soul of this child. You must do this for my sake."
> I: "I don't understand, but I'll believe you and do this horrific and absurd deed." (p. 321)

Here we see Jung confronted by a dilemma he would not face in the concrete world. The woman's request was beyond sense. Jung was not asked to take part in a religious ritual but to remove a girl's liver from her corpse. To describe this experience as *symbolic*, we run the great risk of distancing ourselves from the experience. From another vantage, however, we might understand this passage as correcting the misuse of the term. All experience is symbolic in that it is charged with irreducible, indeterminate meaning. Jung's ethical obligation is to engage in the experience and understand (in Schenk's sense) how it also—not merely—symbolic.

> I reach into the child's visceral cavity—it is still warm—the liver is still firmly attached—I take my knife and cut it free of the ligaments. Then I take it out and hold it with bloody hands toward the figure.

> S: "I thank you."
> I: "What should I do?"
> S: "You know what the liver means, and you ought to perform the healing act with it."
> I: "What is to be done?"
> S: "Take a piece of the liver, in place of the whole thing, and eat it."

I: "What are you demanding? This is absolute madness. This is desecration, necrophilia. You make me a guilty party to this most hideous of all crimes."

S: "You have devised the most horrible torment for the murderer, which could atone for his act. There is only one atonement: abase yourself and eat."

I: "I cannot—I refuse—I cannot participate in this horrible guilt."

S: "You share in this guilt."

I: "I? Share in this guilt?"

S: "You are a man, and a man has committed this deed."

I: "Yes, I am a man—I curse whoever did this for being a man, and I curse myself for being a man."

S: "So take part in his act, abase yourself and eat. I need atonement."

I: "So shall it be for your sake, as you are the soul of this child."

I kneel down on the stone, cut off a piece of the liver and put it in my mouth. My gorge rises—tears burst from my eyes—cold sweat covers my brow—a dull sweet taste of blood—I swallow with desperate efforts—it is impossible—once again and once again—I almost faint—it is done. The horror has been accomplished.

S: "I thank you."
    She throws her veil back—a beautiful maiden with ginger hair.

S: "Do you recognize me?

I: "How strangely familiar you are! Who are you?"

S: "I am your soul." (pp. 321–322)

The event has taken on the feeling of a ritual. Jung was asked to eat of the innocent body as orthodox Christianity congregants are asked to eat of the body and blood of the innocent Christ. Jung's experience, however, was brutally real. He cut out the liver with his own knife and offered it to the woman, who insisted on drawing him radically into the reality of the girl's death. His participation was a healing act that promised atonement. Etymologically, at the root of *atonement* is a contraction of the words *at one* (Atonement, n.d.). Jung literally became *at one* with the girl's corpse by eating the liver. He integrated the violent result of this profound conflict into himself.[4]

One of the most striking elements of this passage is the detail Jung employed to describe the act of eating the liver. Giegerich's (1993) reminder that religion and culture were not born just "from the spirit of killing but from actual killings" (p. 8) is vividly evoked by this passage. Imaginal experience is real experience, and actual killings occur in the psyche. Our horror at personally witnessing violence in the concrete world is mirrored by our own experience of intrapsychic conflict. It is significant that Jung's first encounter with his soul depended on his participation in an act of atonement or of acceptance of his ethical obligation within the psychic community. Jung did not just witness the violence; he participated in it and understood his responsibility for it. The human psyche itself is an ethical gray zone, in which violence occurs below our awareness but within the domain of our duty. We are always already guilty bystanders.

Jung (2009) titled this chapter "The Sacrificial Murder." The hooded woman told him that he had devised "the most horrible torment for the murderer," which he himself must undergo. An ambiguity lurked in her statement, "You are a man, and a man has committed this deed" (p. 322). Resolution depended on Jung accepting responsibility for the murder and in so doing, perhaps, understanding that he was indeed the murderer. Paradoxically, however, the murder itself was sacrificial: it was a making-sacred that culminated in the soul's revelation of itself to Jung. Did this murder have to occur for Jung to encounter his soul? Did it make Jung sacred? The conflict had to enter discourse, and the only way for this to happen in Jung's life was in the form of this highly charged experience. He had to see the effect of his unconscious inner conflict. It had to rise to the level of a horrible act against nature—an *opus contra naturam*—to become conscious and assimilable. The act was against himself. The woman first introduced herself as the girl's soul and only later revealed herself as Jung's soul. She did not revoke her earlier statement: the girl was also Jung, he suffered her murder, and he came to self-knowledge as a result of the unconscious act.

Jung's (2009) encounter with his soul illustrates several themes that have appeared across the texts we have considered and that together suggest an emerging set of principles that can guide an ethical approach to the imagination:

1. Ethical codes are provisional and temporary expressions of an ethical impulse that serves a developmental purpose.
2. That ethical impulse is to respect and safeguard the experience of the Other and reflects the fundamentally relational nature of the psyche.
3. Following Levinas (1985, 1989/1984, 2008), an ethical impulse involves recognition of pre-existent responsibility for our participation in the entire field.
4. Ethical response from a Jungian perspective is inherently interpretive. We are called to engage our experience symbolically. To interpret is not to engage semiotically but to understand that multiple interpretations of a situation are correct and that multiple, contradictory actions could be required.
5. The ethical response may directly contradict traditional ethical codes. Jung's (2009) initial objections in the "Sacrificial Murder" passage above are based in traditional ethical codes; they functioned to shield him from ethical action in the situation and must be transcended.

6. We have an ethical obligation to bring into consciousness the intrapsychic violence that we encounter. Violence in the psyche occurs below the level of discourse and can emerge as charged images. To resolve the conflict, we have to understand it.
7. The *ethical imagination* is both a description (i.e., the imagination is inherently ethical, in the sense that it is a matrix of relationship) and an imperative (i.e., we need imaginative ethics that respond to the complexity of our experience).
8. The course of human psychological development can be described as the increasing integration of separate elements of the psyche. This process depends on one's opening oneself to Otherness within, genuine curiosity regarding the intrapsychic Others we encounter, respect for their autonomy, and cultivation of relationship and collaboration with them. Thus a dimension of increasing psychic integration is the development of a sensitive, sophisticated ethical orientation. Human development depends on one's relating to intrapsychic Others with respect, compassion, and concern.

Building a container for our fantasies

As abstracted principles, these ideas sound noble and unattainable, if not outright naïve. If the psyche is inherently ethical, why do we behave so unethically? Why do good people do bad things? The position that unethical behavior is a failure to attend to our fundamental ethical obligation to the Other sounds insufficient. As I mentioned in chapter 4, Jung clearly understood evil to be something more tangible, or ontologically grounded, than the *privatio boni*. Whether it is something other than the absence of the urge—or the capacity—to achieve psychic integration is another question. Yet, as noted by Jung, the course of human development may need to lead through difficult, morally questionable passages (he noted that evil is unmistakable but "for this particular person in this particular situation at this particular stage of development it may be good" (Jung, 1964/1960, para. 883). As suggested by Ulanov (2013), "We also need evil to help us do the unthinkable, the unbearable that we are helpless to do by ourselves" (p. 36). By no means is integration ensured, nor is it ideally achieved in any lifetime. Only the smile of the Buddha suggests its possibility.

It will be useful for us to consider how ethical conflict appears in the imagination and plays out in a human life. Let's return to the example of Morgan, whom we discussed in the introduction. In a long-term, ostensibly happy relationship, Morgan found that she was persistently dogged by erotic fantasies about a neighbor. She would have preferred to have no erotic feelings for anyone but her partner, and the fantasies were increasingly disruptive. She engaged the neighbor in conversation one morning, and although the conversation was brief and innocuous, she replayed it for days afterward and felt a mix of guilt and excitement. She felt compelled to seek him out and helpless when the fantasies emerged. Her partner noticed her preoccupation and commented on her distractibility.

She did not know what the fantasies meant. She wondered whether she should pursue this neighbor further, whether the fantasies were signs that something was wrong with her current relationship, and whether they demonstrated her immaturity (i.e., do they reflect a developmental task that she failed to master when younger?). Was she using the fantasies to escape the difficult work of long-term relationship? Or did they mean that her current partner was not her soulmate and that she needed to leave the relationship to live in integrity? Would staying in the relationship actually inflict damage on both herself and her partner? Finally, we must ask, how does one go about discerning the answer to any of these questions?

Morgan felt helpless before the questions and before the increasing insistence of her fantasies. Her choices all seemed to involve action or inaction; she had no road map for this kind of crisis, and she did not know how to reflect on the interpretations in a consistent and helpful way. She blamed herself for the fantasies and also felt completely out of control of them.

The king in his sweat-bath

Control is impossible; the unconscious will force itself into awareness using disruptive means if necessary. What is needed is a way to host the fantasies that both honors their autonomy and offers us the chance to engage with them interpretively. One possible model for this process appears in Jung's late work *Mysterium Coniunctionis* (1963/1954), in which Jung briefly discussed an alchemical image: the king in his sweat-bath. In his *Mysterium Lectures,* Edward Edinger (1995) reproduced an engraving that Jung seems to have referenced in a footnote (Jung, 1963/1954, p. 40, n. 227). The image depicts a naked man in a large wooden box with transparent sides. The box is raised off the ground on a short frame, and heat rises from below the box. Steam escapes from the edges of the box.

The reference to the sweat-bath appears in Jung's (1963/1954) discussion of alchemy and Manichaeism. Perhaps the most valuable contribution made by Edinger (1995) in his study of this passage was his inclusion of a correction to the current English translation of *Mysterium* (Jung, 1963/1954) by R.F.C. Hull. Edinger (1995) reported that a student had informed him that Hull's choice of "pernicious heresy" (Jung, 1963/1954, para. 31) to translate Jung's description of Manichaeism had an important qualification in the original German. Retranslated, the line would read: "It is said, according to Christian tradition, that from these books Mani concocted his pernicious heresy" (Edinger, 1995, p. 47). Jung's thought has at times been accused of Manichaean tendencies, notably by Jung's longtime correspondent and friend, Fr. Victor White, who accused him of "quasi-manichaean dualism"

(Lammers & Cunningham, 2007, p. 140, n. 26). That Jung's expressed position toward Mani is more ambiguous than it initially seemed in the text colored Jung's discussion of Mani, as we will see.

Mani appeared in Jung's text as "the best-known example of the 'son of the widow'" (Jung, 1963/1954, para. 31). This relates to his origin story; Manichaeans, Jung stated, are known as "children of the widow" (para. 14). Jung amplified this symbolism by referencing the alchemist Trismegisthus, Hermes, Thrice Greatest, who referred to the philosopher's stone as a specific kind of orphan that was in relationship to a mother whose husband had died. The orphan was fatherless but not motherless. Jung suggested that the "son of the widow" (para. 31) refers to the necessary relationship between the *lapis philosophorum* and its *prima materia*. This codes the *prima materia* as feminine and virginal, in Jung's thought. In psychological language, the *prima materia* may be understood as the unconscious matrix from which the ego individuates or from which an unconscious content emerges into consciousness.

Son/widow is the foundational dyad of a system of thought that is fundamentally dualistic. Evil has the same power and reality as good in Manichaean thought, and it is an independent force at work in the world. Mani believed that there were two deities (i.e., a god of darkness and a god of light) and that "the god of darkness had stolen sparks of divine light and imprisoned them in human material bodies" (Edward, 1980, p. 32). Our task as humans, then, is "to release those sparks of divinity by rigorously suppressing bodily pleasures" (p. 32). One wonders what drives this fantasy and what psychological costs it might continue to have across the millennia.

The parallels between Jungian psychology and Manichaean thought begin with Jung's articulation of archetypal evil, which, although Jung framed it as simply a phenomenological observation, suggests that evil is both real and transpersonal. Jung also famously understood psychic structure to be expressed in paired opposites: ego/Self, archetypal mother/father, senex/puer, and so on. Indeed, the subtitle of *Mysterium Coniunctionis*—"an inquiry into the separation and synthesis of psychic opposites in alchemy"— suggests how important these polarities were to Jung's understanding of the psyche. The archetypes themselves have dual natures, positive and negative, because, as Jung stated in *Aion*, "there can be no reality without polarity" (Jung, 1969, para. 423). Jung's thought, however, was not strictly Manichaean. He wrote that good and evil "spring from a need of human consciousness and that for this reason they lose their validity outside the human sphere" (para. 423). To perceive, we must see difference, and the first difference always is that/not-that.

We now return to Jung's discussion of Manichaean symbolism in *Mysterium* (1963/1954), as we slowly circumambulate the image of the sweat-bath. Perhaps the most famous disciple of Mani was St. Augustine, whose later Christian thought—particularly the doctrine of the *privatio boni*—could be seen as a reaction to his experience with Manichaeism and possibly also to the dualist and eschatological theology of Persian Zoroastrianism, which was influential in Augustine's time. Jung related that the Manichaeans understood matter to be symbolized by "the dark, fluid, human body of the evil principle" (Jung, 1963/1954, para. 53) and Augustine wrote that "they assert that all flesh is the work, not of God, but of an evil mind" (as cited in Edward, 1980, p. 38). For the Manichaeans, the spirit imprisoned in the evil body must be released "by angelic beings who dwell in the sun and moon" (Jung, 1963/1954, para. 53). Jung described the process as follows:

> Assuming alternately male and female form [the angels] excite the desires of the wicked and cause them to break out in a sweat of fear, which falls upon the earth and fertilizes the vegetation. In this manner the heavenly light-material is freed from the dark bodies and passes into plant form.
>
> The inflammation by desire has its analogy in the alchemist's gradual warming of the substances that contain the *arcanum*. Here the symbol of the sweat-bath plays an important role, as the illustrations show. Just as for the Manichaeans the sweat of the archons signified rain, so for the alchemists sweat meant dew. (paras. 33–34)

Jung (1963/1954) discussed the significance of removing moisture in an earlier passage. He quoted a passage which was attributed to Ostanes, a legendary Iranian mage who was often cited as an authority in Greek literature and later alchemical works. Smith (2003) suggested that Ostanes' work continued to grow long after his death, particularly in the period of medieval alchemy. He suffered because he stood "between two exalted brilliancies known for their wickedness, and between two dim lights" (Jung, 1963/1954, para. 5). He was directed,

> Take the child of the bird which is mixed with redness and spread for the gold its bed which comes forth from the glass, and place it in its vessel whence it has no power to come out except when thou desirest, and leave it until its moistness has departed. (para. 5)

This is one of many alchemical procedures for bringing about the union of four elements, which Jung (1963/1954) stated was "one of the main preoccupations of alchemy" (para. 6). Jung identified Ostanes' bird as related both to the *aurum philosophorum* and to Hermes; the advice described an alchemical process of heating the substance until the "moistness" (para. 5) has left. That *moistness* Jung identified as the "radical moisture," the "*prima materia*, which is the original chaos and the sea (the unconscious)" (para. 6). Jung wrote, "Some kind of coming to consciousness seems indicated" (para. 6). The theme of drying moisture appeared more ominously in a later passage, in which the transformation involved the dismemberment of a dragon by "weapons which are fashioned in the body of the woman" (para. 15). The dragon became nothing but blood, which then dried and released poison. The "hidden wind" could then appear, which Jung stated in a footnote was "the pneuma hidden in the *prima materia*" (para. 15, n. 104).[5]

These motifs—the sweat that becomes dew and the blood that dries, releasing the pneuma—are mixed in a striking way in an alchemical text quoted by Jung in a footnote. After an alchemical heating process, "That body becomes moist, and gives forth a kind of bloody sweat after the putrefaction and mortification, that is a Heavenly Dew, and this dew is called the Mercury of the Philosophers, or Aqua Permanens" (Jung, 1963/1954, para. 34, n. 229). Much later, Jung described the *aqua permanens* as bitter, difficult to acquire, and ultimately "the primal water which contains the four elements" (para. 341). The unconscious emerges spontaneously into the psyches when the traditional religious containers have failed: "We know from numerous hints that man's inner life is the 'secret place' where the *aqua solvens et coagulans*, the *medicina catholica* or *panacea*, the spark of the light of nature, are to be found" (para. 344).

Jung (1963/1954) commented in the epilogue of *Mysterium* that the entirety of the individuation process cannot be conveyed by a single case. Different aspects of the process are more apparent in different cases, psyches differ, and analysts encounter individuals at different stages in their development. Alchemy provided him a platform from which to survey the vast range of symbols and processes that appear during human psychic development. He ultimately viewed the goal of alchemy as bringing the "antagonistic forces" at work in the psyche "into harmony and, out of the multitude of contradictions, produce a unity, which naturally will not come of itself, though it may—*Deo concedente*—with human effort" (para. 791). In the section on Mani and alchemy, Jung was more specific: "It is the moral task of alchemy to bring the feminine, maternal background of the masculine psyche, seething with passions, into harmony with the principle of the spirit—truly a labour of Hercules" (para. 35).

A vessel for psychological transformation

The king in his sweat-bath suggests a way of imaging the imagination as we navigate the process of ethical interpretation. The fantasy must be allowed to emerge into our awareness and understood as a symbolic request, in the full sense of *symbolic*, which we have discussed. The appearance of the fantasies does not have one single meaning but a multiplicity of meanings that have unclear implications for one's life. A truism among scholars of myth is that all versions of the myth are true. Each reveals a different aspect of the topography and thus the more versions, the more complete the view. In Morgan's case, the image of the sweat-bath suggests that she must suffer the emergence of these fantasies without trying to avoid them or enact them. The energy must be brought into awareness and held.

The way of the sweat-bath is not kind. It represents a choice to suffer the conflict by holding all options close, by understanding all impulses and desires to be, in their way, true. Jung's (1963/1954) suggestion that this process comes after putrefaction and mortification evokes the death endured by the personality as it enters this process. The king/ego will emerge diminished. It is worth noting that the (erotic) excitement is necessary to the process. The sweat cannot emerge until the king is excited by desire (specifically by male and female forms). These angels serve an angelic purpose.

Morgan's story remains unresolved; a coda might imply that one interpretation is more valid than another; however, it is worth examining the reproduced image of the king one more time to suggest other elements that may be worth considering. Steam emerges from the corners of the box and rises, unlike the description of the Manichaean sweat that falls like rain or the alchemical dew that fertilizes the earth. One interpretation of this in a clinical context is that the steam's escaping from the container suggests the necessary release of heat and pressure that occurs in psychotherapy and in relationship with others. When we undergo crises of the imagination, we allow some of that pressure to escape by sharing the experience with a therapist or trusted others to maintain the integrity of the container. Otherwise, the sweat-bath will explode. Similarly, Jung's (1963/1954) suggestion that the alchemical heating of the substances happens gradually underscores the need to maintain the integrity of the container. The presence of a clinician can help the client understand the nature of the process and encourage the release of pent-up affective pressure in session.

The imagination in this sense functions as a location of intrapsychic experience and is expressed in visual terms. Morgan experienced her conflict as between material Others that appear visually in nonmaterial ways. It is a mistake to focus only on the visual. Fantasy has auditory, kinesthetic, and sensual qualities. The king exists in a three-dimensional box, and the primary sensory experience is tactile: the heat and steam, the rough wood at his back, the sweat and blood pouring from his skin. As discussed in chapter 3, the imagination is not simply a neural screening room for visual narrative but an experience that engages the entire sensorium. To hold a fantasy in one's awareness with integrity is a physical act. This is perhaps easiest to grasp when the tone of the fantasy is erotic. Biologic responses are a normal part of erotic fantasy. The son who has recurring fantasies of leaving his father's business and beginning a new life overseas, however, also experiences biological reactions. Excitement and anxiety appear in real-time floods of adrenaline, tightening bowels, opening pores, and rising blood pressure. Within the imaginal moment, the son experiences the spray of salt water on his skin, the smell of fresh fish grilled over hot coals, and the sound of alien insects buzzing at the threshold of awareness. It is no wonder that, with rare

108 Eating the liver, killing the tortoise

exceptions, we experience our dreams as real when we are dreaming. We are not in an inner theatre, passively watching, but exploring an inner world. It is also useful to remember Hillman's (1977) suggestion that we understand *image* in this sense to refer to a much broader category of experience than usual. A passing worry, a momentary loss of focus, a sudden elation, and a mood that settles on us and refuses to leave are all images and imaginings or Others in the psychic world.

The process I have described does not have strict boundaries or necessary steps for success (*success* is a dubious idea in any case). We can, however, list some elements that reflect the psychological dynamics that may guide us in building our imaginal container and engaging in the ethical gesture of holding fantasies consciously:

1. *Make room for imaginal experience.* This is perhaps the hardest task. Our culture is oriented decisively toward the material; meaning and image are illusory or afterthoughts (and thought rather than experience is the only acceptable vehicle for meaning, among other reasons, because it gives the illusion of transmissibility). By *make room*, I mean the creation of space in time, dwelling, and psyche. We create the imagination in material ways, by establishing it in our schedule and locating the few concrete circumstances that we need to have the experience (i.e., whatever may be required to bring our attention inward, such as a quiet room, a park bench, a space apart from our usual routines). We also need to make psychic space for it by the simple act of choosing to value what arises when we are quiet.

2. *We have to learn to notice what we avoid.* This includes the thoughts that are censored, the moments of anger that we immediately stifle, the impulses that we fight, and the means of distraction we employ. This is an essential element of the hard work of self-knowledge that accompanies psychotherapy.

3. *Let the fantasies come.* In his memoir *Memories, Dreams, Reflections,* Jung (2011) famously described the blasphemous fantasy that appeared when, as a child, he walked past the cathedral at Basel. He attempted to resist the fantasy; he was able to keep it from continuing for three days. He could not, however, hold it away indefinitely, and his decision to allow it to move to its natural conclusion was a key developmental moment. The turd that crashed through the cathedral's roof ended his naïve acceptance of his father's faith and further shaped his explorations of the objectivity of the psyche. Our fantasies are not right or wrong. They express psyche, and those we resist, surely signal a part of the system that needs to be brought into awareness and relationship.

4. *We imagine when we act, but we do not have to act when we imagine.* Our dreams do not necessarily foretell the future, and our fantasies do not indicate that we should take one path over another. Our keeping this in

Eating the liver, killing the tortoise   109

mind allows us to collaborate with the unconscious in developing a relationship. Image is the language of the psyche, and psyche speaks using fantasy; it does not impose itself on us as fate.

5. *Allow multiple interpretations to arise from the fantasies that appear.* We may be able to get the psychic need met by the actions depicted in the fantasy. Those actions are also always a metaphor for psychic process, and there may be multiple paths to get the need met. The new mother who helplessly fantasizes forcing her infant under the water in the bathtub does not need to drown her baby to find relief from her suffering. The psyche asks for the death of the child because the circumstances in which the mother finds herself are intolerable and must be changed. Support from parents, friends, a spouse, or others who can share the caregiving burden, as well as the help of the therapeutic and medical professions, can help with her experience of postpartum depression and can end the crisis. The intensity of the imagery indicates the intensity of the mother's emotional distress rather than the recommended course of action.

6. *Reflect on the quality of the relationships in the fantasy.* How do the figures relate to each other? What do you notice about the emotions of the people involved? What are the power dynamics? Does one person have more power or authority than others? If the fantasy involves people in the material world, how might they differ from your experience of them in life? If the fantasy were to occur in the material world, how might the relationships change? How might relationships outside of the fantasy be affected? Ethical discernment involves understanding ourselves as inextricably related both intrapsychically and interpsychically. We are always already related, and every action we take affects others for good or ill.

7. *Intend no harm but understand that harm will inevitably occur.* Although its origins are modern and not directly attributable to Hippocrates (whose oath includes the injunction to do no harm (Smith, 2005)), the maxim *primum non nocere*—first, do no harm—reflects a core ethical value in health care during the last 500 years. Sometimes, we must risk harm to enable growth. This is true both in personal and clinical contexts. We also must accept that choices between our relative good and the relative goods of others will need to be made as will difficult choices in which an apparent good is dependent on circumstances outside of our control. If a husband has an intense desire to maintain a marriage, and his wife is suffering in the relationship, it may well be best for both partners to end the relationship, although suffering will undoubtedly follow for the husband. The choices made by the wife regarding her fantasies of leaving the relationship must include the awareness that what her husband desires may not in fact reflect the course that will lead to his growth.

8. *Hold the tension of apparent opposites.* As discussed briefly in chapter 4, Jung (1969) understood consciousness to discriminate experience into binaries. When a conflict is experienced in fantasy as a choice between multiple courses of action (or multiple potential lives) all courses must be acknowledged as valid in some psychological sense, regardless of their apparent ethical coding. The depressed man who experiences suicidal fantasies opens them to understanding when he understands that the psyche is making a valid and necessary request. A way of living needs to end. Acknowledgment of the validity of the experience and one's allowing it to exist in the sweat-bath of imaginal experience enables its transformation from an impossibly compelling impulse into profound meaning. A binary can become a multiplicity. The conflict between living in intolerable suffering or killing oneself can transform to include other options (e.g., beginning or ending a long-term relationship, leaving an abusive employment situation, emancipating oneself from the destructive force of a negative parental complex).

9. *Talk about it.* Bring the conflict into discourse before it can become violence. The steam that escapes from the sweat-bath is a necessary release of pressure. The analytically informed therapist can be a valuable resource who is obliged to hold the material in confidence, is trained to approach the content without judgment, and is aware of how the fantasy might reflect the development of the psyche. Carefully chosen others (e.g., friends or relatives) who can be trusted not to share the content with others and who will listen compassionately also can be helpful. The choice requires discernment, as holding the information may incur a cost for the person who hears it, particularly if actions that result from the conflict might affect significant others in the listener's life. Our ethical concern extends to those who support us in our suffering.

10. *Accept that the chosen course of action is one among many and that none is the right answer among wrong answers.* Ethical action is always an interpretation, and depth psychology states that many interpretations are true in different ways. This does not mean that there are no false interpretations or unethical actions. Any action, however, even those that are followed by a sense of equilibrium and satisfaction for everyone involved, reverberate in ways we cannot control and for which we bear responsibility.

11. *Be aware of, and respect, the gravitational pull of fantasy.* Fantasy is real psychic experience, and the experience can be pleasurable and rewarding. The classic example of this is erotic fantasy; we can return again and again to an intensely pleasurable experience that does not involve or depend upon material others. For someone in a sexual relationship with a material partner, there is nothing intrinsically wrong or unhealthy about also having erotic fantasies of imagined others. Repeated experiences of such fantasies, however, may reflect changes in the dynamics

of our material relationships, and engagement in fantasy also may serve the function of avoiding difficult work in the relationship. The fantasies do not have to be erotic. Consider the partners who sit together in a room, playing online games for hours at a time on separate computers, in separate virtual domains. It is neither healthy or unhealthy. If an effect of logging in, however, is that the partners do not have to confront and work through troublesome issues in the relationship, the online fantasy space becomes a place where one can avoid important psychological development.

Notes

1. Shakespeare captured this from the perspective of the tortoise in *King Lear*: "As flies are to wanton boys, so we are to the gods./They kill us for their sport" (Shakespeare, 1608, Act 4, Scene 1).
2. See chapter 3.
3. It is beyond the scope of this study to speculate on the intrapsychic conflict in Jung's life that was imaged in the girl's death. My position is that this violence reflects an unresolved conflict; in this context, the nature of that conflict cannot be pursued.
4. The liver also is historically associated with the seat of the passions, especially courage.
5. The tracking of the movement of the invisible world as it moves through the forms of the visible—the traditional theological project—has perhaps been taken over by the project of depth psychotherapy. As Jung (1967/1938) stated, "The gods have become diseases" (para. 54).

References

Atonement. (n.d.). Dictionary.com Unabridged. Retrieved from http://dictionary.reference.com/browse/atonement

Bauman, Z. (1993). *Postmodern ethics.* Malden, MA: Blackwell.

Burnham, G., Lafta, R., Doocy, S., & Roberts, L. (2006). Mortality after the 2003 invasion of Iraq: A cross-sectional cluster sample survey. *The Lancet, 368*(9545), 1421–1428. doi:10.1016/S0140–6736(06)69491-9

Edinger, E. (1995). *The mysterium lectures: A journey through C. G. Jung's mysterium coniunctionis.* Toronto, Canada: Inner City.

Edward, P. (1980). *Heresy and authority in medieval Europe: Documents in translation.* Philadelphia, PA: University of Pennsylvania Press. Retrieved from http://web.ebscohost.com.ezproxy.humanisticpsychology.org:2048/ehost/ebookviewer/ebook/

Giegerich, W. (1993). Killings. *Spring, 54*, 1–18.

Hillman, J. (1977). An inquiry into image. *Spring, 44*, 62–88.

Hillman, J. (1978). Further notes on images. *Spring, 45*, 152–182.

Hillman, J. (1979). Image-sense. *Spring, 46*, 171–185.

Jung, C. (n.d.) *The black books.* Unpublished manuscript.

Jung, C. (1963). *Mysterium coniunctionis: An inquiry into the separation and synthesis of psychic opposites in alchemy: Collected works, Vol. 14.* Princeton, NJ: Princeton University Press. (Original work published 1954)

Jung, C. (1964). Good and evil in analytical psychology. *Civilization in transition: Collected works, Vol. 10* (pp. 456–465). Princeton, NJ: Princeton University Press. (Original work published 1960)

Jung, C. (1967). Commentary on "The secret of the golden flower." *Alchemical studies: Collected works, Vol. 13* (pp. 1–55). Princeton, NJ: Princeton University Press. (Original work published 1938)

Jung, C. (1969). *Aion: Researches into the phenomenology of the self: Collected works, Vol. 9ii.* Princeton, NJ: Princeton University Press.

Jung, C. (2009). *The red book: Liber novus.* New York, NY: W.W. Norton.

Jung, C. (2011). *Memories, dreams, reflections* (Aniela Jaffe, Ed.). New York, NY: Random House.

Kerenyi, C. (1951). *The gods of the Greeks.* London, UK: Thames and Hudson.

Lammers, A., & Cunningham, C. (2007). *The Jung-White letters.* New York, NY: Routledge.

Levinas, E. (1985). *Ethics and infinity: Conversations with Philippe Nero* (R. Cohen, Trans.). Pittsburgh, PA: Duquesne University Press.

Levinas, E. (1989). Ethics as first philosophy. In S. Hand (Ed.), *The Levinas reader.* Malden, MA: Blackwell. (Original work published 1984)

Levinas, E. (2008). *Otherwise than being or beyond essence* (A. Lingis, Trans.). Pittsburgh, PA: Duquesne University Press.

Ricoeur, P. (1981). *Hermeneutics and the human sciences* (J. Thompson, Trans.). New York, NY: Cambridge University Press.

Ricoeur, P. (1999). Imagination, testimony, and trust: A dialogue with Paul Ricoeur. In R. Kearney & M. Dooley (Eds.), *Questioning ethics: Contemporary debates in philosophy* (pp. 12–17). New York, NY: Routledge.

Shakespeare, W. (1608). *King Lear.* Retrieved from http://www.william-shakespeare.info/act4-script-text-king-lear.htm

Smith, C. (2005). Origin and uses of *Primum Non Nocere*: Above all, do no harm! *Journal of Clinical Pharmacology, 45*(4). doi: 10.1177/0091270004273680

Smith, M. (2003). Ostanes. *Encyclopædia Iranica* [online ed., 2012]. Retrieved from http://www.iranicaonline.org/articles/ostanes

Ulanov, A. (2013). *Madness and creativity.* College Station, TX: Texas A&M Press.

Zoja, L. (2007). *Ethics and analysis: Philosophical perspectives and their application in therapy.* College Station, TX: Texas A&M Press.

Chapter 6

A dream of the desiring imagination

By now, it should be apparent that a simple question—should we apply ethics to fantasy?—cannot be answered in a simple way. The foundations of these ideas have been considered, and I hope that I have established that fantasy is at least as ethically complex and nuanced as waking experience. Neu (2002) pointed out that philosophical and popular ethics "tend to focus on action" (p. 134), or on questions of behavior rather than reflection, which is artificially segregated from our typical understanding of action. For the psychoanalytically-informed Neu, our fantasies are subject to critique on the grounds that "fantasies like symptoms may reflect potent desires rather than ineffectual wishes" (p. 154). What does it mean to critique desire, as suggested by Neu? Even if critiqued, is it possible then not to want what we want or to choose not to desire? Is it more a matter of becoming ethically informed about our desire? In this chapter, we will track erotic desire across a literary narrative with the hope that some of the nebulous ambiguity of these lines of exploration will come into sharper focus.

Fridolin's fantasy; Albertine's dream

The Viennese writer Arthur Schnitzler worked on his novella, *Dream Story*, from 1907 to 1925 (Helmetag, 2003), during the period of his fellow Viennese Sigmund Freud's ascension to international renown. The two were friends, and Freud legendarily distanced himself because he was afraid that Schnitzler's worldview was too deeply influencing his own (Simon, 2002). Freud wrote approvingly of Schnitzler's work prior to the publication of *Dream Story*: "At the root of your being, you are a psychological depth explorer as honestly unprejudiced and unafraid as anyone ever" (Simon, 2002, para. 9).

Schnitzler's (2002) *Dream Story* is a dreamlike movement through jealousy and erotic fantasy, played out in *fin de siècle* Vienna, near the end of Mardi Gras celebrations (Helmetag, 2003). The aristocratic physician Fridolin was married to his beautiful wife Albertine, and they had a young daughter. During the course of three days, the foundation of their marriage was shaken as Fridolin encountered the compelling power of unconscious fantasy, jealousy, and erotic attraction. The issues explored by Schnitzler in the film lost none of their relevance at the end of the century, when the late British filmmaker Stanley Kubrick adapted *Dream Story* for his last film, *Eyes Wide Shut* (1999), which starred the real-life couple Tom Cruise and Nicole Kidman (Kubrick renamed the characters Bill and Alice).[1] Although I focus the following discussion on Schnitzler's (2002) characters, when relevant I refer to Kubrick's masterful recasting of the material in a contemporary New York, which Kubrick re-created on a London soundstage. *Dream Story* lushly illustrates: the ethical conflicts posed by fantasy; the interpenetration of imaginal and material reality; the violence that can arise from unresolved psychic conflict; the ways in which ethical response may directly contradict traditional ethical codes; the ways in which every action we take affects others, for good and ill; and the importance of bringing unresolved conflicts into consciousness to further the individuation process.

Fridolin and Albertine kissed their young daughter goodnight and headed anxiously to their bedroom, where they could discuss their experiences at a masked ball the previous evening. Each had charged encounters with strangers: Fridolin with two young, masked women who teasingly suggested that they knew him intimately from his student days; and Albertine with an older, charming foreign man who danced with her and made an indecent remark. In his version, Kubrick lingered on these flirtations, both of which seem closer to consummation than Schnitzler suggested in the original. Schnitzler (2002) highlighted the way that jealousy can charge erotic feeling; after leaving the ball, "they had sunk into each other's arms in lovemaking more ardent than they had experienced for a long time" (section 1, para. 4) and returned to the conversation the following evening, as they began to intimate "those hidden, scarcely suspected desires that are capable of producing dark and dangerous whirlpools in even the most clearheaded, purest soul" (para. 5).

It was during this conversation that Albertine told Fridolin about an encounter she had with a military officer while the family was on vacation in Denmark the previous summer. She found herself overwhelmed with desire for him and knew instantly that she would leave Fridolin and their daughter if he asked. He did not; he left before the two even exchanged greetings. The encounter, however, shook her, and her recollection of the experience possessed Fridolin throughout the rest of the story. He related his own temptation on the seashore, with a young girl whom he had encountered on the beach in the early morning hours. He reached out to her, and the girl was initially drawn to him but waved him away. Albertine made Fridolin promise that, in the future, the two would "always tell each other these kinds of things at once" (para. 14). Fridolin made the promise, but his fantasy of her memory launched the dark, unsettling journey to come.

Before we continue, it is worth making a few preliminary observations about the context of Fridolin's fantasy. As vividly rendered by Kubrick

A dream of the desiring imagination   115

(1999), Fridolin/Bill (and the viewer) see Albertine/Alice caressed by a naval officer in dress uniform. The fantasy evolves over the course of the film. Shot monochromatically in blue tones and divided into sections, first Alice and then the officer disrobe and, by the last segment near the end of the film, make intense love. Kubrick was aware of the moviegoer's voyeuristic participation in the fantasy and of the role played by the actors' marriage in the viewers' experience of the film. Bill's fantasy was inherently visual (i.e., the brief scenes are scored but include no dialogue or sound from the actors), and it was both his fantasy and the viewers'. It reflects the endless public appetite for access to celebrity lives; the age of the celebrity sex tape had just dawned and would explode over the coming decade as the internet became increasingly powerful. It is also worth noting that, in Kubrick's version, the lovers did not actually see each other. As Bill initiated lovemaking with Alice following the holiday party they attended together (standing in for the masked ball in the original), his eyes were closed and hers returned again and again to her reflection in the nearby mirror, in which she examined herself throughout the film. Later, in Bill's fantasy of Alice's infidelity, Alice never looked the officer in the eyes but peered briefly in the direction of the audience and seemed trapped in her internal experience. Real connection eluded them, and the characters struggled throughout to see themselves.

The sequence of events that led to Fridolin's fantasy are worth reviewing: Fridolin and Albertine engaged in actual flirtatious contact with others outside of their marriage, which led both to increased desire and to increased jealousy as they shared the experiences with each other. Albertine shared her memory as a way of confessing and relieving the tension that had built between them.[2] Fridolin's fantasy was birthed, then, of Albertine's memory of her own fantasy,[3] and it serves not to alleviate tension but only to inflame it. Both experienced desire for partners outside of the marriage, and they both acted on that desire. Acknowledgment of the fact of that extramarital desire had consequences for the relationship.

Walking backward through time

A call interrupted the couple, and Fridolin had to leave to visit the family of a deceased patient. While there, he encountered Marianne, the bereaved daughter of the patient, who had been taking care of her ill father for some time. He found that grief and time had dulled her beauty, and he had the curious, passing thought that she "would certainly look better if she were his mistress. ... Her hair would be less dry; her lips would be fuller and redder" (Schnitzler, 2002, section 2, para. 5). Unexpectedly, she confessed her love for Fridolin, who was not surprised by her feeling for him but by her decision to tell him. He was saved from the awkward situation by the appearance of her fiancée, and Fridolin left the house feeling that "he had

116   A dream of the desiring imagination

escaped from something, not so much from an adventure but from a melancholy spell that he must not let overpower him" (section 3, para. 1).

His encounter with Marianne was the first of a series of strange erotic encounters with women over several hours. Still troubled by Albertine's revelation and unable to escape his fantasy of her nonexistent infidelity, he wandered the streets of Vienna. He encountered a group of drunken students, and one deliberately bumped him, silently challenging him to respond. Fridolin wanted to confront the young man but was struck by the ridiculousness of the challenge: "Should I go and confront a drunken student, I, a man of thirty-five, a practicing physician, married, and the father of a child! Formal challenge! Witnesses? Duel!" (Schnitzler, 2002, section 3, para. 2). Unsettled, feeling cowardly, he imagined with what grim enthusiasm he would challenge Albertine's Danish officer, concluding "Well, really, she might just as well really have been his mistress! It wasn't any different. Even worse" (para. 2). He did not explain how it might be worse. Reality was blurring with fantasy, imagination becoming in Fridolin's experience more potent than reality. Albertine and his daughter, sleeping in their beds, "had now moved into the realm of specters" (para. 3). This sensation calmed him, "as it appeared to free him from all responsibility, to absolve him from all human connection" (para. 3).

Fridolin encountered a young prostitute and found himself drawn to her. We hear Schnitzler's (2002) conversation with Freud and psychoanalysis clearly in Fridolin's concern that this attraction means "that he was suddenly regressing to adolescence" (para. 7). Indeed, his path from his home to the door of the evening's final destination was marked by its trajectory backward in time, from the younger but more age-appropriate Marianne to the encounter with his college days via the fraternity brothers to the prostitute Mizzi, who was 17. Fearing that he lacked courage, Fridolin followed her into her apartment, drawn both by desire for her and for revenge against Albertine. After Mizzi undressed and he discovered how young she was, he changed his mind. She told him he was afraid, and after his protests, gently corrected him: "You can never tell, some time or other it's got to happen. You're completely right to be afraid. And if something were to happen, you would curse me" (para. 25). Fridolin was deeply touched by her guileless honesty; he offered to pay her, but she refused.

In these three encounters—Marianne, the fraternity brothers, and Mizzi—we can see Schnitzler sketching a descent or a deliberate but seemingly involuntary movement away from the world of Fridolin's persona as physician and loving husband into "the dark and dangerous whirlpools" (Schnitzler, 2002, section 1, para. 5) that Fridolin also carried within. His experience of privilege appears at points as outright hauteur; he assured himself that "indeed he was still in the prime of youth, had a charming and lovable wife, and could still have another woman or several other women in addition, should he choose to" (section 3, para. 1). It is a common affliction.

Mizzi commented that she knew he was a doctor because "in this district, they're all doctors, aren't they?" (para. 5). He was a man of power, and his ability to relate authentically to others (i.e., to see their desires and trajectories as independent from his) had not developed in the shadow of the power afforded him by his position. Others are objects with which to reinforce his self-worth or to gratify himself. Albertine's desire had shaken his fragile security.

We can see vividly in these passages the interpenetration—even the reversal—of fantasy and reality. Fridolin entered his own fantasy and was powerless to leave it. His walk through Vienna was the continuation of his fantasy of Albertine with the Danish officer, in which Fridolin struggled to master his conflicted feelings and to understand the primal impulses rising within him. He wanted revenge and an answer to the sudden loss of equilibrium he experienced.

We also can see the first intimations of violence emerging from the unconscious, reflecting a core unresolved conflict. Fridolin's encounter with the fraternity brothers foreshadowed darker encounters to come and served as a warning that went unheeded. Fridolin wondered whether he had regressed, but an equally compelling interpretation is that Fridolin had not actually developed past late adolescence in a fundamental way. When the fraternity brother deliberately bumped Fridolin, his shock was more about his impulse to react like an offended student than it was about the challenge itself. I think we also will find that the violence he encountered was not as a result of his trespass into this dark realm within him. The acts and artifacts of violence reflect conflicts that came into his awareness because of the journey he took.

Securing the mask

Sitting in a café, Fridolin encountered another echo of his youth in the form of Nightingale, a pianist who was taking a break from playing in the cellar bar. Nightingale went to medical school with Fridolin, and the two discussed Nightingale's life since they had last seen each other. He dropped out of medical school and became a full-time pianist. He impulsively told Fridolin about a gig, a private party at a still-unknown location, where he was scheduled to play later that night. The job was mysterious, the party more so, and Nightingale told Fridolin that the hosts made him play blindfolded, so he could not witness what was happening in the room. Nonetheless, Nightingale had seen enough to titillate Fridolin: naked women in a room with men wearing masks and cloaks. "Do you have courage?" Nightingale asked Fridolin (Schnitzler, 2002, section 4, para. 34), who protested "in the tone of an offended fraternity student" (para. 35). Fridolin convinced Nightingale to help him gain entry to the party. He would need a costume, a mask, and the password, which Nightingale had yet to be told. Fridolin quickly created

118 A dream of the desiring imagination

a plan, assured Nightingale that he could acquire a costume in the middle of the night, and returned to the streets.

Not far away, he arrived at the shop of the costumer Gibiser, who seemed unsurprised at the late request. As Fridolin selected his costume—a monk's cloak with a dark mask—a commotion broke out in the store. At the end of a darkened hallway, two men dressed in red inquisitors costumes appeared, along with "a graceful, very young girl, still almost a child, wearing a Pierrette costume with white silk stockings" (Schnitzler, 2002, section 4, para. 71). Gibiser raged at the men and told them they must stay until he turned them over to the police for taking advantage of a "lunatic" (para. 74) and a "depraved creature" (para. 82). The men protested that they were there "at the lady's invitation" (para. 73). Meanwhile, the girl ran to Fridolin and pressed herself against him; Fridolin noticed that "from her delicate breasts there arose an odor of roses and powder—mischief and desire laughed in her eyes" (para. 71). His impulse was to stay with the girl, perhaps out of a desire to protect her, and he protested to Gibiser that he was a doctor and that she needed care. Gibiser showed him to the street, laughing "mockingly" (para. 93) at the suggestion that they would discuss it further the next day.

In these two encounters, Fridolin's descent continued. It is worth briefly reflecting on Schnitzler's (2002) choice of the name *Nightingale*, which is perhaps the most openly allusive name in the novella. The male nightingale sings at night, both as part of his courting behavior and as a way to establish and defend his territory (Likoff, 2007). He also chooses a new mate each year (Likoff, 2007). Nightingales appear throughout myth and literature and are often associated with love. In Milton's "Sonnet to a Nightingale," the poet hears "thy liquid notes that close the eve of day/first heard before the shallow cuckoo's bill/portend success in love" (p. 39). The implied contrast with the cuckoo (which is connected etymologically to the later "cuckold" (Safire, 1998)) suggests the nobler and hopeful cultural associations with the nightingale.[4] Although Schnitzler (2002) did not seem to have been alluding directly to Milton's sonnet, the superficial parallel is interesting: Fridolin, the cuckold in fantasy, and Nightingale, the married father of four children who sings of love at night, and (as shown below) reluctantly initiates him into a dark underworld that affirms a primitive male power over women.[5]

Later in the story, Fridolin referred to the young daughter of Gibiser as the Pierrette, a stock character in *commedia dell'arte* who evolved from an earlier character, Columbine. Green and Swan (1985) explained that the three central characters of later *commedia dell'arte* are the "love-struck simpleton and victim of life," Pierrot; the "light-minded sex object," Columbine; and the "brutal and cynical trickster," Harlequin (p. 3). Schnitzler (2002) devoted one of his puppet plays, *The Veil of Pierrette,* to the character. The plot reflected common themes in the Pierrot/Pierrette story: Pierrette left Pierrot for a wealthy, older man; Pierrot, stricken, agreed to Pierrette's suggestion that they commit suicide together; Pierrette, however, did not follow through on the plan, and Pierrot haunted her on her wedding day; she was driven insane and danced until she collapsed and died next to his body (Weinberger, 2003). Weinberger (2003) also suggested that Schnitzler's (2002) puppet plays reflected a "lifelong concern with the element in human nature that seeks to control the other, be it for the satisfaction of some drive for power or to do something for another person's 'good'" (Weinberger, 2003, p. 205).

The Pierrette of *Dream Story* (Schnitzler, 2002) reappeared later in the novella, as Fridolin returned the costume the following day. She was perhaps, as Green and Swan (1985) suggested, a "light-minded sex object" (p. 3). Schnitzler (2002) alluded to her light-mindedness in Gibiser's description of her as a lunatic. She also was drawn to the older, wealthy Fridolin, and he was drawn to her in ways that were opaque and troubling to him. She was a bad omen or a reflection of his desire to control and intervene, even, as Weinberger (2003) suggested, for her "good." Her desire was her own, uncontrollable and disturbing, "depraved" (Schnitzler, 2002, section 4, para. 82) and "lunatic" (para. 74). Fridolin again encountered the problem of female desire, of the Otherness of the Other. He left with the problem unsolved and worried about what her appearance portended.

Denmark

Fridolin returned to the café, where Nightingale told him the password: Denmark. Fridolin was clearly startled but did not explain the significance to Nightingale. He followed behind Nightingale in a hired coach and, after a long journey, arrived at the gates of a villa. Armed with the password, he was welcomed into the main house and left his overcoat with the staff. Everyone was masked; men and women were dressed as monks and nuns. Fridolin heard the playing of a harmonium, joined by a woman's voice singing an aria. He felt slightly out of place and exposed, and he wondered whether he was among "lunatics," "conspirators," "the meeting of a religious sect" (Schnitzler, 2002, section 4, para. 108) or was the victim of an elaborate prank. He stopped, as did the others, to listen to the aria, and as he stood there, a woman's voice warned him, "Don't turn around to look at me. There's still time for you to leave. You don't belong here. If they discover you it will be very bad for you. ... I would be sorry if something happened to you" (Schnitzler, 2002, section 4, paras. 109, 111). Filled with "curiosity, desire, and above all pride," (para. 110) he refused to leave.

The nuns left the room as the music changed, and Fridolin heard Nightingale's distinctive playing. He surveyed the room:

> On one side Fridolin recognized Nightingale's indistinct outline at the piano, but the room opposite was radiant with a blaze of light. All the women stood there completely motionless, with dark veils around

120 A dream of the desiring imagination

their heads, face, and necks, and black lace masks over their faces, but otherwise completely naked. Fridolin's eyes wandered thirstily from voluptuous bodies to slender ones, from delicate figures to luxuriously developed ones and the fact that each of these women remained a mystery despite her nakedness, and that the enigma of the large eyes peering at him from under the black masks would remain unresolved, transformed the unutterable delight of gazing into an almost unbearable agony of desire. (Schnitzler, 2002, para. 112)

Fridolin also noticed, to his discomfort, that he was the only man left wearing a monk's costume; the other men were in brightly colored cavalier outfits. They rushed to dance with the naked women, and he was alone. Then a woman was by his side, and, happily and loudly, she claimed to recognize him as she moved him away from the increasingly suspicious gaze of other men. This woman, still masked, warned him that her deception would only work briefly and that he must leave immediately: "You will have no peace or quiet for the rest of your life if they find out" (Schnitzler, 2002, para. 115). Fridolin, however, was possessed with desire for her and refused to leave if it meant he could not see her again:

> He laughed and heard himself laughing, as one does in a dream. "I can see where I am. You're not here, all of you, just to drive men crazy with looking at you. You're just playing with me in order to drive me completely mad with desire." (para. 122)

She pleaded with him, telling him that he cannot consummate his desire (there were no secret rooms) and that if anyone pursued her outside of this context, both of them would lose their lives. Then she was swept away by another cavalier for a dance, and Fridolin was left alone.

Unsure what to do, Fridolin could not believe that his staying would cost him his life. He imagined that this might be a test of courage to determine his worthiness for the woman. He was desperately uncertain about what it meant. Staying and preparing to deal with any further challenges in a way that conformed to his sense of civilized conduct and chilvalry was the only way to keep alive the hope that the evening would "amount to something more than an unreal and chaotic succession of dismal, miserable, scurrilous, and lascivious adventures, not one of which he had been able to bring to a satisfactory conclusion" (Schnitzler, 2002, para. 140).

Fridolin was challenged again. The dancing and music stopped as he was asked for the password. He supplied it, but the cavaliers insisted that he supply a second password, which he told them he had forgotten. They demanded that he remove his mask, which Fridolin felt to be "a thousand times worse" than if he were "the only one naked among people who were dressed" (Schnitzler, 2002, para. 149). He refused and offered them "satisfaction in the usual way" (para. 149; i.e., via a duel, the mechanism of the code of chivalry). A cavalier responded, "It's not a question of satisfaction ... but of expiation" (para. 150).

As someone attempted to remove Fridolin's mask, a woman in a nun's habit—the one, Fridolin knew, who has been warning him throughout—appeared on the balcony and told the assembly, "Leave him alone. ... I'm prepared to redeem him" (Schnitzler, 2002, para. 154). The room filled with silence "as though something monstrous had happened," and one of the cavaliers asked the woman, "You know what you're taking upon yourself in doing this" (para. 155). She confirmed that she did, and "There was a general sigh of relief in the room" (para. 157). No one would respond to Fridolin's request for more information about the nature of the redemption, and he attempted to convince the gathering that he should pay his own price. The cavalier responded that nothing could help her now, that "there is no turning back" (para. 161) from a promise made in this place. As he protested and began to take off his mask, she distracted the group once more, dropping her habit and crying to the men, "Here I am, take me—all of you!" (para. 164).

Fridolin was forcibly removed from the room, packed into a carriage with covered windows, and delivered to an open field, unaware of his location and still unsure what he had just witnessed. Thoroughly confused, trying to make meaning of the "absurd, unfinished adventures" (Schnitzler, 2002, para. 171) of the night, he vowed to find the woman from the villa and also felt that he must win back Albertine, "as though she could not, must not, be his again before he had betrayed her with all the other women of this night, with Pierrette, with Marianne, and with the hooker on the narrow street" (para. 171). He wanted to find the fraternity students as well and settle matters with a duel. His life's meaning suddenly seemed to vanish: "Should one always stake one's life only out of a sense of duty and self-sacrifice, never out of a whim or a passion, or simply to match oneself against fate?" (para. 171).

As readers and viewers of Kubrick's (1999) retelling of this story, which was remarkably faithful to the novella throughout this section, we are in the same open field, in a parallel place of confusion and uncomprehension. We are left to interpret, knowing that our interpretations are never final or definitive. Therefore I suggest some ways to understand this densely symbolic passage, interpreting, as suggested by Ricoeur (1974, 1981), in front of the text, with an eye to how Schnitzler's (2002) vision reflected and illuminated contemporary experience.

The password *Denmark* presented a moment of synchronicity for Fridolin that suggested Fridolin was returning to explore the heart of the ungovernable, alien desire that is also in each of us. When he entered the villa, he brought with him his code of civilized conduct (i.e., his ethics, which he never fully relinquished) and called on it to protect him as he was confronted for his intrusion. It structured his experience; even his intention to betray Albertine fits in a larger cultural expectation that men will take mistresses.[6]

Although he may have understood himself to have been transcending that code in his pursuit of these women, the true transcendence would occur only when he made room for a female desire outside of his control.

The proceedings at the villa were a ritualized expression of the era's power arrangements, distilled to their brutal essence. It was a carnival of male desire; there was no overt indication that the women were turned on, and the women's lives are at stake simply for being pursued outside of the ritual context. The situation is strongly reminiscent of the play of desire in most pornography, which is primarily made for and consumed by men. Fridolin's overwhelming experience of desire at the open display of naked female bodies suggests a fundamental truth about male sexuality: men's sexuality is neurologically tied to the visual system. As Ogas and Gaddam (2011) stated, neuroscience suggests that "what you may have long suspected is true: men's brains are designed to objectify females" (chapter 3, para. 7).

The context is also important. The men were dressed as monks and the women as nuns. This ritualized transgression shows the experience of desire intensified because it flouts civilized codes. Kubrick's (1999) vision of this scene amplified the religious, ritual element, with a male figure in red robes moving among a circle of women, stopping at each to waive a smoking thurible. The scene is a parody of making-sacred and is also rigorously impersonal. The women were not people but abstractions or objects of male desire. Kubrick explicitly identified the women as hookers,[7] but Schnitzler (2002) suggested that these women were part of the aristocracy: after a man tried to remove her veil at an earlier ritual, one woman was forced to take poison the day before her wedding to an Italian prince (section 4, para. 137). In Schnitzler's view, it was not a single class of women who are disposable in this dark parlor of the male psyche—all women are. The religious gestures were failed attempts to elevate this strange gathering to the level of the symbolic or to grant it a meaning beyond its primitive expression of power and submission. The scene reveals the dark secret of the culture and of the male psyche.

The scene is also an expression of the truth of Fridolin's psyche and what he must discover and understand. The situation gave lie to his persona of the devoted husband and compassionate, respectable physician. Fridolin's predicament exposed the deep cracks in his ethic. His fantasy of Albertine's desire led him to a reckoning with his own unruly desire, and he continued to operate with an illusion of his own power and control. The line between reality and fantasy is meaningless; the villa was an expression of his unconscious and his unconsciousness. The cost of his unconsciousness would be severe.

Kubrick's (1999) retelling of this section of the story varied in a significant way. The woman in Schnitzler's (2002) version was adamant that there were no places in this villa for consummation. Kubrick (1999), however, depicted open copulation in an orgy at which some were participants and some were spectators and all were hidden behind their masks. The difference is important. The woman might have been lying to Fridolin for a variety of reasons. Schnitzler's (2002) version maintained the focus on arousal or on desire as such. The ritual celebrated male desire and gave the course of Fridolin's evening a different cast. Rather than one more failure to consummate, the villa presented a distillation of the entire experience. Fridolin must experience his desire as a fact of his existence; to sate it would not eliminate it. The desire was not the problem; what he did with it was. It was his pursuit of satisfaction, of escaping desire in the release of orgasm, that led to his ethical failure in the domain of the imagination.

It is worth noting, as well, that Fridolin's suspicion that he was regressing over the course of the evening can be read a different way. His experience in the villa was with an idealized, adult woman, so it is not a precisely linear age regression. It is, however, a relational regression, from Marianne, whom he had known for many years, to Mizzi, with whom he shared a brief moment of personal connection, to the Pierrette, whose name he did not even know, to this final woman, whose face he did not see. Mutuality evaporated over the course of his descent, as did his ability to attune to the needs of the Other.

The moment of Fridolin's redemption by the woman reflects what was absent in Fridolin. She behaved ethically in a purely Levinasian sense: his existence was more important than her own, for no material reason and with no hope of gain.[8] Bauman (1993) quoted Wladyslaw Bartosewzki, the rescuer of Nazi victims: "Only those who died bringing help can say that they have done enough" (p. 80). This response is radical, that of a saint, and without context; we know nothing of the woman's life, and Schnitzler (2002) provided no details. She was a pure exemplar or an ethical object to highlight Fridolin's developmental challenge. His inability to see the need of the Other led to his defeat and to an ominous fate for the woman. This defeat is a failure to master the developmental moment.

Fridolin's struggle to understand what happened in the villa also reflects the challenge of ethical interpretation. He remained hopeful that what he had witnessed conformed to his chivalrous code, by which his resolve was tested and for which he would soon be awarded the woman as prize. The world of the villa—the depths of his psyche—obeyed a different set of rules that preceded moral codes and to which he owed an inescapable obligation. His encounter with the unconscious in this way is understandably, and necessarily, disorienting. In one sense, Fridolin understood the task before him. His belief that he could not return to win back Albertine until he had sex with all of the women of the night suggests an urge to upend the moral code that cannot make sense of Albertine's desire and his own unknown depths. The situation remains toned with revenge, hurt, and a desire to restore equilibrium under the old ethic. In a psychological way, Fridolin found himself challenged to a duel.

124 A dream of the desiring imagination

Albertine's dream

Fridolin returned home, exhausted and preoccupied with the evening's events. After hiding his costume in a cabinet in his office, he made his way to his bedroom, where he found Albertine dreaming and laughing in a way that frightened him. He awakened her, and, after she resisted initially, she told him her dream.

Albertine was at the waterfront home of her parents, where she lived when she became engaged to Fridolin. Her parents were gone, and Fridolin arrived as a prince on a boat rowed by slaves (significant because the novella opened as they listened to their daughter read a fairy tale in which a prince arrived on a boat rowed by slaves). Albertine understood what followed— an ascent to a bridal chamber atop a mountain under an impossibly beautiful night sky—to depict their honeymoon. However, "our love was very melancholy, as though with a premonition of future sorrow" (Schnitzler, 2002, section 5, para. 21). As they returned to the world, they found themselves naked, and Albertine was consumed by terror, shame, and rage at Fridolin. His reaction was to leave to find clothes for them, and she was relieved and happy to be by herself. She explored this intermediate place and reclined under the sun in a meadow, where a young man like the Danish military officer approached her. As she watched Fridolin attempt to return to her, pursued by an angry mob, she encountered the young man again and again. He circled the earth each time and returned different each time. Finally, he reached out to her, and although she wanted to run away, she stayed where she was and he reclined beside her. After countless days, during which "nothing in our conscious existence can match the feelings of release, freedom, and ecstasy that I felt" (para. 24), Albertine saw Fridolin captured by soldiers and held for execution. She felt nothing for him, as she and the young man reclined naked in the meadow with many couples around them. Fridolin could see her and the young man and "saw this infinite sea of nakedness which foamed about me, of which I and the man who held me in his embrace were but a wave" (para. 24).

As Albertine dispassionately watched Fridolin's fate unfurl from a distance, she noticed "a young woman with a crown on her head and a purple cloak ... the queen of this country" (Schnitzler, 2002, section 5, para. 24) appear in a window high above Fridolin. If Fridolin would have accepted her and become her lover, she would have pardoned him and his death would have been averted. Fridolin, however, refused to be disloyal to Albertine, and he began to be whipped. After a second attempt, in which the naked queen attempted to hand Fridolin her diadem, Albertine recognized her as the young girl that Fridolin encountered on the Danish beach. His second refusal led to the erection of a cross, and he made his way slowly toward Albertine, bearing all that he felt she needed, "clothing and shoes and jewelry" (para. 24). Albertine, however, could not understand: "I thought your gestures stupid and senseless beyond belief, and I was tempted to make fun of you ... because you had refused the hand of a queen out of loyalty to me" (para. 24). The dream ended with her shrill laughter at him, which she hoped he would hear "just at the moment when they were nailing you to the cross" (para. 24).[9]

As the dream ended, Fridolin found that he wanted more than ever to return to all the women of the evening and consummate the relationships, then return and admit to it all as an act of revenge against Albertine, "who in her dream had revealed herself as that which she was—faithless, cruel, and treacherous, and whom he now believed he hated more than he had ever loved her" (Schnitzler, 2002, section 5, para. 25). Yet he found himself caressing her hand and could feel "only the same, unchanged tenderness— if anything, a more painfully acute tenderness" (para. 25) for Albertine. Deeply conflicted, he fell asleep next to her.

Albertine's dream neatly summarizes the couple's relationship as they found themselves in this midlife passage. After an idealized beginning, the couple's illusions evaporated in the complexity of long-term relationship. The story of the Danish officer might have catalyzed the current crisis, but their experience of extramarital desire preceded it; they found themselves naked and diminished, without the shallow resources of persona to sustain their relationship. Fridolin desperately tried to retrieve these old markers of security, leaving Albertine vulnerable but also able to explore this new freedom. Albertine acclimated to her experience of desire, and the Danish officer is a worthy partner. He had deeply explored his psyche (circled the world many times) and was able to recline with her in shared vulnerability. What had seemed to offer her security—her identity as a faithful, devoted, aristocratic wife—was a prison from which she was then freed. She knew herself in ways Fridolin did not, and in his adherence to the old ethic— to the image of the relationship that they have outgrown—he abandoned her to a vulnerability in which he could have discovered a new image of relationship.

We also could apply a Jungian shorthand here: Albertine cultivated a relationship with her anima/us, whereas Fridolin was not yet capable of it, which put their marriage in jeopardy. We see this most vividly in his inability to see the woman at the villa as authentically inviting him into re-lationship. By recognizing her insistent reality—by accepting her Otherness and safeguarding it—he would have accepted the hand of the queen, even though it would have foreclosed even the fantasy of consummation with her. It never occurred to Fridolin, given his chivalric code, that his trust-ing and respecting the woman would have represented an ethical victory worthy of reward, even perhaps in the form of sexual consummation. She could not be anything other than a prize to be won. In a vivid way in this passage, an intrapsychic ethic is also an interpsychic ethic, and his inabil-ity to see the Other as anything but an object was reflected in Albertine's

126 A dream of the desiring imagination

dream. The invitation of his psyche was extraordinary and frightening, and Fridolin lacked the courage to accept it. His punishment at the hands of the angry mob implicitly occurred because he had raced away from his relationship and from his true obligation to share Albertine's shame and experience her rage. In the dream, he failed at a second opportunity for relationship.

Denouement

The next morning, Fridolin left to attend to his medical rounds and to try to make sense of the previous evening. At each turn, he was thwarted. He searched for Nightingale and discovered that, agitated, he checked out of his hotel in the early morning hours in the company of two men and was driven to a train station. Fridolin next took his costume back to Gibiser's. There, one of the men whom Gibiser had vowed to turn over to the police was leaving the flat and, Fridolin believed, Pierrette's room. When Fridolin confronted Gibiser about the need for the girl to be treated medically, Gibiser scornfully implied that Fridolin would want to treat her himself as a pretext for sleeping with her. Fridolin was incensed by the implication, which reflected some measure of the truth. Gibiser explained to Fridolin that, rather than turn him in, he and the other man "came to another agreement" (Schnitzler, 2002, section 6, para. 14).

Fridolin left Gibiser's and next went in search of the villa, uncertain what he wanted to achieve there. As he approached the gate, a valet appeared and handed him a letter warning him by name that his investigations would come to nothing and should be dropped at once. Disappointed but still secure in the illusion that this might be yet another test of his courage and that the woman from the previous evening was unharmed, Fridolin returned home for lunch. Although in spite of himself he enjoyed the time spent with his daughter and the woman "who last night had calmly let him be nailed to the cross" (para. 30), as he left for the afternoon, he felt that "all this order, all this regularity, all this security of existence was nothing but an illusion and a deception" (para. 32).

He returned to Marianne's house, where he fantasized living "a kind of double life" as a family man and respected doctor and secretly as "a libertine, a seducer, a cynic who played with people, with men and with women, just as the spirit moved him" (Schnitzler, 2002, section 6, para. 33) and was still motivated by the fantasy of using this double life as a way, much later, to exact revenge on Albertine. When he encountered Marianne, however, he dealt with her brusquely rather than seductively, looking to escape the house as quickly as possible.

He wandered the street aimlessly, unwilling to return home and unsure where next to go. He found himself near Mizzi's apartment and sought her out, but a roommate informed him that Mizzi has been diagnosed with some vague illness and taken away with the hope that she would return in six to eight weeks. Although he was briefly drawn to Mizzi's roommate, he left her as well, unsure whether to understand this as yet another failure or "a sign that he had escaped a great danger" (Schnitzler, 2002, section 6, para. 54). He arrived at a café, where he picked up a paper and read of the strange poisoning of a woman, Baroness D., who had returned to her hotel at four o'clock in the morning in the company of two men. Concerned that this was the woman from the villa, Fridolin sought her out, first finding her hotel, then locating the hospital to which she was taken. On arrival, he discovered that she had died and that the death was ruled a suicide. Because of his standing, he was allowed to visit her body in the morgue, where he hoped to discern whether this was the woman from the villa. He had never seen her face, however, which had not occurred to him "because, up to this moment, in the last few hours since he had read the notice in the newspaper, he had envisaged the suicide, whose face he didn't know, with Albertine's face" (para. 65). It suddenly came to him that he had been pursuing Albertine. When he viewed the corpse, he realized he would never know whether this was the woman from the villa.

He returned home and entered his bedroom, where he discovered Albertine asleep and his mask from the previous night on his pillow. He collapsed onto the bed and sobbed to Albertine, "I'll tell you everything" (Schnitzler, 2002, section 7, para. 3). When he was done, he asked Albertine what they should do:

> "I think that we should be grateful that we have come away from all our adventures unharmed—from the real ones as well as from the dreams."
> "Are you sure we have?" he asked.
> "Just as sure as I suspect that the reality of one night, even the reality of a whole lifetime, isn't the whole truth."
> "And no dream," he said with a soft sigh, "is entirely a dream."
> She took his head with both her hands and pressed it warmly to her breast. "But now I suppose we are both awake," she said, "for a long time to come."
> Forever, he wanted to add, but before he could say the word she put a finger on his lips and whispered almost as if to herself, "Don't tempt the future." (paras. 6–12)

In this passage, the two lovers finally saw each other. Fridolin's mask had to be symbolically removed; he had to become vulnerable and reveal himself to Albertine, who had been waiting for him. They are both *awake*. As throughout the book, Schnitzler in this passage presented dream and fantasy as blurring together. Both represent unconsciousness of a psychic reality that is present symbolically. An act of interpretation was required, or, more directly, an act of ethical relatedness or of concern for all elements of the experience. Fridolin's groping search for satisfaction across

128 A dream of the desiring imagination

three evenings was driven by forces he could not understand and refused to acknowledge. His jealousy of Albertine's fantasy of the Danish officer was a shield against his true feelings of profound insecurity. The foundations on which he lived his comfortable life were nothing but "illusion and deception" (Schnitzler, 2002, section 6, para. 25).

The poisoning of Baroness D. remains a mystery. Although the woman at the villa alluded to an earlier poisoning of an aristocratic participant in these rituals (about whom Fridolin had read in the paper), Fridolin did not know whether the same fate befell the woman at the villa because of his presence there. He was haunted by the possibility and by his fantasy that the woman in the morgue might wear Albertine's face. This could reflect his deeply passionate feeling for his wife as well as his jealous aggression toward her; likely, it is both. Fridolin did not come to a clear realization that his inability to see the woman at the villa as more than a body to be desired likely led to her death. In the end, he continued to resist accepting responsibility for her. He knew at least that he had gotten in over his head. In the end, he knew that he did not know, that fantasy is real in ways that he could not have understood before, and that reality is charged with symbolic, synchronistic life. The only security is in remaining awake to symbolic experience and knowing that it is inevitable that one will fall asleep again, fall into unconsciousness, and reach for an ephemeral security in status, tribe, and wealth.

In one way or another, all of the women encountered by Fridolin suffered his unconsciousness. He was emotionally brutal with Marianne and unable to acknowledge or empathize with her suffering (which was expressed in the most flattering way to Fridolin, as love); Mizzi, the victim of a tragic disease, disappeared; the Pierrette's father, it was implied, became her pimp. In each case, Fridolin could have done something to mitigate the suffering. At minimum, he could have used his credentials (so quickly flashed at other convenient moments in his travels) to find and visit Mizzi, and he could have chosen to stay with the Pierrette to ensure that she would not be victimized.

We have been operating with a dual understanding of fantasy in analyzing Schnitzler's (2002) work. The first is a literal understanding of fantasy's appearances in the text. Fridolin's fantasy of Albertine's sexual experience with the Danish officer—which was itself a fantasy (but not also a memory)[10]—is the chief example. The second is suggested by Schintzler's (2002) deliberate overlay of Fridolin's experience and Albertine's dream. The dream did not happen in reality, yet it reflects fundamental psychic truths that shocked Fridolin: it was more than a *dream* in the common sense of something evanescent and illusory.[11] Likewise, Fridolin's experience was more than reality in that he experienced it as containing symbolic depth. When contemplating the possibility of living a double life, he wandered into a reflection on the variable intensity and reality of dreams and noted that some dreams are remembered whereas others are forgotten: "One remembers the dream only later, much later, and then no longer knows if one has really experienced it or only dreamt it" (section 5, para. 53). This line underscores the epistemological uncertainty at the heart of these distinctions. Dream may be reality; reality may be dream. So we also have read Fridolin's experience after Albertine's confession as itself a fantasy.

If we keep to the stricter understanding of fantasy (i.e., to the charged images of Albertine in the Danish officer's arms), we can see that it has ethical implications. Although they may not have been apparent to either in the moment, Albertine and Fridolin both faced key decision points. Rather than hold the increasing tension between the two of them (i.e., rather than notice the affective intensity and reflect together on what was happening between them), Albertine communicated her fantasy to Fridolin as a way to release tension. This was a moment of unconsciousness for both of them. Albertine could have made a different choice. Fridolin also could have interrogated his own feelings of hurt, anger, and jealousy. Why was Albertine's fantasy so threatening to him? Why did he imagine it was a betrayal? Can anyone control who or what they desire? This lack of ethical relatedness did not cause the death of the woman at the villa, but it was a moment when Fridolin's conflict could have been interrogated and integrated without his leaving the relationship. Instead, the conflict remained embedded in his fantasy of Albertine in the arms of the Danish officer.

To understand fantasy in a fuller sense—that Fridolin's experience *in reality* was simultaneously an intrapsychic journey—opens his travels through the Viennese streets to ethical interrogation in a psychological mode. It was not just the way he treated material others but the way he treated them within himself that affected them. His capacity to hold them internally mirrored his conduct externally. This may seem to be an academic point, but it affects how we understand ethical codes. There is a difference between a prohibition against killing and a commitment to understand and accept the desire to kill. The desire to kill is acceptable; indeed, is a natural expression of anger and aggression. Our ethical response toward fantasy is first to allow it and then to stand under it. This is a point made clearly by the fate of the woman at the villa. Fridolin did not kill her; he desired her. Had he known himself better, however, he would have taken her pleas seriously and understood the real danger she faced because of her ethical gesture toward him. Because we imagine Others, our engagement with those images matters for ourselves and for those Others. It also mattered for Fridolin. He risked divorce, disgrace, and death. His intrapsychic conduct had significant intrapsychic consequences, in the form of anxiety, fear, anger, guilt, and profound confusion. He could not see beyond the walls of his narcissistic prison and had to be released by Albertine, who could see him for who he was and had compassion for him.

We could spend much more time with Schnitzler's (2002) densely symbolic and thought-provoking work. This brief overview I hope has communicated

130 A dream of the desiring imagination

the complexity of ethical inquiry into fantasy. The imagination is inextricably bound with the physical world, but the imagination also remains distinct. How we engage with our imaginal experience impacts material and imaginal Others and is the domain of our individuation. Fantasy also may upend ethical codes that have constrained our growth; the compelling fantasy demands not that it be enacted but that the conflict be acknowledged and integrated.

Notes

1. The famously exacting Kubrick kept Cruise and Kidman from working on other films for the 18 months of the shoot, which is an extraordinarily long time for two of the world's highest profile stars to be unavailable for other projects and unseen by the public in new material. That two actors of their stature would marry the project for such an unusual length of time suggests both the prominence of Kubrick and the perceived import of the project.
2. "Anxiously drawing closer to each other, both searched for an event, however indifferent, for an experience, no matter how trivial, that might count as an expression of the inexpressible and whose honest confession now could perhaps free them from the tension and mistrust that was gradually becoming unbearable" (Schnitzler, 2002, section 1, para. 15).
3. Albertine had no contact with the officer, other than a brief glance outside the hotel. Her reflections on their contact suggest that she believes he felt as much desire for her as she did for him, but it was never confirmed.
4. This interpretation of Milton was aided by Potter (2014).
5. The Greek myth of Philomela is also worth mentioning in this context. As told by Ovid in his *Metamorphoses* (1955), Philomela was imprisoned, mutilated, and serially raped by her sister's husband, the king Tereus. After she orchestrated her escape, she exacted a gory revenge during the festivals of Bacchus. As she escaped, she transformed into a nightingale. Here we have the nightingale associated with orgiastic ritual and the subjugation of women.
6. In Kubrick's (1999) vision of the conversation between Bill and Alice, in which Alice confessed her attraction to the military officer, Bill did not confess a parallel experience of his own. Alice raged at Bill ("If you men only knew"), pointing directly to Bill's double standard. Fridolin's vengeful confession regarding the girl at the beach at least established a parity; Alice's tone, which seemed far harsher than Albertine's appeared on the page, seems to reflect Bill's even deeper unconsciousness and greater sense of entitlement (as well as the changes in culture that accompanied feminism; Alice can acceptably be angry with Bill's lunkheadedness). Perhaps Kubrick was communicating that it is now simply assumed that extrarelational attraction is a normal male experience. Alternatively, perhaps he understood Bill to be dimmer and less evolved than Fridolin, which are traits that the actor Tom Cruise performed ably.
7. This is perhaps a nod to the shifting balance of power in post-feminist gender politics—all women can be objectified, but not all women can be controlled.
8. Kubrick (1999) opted out of this tension by suggesting in a later scene that the woman was a beautiful hooker for whom Bill had cared in an early scene of the film; she knew who he was and was in a symbolic way indebted to him.
9. Kubrick's (1999) version of the dream was a sketch of the original, with important changes in emphasis. He omitted the honeymoon—the authentically happy beginning to the relationship—and placed the couple naked in a foreign city.

The naval officer appeared to Alice, reclined naked in a garden, and laughed at her. Then they made love. Alice told Bill, "Everyone was fucking. And then I was fucking other men ... so many ... and I knew you could see me in the arms of all these men ... and I wanted to make fun of you, to laugh in your face, and so I laughed as loud as I could". Again, in Kubrick's version, consummation was foregrounded, and Alice mocked him not for his failure to follow his desire but simply for his failure to see and respect her ungovernable desire.

10. Actually, Schnitzler (2002) did not suggest that Albertine's experience of the Dane was a fantasy in the sense that Kubrick (1999) visualized Fridolin/Bill's fantasy of Albertine/Alice's sexual experience. Albertine recounted a memory of desire rather than a visually described imaginal experience that was separate from the material encounter with the Dane. That memory is also, however, a fantasy, as is all memory. Her imaginal experience was of the encounter with the Dane, and she had tended that imaginal experience (i.e., memory, fantasy) during the year since it happened. To discriminate it from Fridolin's fantasy perhaps involves hair-splitting and serves as one more illustration of the complexity of the precise use of these terms.

11. For example, the fifth definition of dream from the Collins English Dictionary is "a vain hope" (Dream, n.d.).

References

Bauman, Z. (1993). *Postmodern ethics.* Malden, MA: Blackwell.

Dream. (n.d.). *Collins English dictionary* (10th ed.). Retrieved from http://dictionary.reference.com/browse/dream

Green, M., & Swan, J. (2010). *Triumph of Pierrot: The* commedia dell'arte *and the modern imagination.* State College, PA: Penn State Press.

Helmetag, C. (2003). Dream odysseys: Schnitzler's *Traumnovelle* and Kubrick's *Eyes Wide Shut. Literature/Film Quarterly, 31*(4), 276–286. Retrieved from http://www.questia.com/read/1P3-522127541/dream-odysseys-schnitzler-s-traumnovelle-and-kubrick-s

Kubrick, S. [producer and director]. (1999). *Eyes wide shut.* London, UK: Warner Bros.

Likoff, L. (2007). Nightingale. In K. Clements (Ed.), *The encyclopedia of birds* (pp. 633–636). New York, NY: Infobase Learning. Retrieved from http://books.google.com/books?id=ILEMaU74oXgC&q=nightingale#v=snippet&q=nightingale&f=false

Milton, J. (1632–1633). Sonnet to the nightingale.

Neu, J. (2002). An ethics of fantasy? *Journal of Theoretical and Philosophical Psychology, 22*(2), 133–157.

Ogas, O., & Gaddam, S. (2011). *A billion wicked thoughts: What the internet tells us about sexual relationships.* New York, NY: Penguin.

Ovid. (1955). *Metamorphoses* (M. Ines, Trans.). New York, NY: Penguin Books.

Potter, L. (2014). *A preface to Milton: Revised edition.* New York, NY: Routledge. Retrieved from http://books.google.com/books?id=siesAgAAQBAJ&dq=milton+cuckoo+cuckold&source=gbs_navlinks_s

Ricoeur, P. (1974). *The conflict of interpretations: Essays in hermeneutics.* Evanston, IL: Northwestern University Press.

Ricoeur, P. (1981). *Hermeneutics and the human sciences* (J. Thompson, Trans.). New York, NY: Cambridge University Press.

Safire, W. (1998, November 29). On language: Touching base with cuckolds. *New York Times*. Retrieved from http://www.nytimes.com/1998/11/29/magazine/on-language-touching-base-with-cuckolds.html

Schnitzler, A. (2002). *Night games and other stories and novellas*. Chicago, IL: Ivan R. Dee.

Simon, J. (2002). Foreword. In A. Schnitzler, *Night games and other stories and novellas* (Kindle ed.; paras. 1–18). Chicago, IL: Ivan R. Dee.

Weinberger, G. (2003). Arthur Schnitzler's puppet plays. In D. Lorentz (Ed.), *A companion to the works of Arthur Schnitzler* (pp. 205–226). Rochester, NY: Camden House. Retrieved from https://books.google.com

Chapter 7

The law of the (imaginal) land

More than 100 years after the dawn of talk therapy, the psychologizing of culture has rewritten our experience and opened—or created—an imagination accessible to public examination. Baudrillard's nightmare of a "forced exteriorization" of individual experience[1] has come true in ways that expose us to a kind of social scrutiny that is unprecedented. We *want* to express our experiences, we are expected to express them, and we understand some aspects of those expressions to be psychologically necessary. Michel Foucault captured the paradoxes at the heart of the psychoanalytic project—ostensibly one of the key forces behind this exteriorization—in the opening pages of his multivolume *History of Sexuality*:

> my aim is to examine the case of a society which has been loudly castigating itself for its hypocrisy for more than a century, which speaks verbosely of its own silence, takes great pains to relate in detail the things it does not say, denounces the powers it exercises, and promises to liberate itself from the very laws that have made it function. (Foucault, 1978, p. 8)

That verbose speech has only been amplified by the internet's transformation of social activity. And the socially agreed-upon conventions to guide behavior—our laws—struggle to guide us adequately. As the philosopher and theologian John Caputo wrote, "Ethics stops short with the law or rule while everything that exists is a singularity of which the coarse lens of the law cannot quite catch sight" (Caputo, 1999). Caputo's "coarse lens of the law" has collided with these exteriorizations in novel ways, with complex results that by their nature cannot wholly satisfy the particular circumstances and context of any given individual. In this chapter, we will explore two contemporary collisions of the imagination and the law—one criminal, the other professional—as a way of teasing out the ethical questions that radiate from our increasingly psychologized, networked imagination.

134 The law of the (imaginal) land

Fantasy, conspiracy, and the digitized imagination

One day in August, 2012, the wife of New York City police officer Gilberto Valle sat staring at their shared computer in disbelief. She had stumbled into a cache of photos her husband had found on a website, darkfetishnet.com, that horrified her. They had been struggling in their marriage, but this was something entirely unexpected and troubling. This was different from S&M, which she'd heard about from the *Fifty Shades* books. She took their daughter, barely a toddler, and ran to her family home in Nevada. She installed software to track his internet use and accessed his email account. What she found led her to contact the FBI (Engber, 2013b).

Among the items the FBI found on Valle's computer was a manual he wrote for "Abducting and Cooking" women (Goldstein, 2012). Images on his computer depicted graphic violence against women. His chats in various online contexts and his email traffic included correspondences with men that described their fantasies about kidnapping, torturing, raping, and killing women. "I was thinking of tying her body onto some kind of apparatus," he wrote in one passage. "Cook her over a low heat, keep her alive as long as possible" (Goldstein, 2012).

What made Valle's wife's discoveries particularly terrifying to her and to law enforcement was their specificity. The fantasies Valle described online involved his wife and other women in his life, some of them long-time friends. He described himself as a budding kidnapper and discussed with his correspondents (including Michael Van Hise and Christopher Lash, who were convicted of conspiracy to kidnap women (Engber, 2014)) his willingness to kidnap women he knew and to deliver them to his correspondents for them to rape, cook, and kill. He visited at least two of these friends and later described these visits as scouting expeditions, trial runs for his planned abductions.

Like Lash and Van Hise, Valle was arrested and charged with conspiracy to kidnap, a federal crime (Goldstein, 2012). Crucially, he was also charged with improperly accessing a police database, which he used to find details about the women he was discussing online. His trial and conviction were a tabloid sensation in 2013, but they also raised difficult ethical issues in the internet age. Who are we when we engage with Others online? Who are they? When we join Others in fantasy, how can we know that those Others understand the experience to be "only" fantasy? And of course the question that has followed us throughout: Can we make a distinction between fantasy and reality? Valle's inner experience retreats from us endlessly; Engber (2013b) suggested that Valle could be a psychopath, or someone who experiences both love and destructive impulses towards these women.

Valle's attorney argued forcefully that the government was prosecuting a thought crime,[2] using what legal scholar Kaitlin Ek called "the fantasy defense" (Ek, 2015). At trial, they argued that his online profile made his

The law of the (imaginal) land   135

understanding of his intentions clear: "I like to press the envelope, but no matter what I say, it is all fantasy" (p. 902). To the prosecuting attorney, Randall Jackson, one's fantasy is subject to the gaze of the legal system: "Gil Valle's fantasy is about seeing women executed. The fantasies that he is engaging in are about seeing women sexually assaulted, executed and left for dead. That's not a fantasy that is OK" (p. 901).

Ek framed the legal issue as a collision between protections under the First Amendment and the established legal understanding of conspiracy. Two exceptions to First Amendment protections that might be applied to Valle's case are obscenity (which has been famously difficult to define from a legal standpoint in American courts) and conspiracy. In the Supreme Court case *Miller v. California*, the court determined that obscenity depends on circumstances in which "'the average person, applying contemporary community standards' would find that the work, taken as a whole, appeals to the prurient interest" (p. 914). The court made a fascinating—and unmeasurable—distinction between "shameful or morbid interest in sex" and "normal, healthy sexual desires" in the choice this hypothetical average person might make (p. 914). Furthermore, the Supreme Court found in *Stanley v. Georgia* that the state cannot regulate the consumption of "obscene" materials by a private individual—it can only address the acts of distributing and receiving them (p. 915). As Ek suggests, "private consumption and expression are not subject to the obscenity exception because there may exist some right to *thought itself* in the First Amendment" (p. 915, original emphasis).

The conspiracy exception, if it applies to Valle's case, hinges on understanding his online exchanges to be "speech that doubles as criminal conduct" (p. 915). Were Valle and his correspondents planning to commit a crime? Or were their conversations expressions of fantasy, a fantasy heightened by speaking *as if* they intended to actually commit the crime? The evidence that the men intended to actually commit crimes is dependent on one's assumptions. Valle's use of a police database to find some of these women was a critical piece of evidence, as were his reports of his visits with some of these women as scouting expeditions for the crime. But it is not so easy to draw a solid line between these acts-in-the-world and criminal intent. Ek related that "It is a cherished maxim in criminal law that 'evil intent alone' may not be punished" (p. 926). The disgust we may feel when hearing Valle's online conversations may contaminate the legal picture: "a criminal prosecution can run a serious risk of punishing a defendant for the unpopularity of his expression" (p. 922). What is required for a conversation to become a conspiracy "is agreement to achieve—rather than proximity to achieving—an unlawful goal" (p. 930). One must both agree with others to commit a crime, and then must also take specific steps toward committing that crime (p. 931).

Some of Valle's actions outside of online discourse can be understood as concrete steps—accessing the database and visiting some of the women he discussed online. But he did not take other steps that were openly discussed. On several separate occasions, the plans hatched and articulated in detail online between Valle and his correspondents never came to pass. They named specific dates and times when kidnappings would occur—and then none of them commented when those dates came and went without action: "Valle supposedly 'agreed' with cyberpals to kidnap three different women on the very same Monday in early 2012—one in New York City, one in Pakistan, and a third in Columbus, Ohio" (Engber, 2014).

This fact was among those cited by the judge in Valle's trial when he took the extraordinary step of setting aside the jury's guilty verdict on the conspiracy count (Engber, 2014). Prosecutors appealed the judge's decision and lost; as of this writing, Valle is a free man, an author of two books who is rebuilding his life. The convictions of Lash and Van Hise stand, though the material issues in all three trials are very similar (Engber, 2014). In her concluding statement about the issues raised in Valle's case, Ek underlined the constitutional conflicts inherent in prosecuting these kinds of crimes, arguing for a revision of the legal system's understanding of what constitutes an overt act: "Even a defendant with the most utterly repulsive fantasies imaginable should not be convicted based on anything less than the jury's belief beyond a reasonable doubt that he committed the acts charged" (Ek, 2015, p. 945).

What does the Cannibal Cop have to teach us about the ethical and the imaginal in the digital age? We can point quickly to the far-reaching effects of an individual's imaginal experience on Others—once they have been expressed and encountered. Valle's wife was traumatized and her life upended by the experience, believing that her husband intended to kill and eat her. The female friends who appeared in his online chats were similarly affected, and Valle's family—particularly his mother—was deeply affected. The case activated a broad regional community who followed the case, and it cost taxpayers considerable expense to have the experiences examined legally. Two other men sit in prison for their participation in these fantasies.

Which raises the next question: Would this have happened before the internet, before its extraordinary power to connect and to amplify reshaped the human community? In simpler terms, would Valle find Van Hise and Lash and the other individuals (upwards of 20 different people (Engber, 2013a)) who engaged with him online about his fantasies? One's imagination has never been fully one's own, of course; however one understands the notion of the archetypal dimension of psyche—whether as a material residue of human evolution, as a transpersonal dimension of experience beyond perception that links us acausally in the present moment, or otherwise—we share stories, images, physiology, environment, psychological patterns and potentials. It seems reasonable to propose that this particular set of fantasies took its extensive form because of its collectivity and its digital context. Mediated by keyboards, screens, and millions of miles of cable, these imaginations found each other and became something larger. They needed each

The law of the (imaginal) land   137

other to breathe together, to conspire. Otherwise there would be no crime and no evidence.

Of course, conspiracies have never required technology to flourish. Whispers can accomplish great hidden projects across vast distances. But embedded in the *Miller v. California* definition of obscenity is a key insight into what has changed since the early 1990s: our capacity to engage covertly in communal behavior that we would experience as shameful if it became public knowledge. The seeming anonymity of online experience makes possible a displacement of the kind of communal judgment that might be internalized as a deterrent. Online, Gil Valle was not "Gil Valle"—he was "GirlMeatHunter" (Engber, 2013c). As we discussed when considering the online world of the Bigs and Littles in chapter 2, online identity is a slippery phenomenon. What emerges in Gil Valle's imagination is an alternate face, one that gains dimension and becomes legitimized in relationship with Others. Who those Others might be outside of the shared fantasies does not need to intrude on either "Gil Valle" or "GirlMeatHunter."

It is in the moment when he visited with his college friend, Kimberly, that these two fantasies of Valle blurred together. Who was he? Kimberly reported a relaxed, pleasurable visit over brunch, and Valle brought his wife and young daughter. At once he was both Gil and GirlMeatHunter, who would return home to report the visit excitedly to an online correspondent. He used her name—Kimberly—in his chats, but he changed many identifying details that might make it easier for his "conspirator" to find her (Engber, 2013c). Gil had a relationship with Kimberly. GirlMeatHunter had a relationship with "Kimberly." The full name of the document on his computer, which emerged at trial, was "Abducting and Cooking Kimberly: A Blueprint" (Engber, 2013c). To which Kimberly did the file refer? And did Valle understand them to be distinct?

After an appellate court upheld the lower court's vacation of the guilty verdict, Valle gave an interview to Daniel Engber, the *Slate* reporter who covered the case extensively. More than three years after his arrest, Valle disavowed his own interest in cannibalism and much of the horrific content of his online chats. His chief explanation for the whole mess? He was a good storyteller: "'You start getting positive feedback, and you want to keep providing for people. It's like this courtesy. If the other guy is into recipes for organ meat, well ... I'm not into that shit at all, but that's the way it works. If he wants to take it that way, you engage him in that way'" (Engber, 2015).

Viewed from a distance, after close to two years in prison, after psychotherapy, Valle understood himself primarily to be pleasing his correspondents, a writer of particularly vivid and entertaining narratives. Since the Engber interview, Valle has published his own work of fiction, *A Gathering of Evil* (2018), which reflects many of the preoccupations of his online chats. His identity as a writer is of course dependent on, inseparable from, his identity as the Cannibal Cop, as GirlMeatHunter.

138   The law of the (imaginal) land

Throughout this brief meditation on Valle's encounter with the legal system, we have been using "fantasy" in a commonsense, imprecise way—as a reflection of experiences that we only know about through his expressions of them in online behavior, and also as "just" fantasies, in the way that the songwriters Norman Whitfield and Barrett Strong (1971) wrote about fantasy in the hit Temptations song "Just My Imagination (Running Away With Me)"—insubstantial, unreal, and evocative of a lonely soul longing for connection. All of these people had imaginal experiences that had significant consequences "in reality," fantasies that were always already real, and that had implications for many people beyond their (lonely) rooms. Encountering an aspect of Valle's imaginal world for the first time on her computer screen, Valle's wife's experienced a (completely reasonable) fantasy of her own: her life was in danger, and she had to flee. And they all were part of a collective fantasy that has a power and an ethic of its own: a fantasy of instant anonymous connection, of guiltless imaginal play, of excitation and release outside of the frame of ethical relatedness. Of an experience that was just their imaginations, running away from them.

Paula and Nathan's *coniunctio*

A therapeutic container informed by the analytic awareness of transference and countertransference can be uniquely attuned to imaginal perception in the moment. The Jungian analyst Nathan Schwartz-Salant (1989) presented a startling transcript of an imaginal experience during a therapeutic session. Below, I reproduce sections of this transcript along with some contextualizing material from Schwartz-Salant's book. His interpretation of the work is useful to explore, but I focus on what I see as the ethical dimensions of the exchange.

A successful professional in her mid-40s, Paula had already completed a year-long Freudian analysis to address borderline personality disorder before her work with Schwartz-Salant. Among her early childhood experiences, Paula's father disciplined her by spanking, and each time she was aware of his sexual arousal during the act. Paula experienced a fear of sexual excitement, which became a focus of treatment shortly before the following exchange, which I reproduce at some length:

> ME: Can you sense a kind of energy field between us, as if there is an imaginary couple here composed of you and your father?
>
> PAULA: I'm not sure. I talked to my father recently. He was so forgetful. I sensed his impotence. I guess that's a loss of the oedipal father. I can sense the couple now, me and my father.
>
> ME: I'm not sure how you and I and the couple connect. I don't sense the fantasy clearly.

The law of the (imaginal) land   139

PAULA: I am lying over your lap on my bed. You are spanking me. I'm feeling the tautness of your arm hitting me, the tautness of your thighs and penis, it's all blended ... the excitement in your body. ... I can't tell whose excitement it is, mine or yours.

My attention was on the imaginal couple between us and also on her. It is essential to grasp the structure of this dual perception. There were two separate objects: a couple composed of the patient and myself and the imaginal couple, whose presence could be sensed and their form imaginally seen in the space between us. My attention was on both couples at once, oscillating between one and the other or hovering between them. In response to her comment, I, too, felt excited and chose to tell her. But then I was surprised to find myself saying, "What do you want to do?"

This last question was a result of imaginally focusing on the transference couple and the drives and fantasies of this dyad. I felt as if I might lose my boundaries, but I also knew that not saying what I did would lead to breaking the field between us. It seemed honest to ask this seemingly seductive question. At the same time, I had a stabilizing reference point through the triangle of Paula, the couple, and myself.

PAULA: I want to see your excitement. I want to undress you, to see it.

At this point the field intensity rose, and I began to feel somewhat identified with the male in the couple. I was again surprised when the following fantasy emerged in me; I told it to her:

ME: I want to penetrate you from the rear.
PAULA: Then do it! I want it too! Don't hide it!

Engaged in my own feelings and vision of the couple, waiting to see what might emerge, the following thought forcefully occurred to me:

ME: What about mother?
PAULA: Fuck her—she doesn't matter. All that matters is us!
ME: I'm scared.
PAULA: I don't believe it! It's incredible! You'd leave me in it all alone because you're scared? Well I'm not! She doesn't count. It doesn't matter what she thinks.
ME: But I'm scared.
PAULA: I feel hate, rage, awe, disbelief. You're a fucking bastard—you can't leave me in it alone! I feel a fury, chaos, a splitting in my mind. Oh God, I don't believe it! I feel fragmented by a tornado inside, like my insides were just taken out of me, sucked out of

140   The law of the (imaginal) land

me. You are denying your feelings and desires, and since we are merged, I have to deny mine, or split them off. I can't trust!

ME: I think that is just exactly what happened to you with your father.

I said this partly because some clarity seemed useful, but also to dampen what seemed to me to be a rising level of unconscious processes that could be overwhelming. In silence, Paula reflected for several minutes, and in an uncharacteristic manner, she said:

PAULA: So all his other denials [of her illnesses and anger] were just a screen for this primary denial. The only way I could remain integrated was to be engaged in a mutually acknowledged sexual relationship. This is powerful! No wonder I've acted it all out— mentors with unresolved mother complexes and unresolved father complexes. I remember one analyst with whom I couldn't collude and I rationalized that he was incompetent. I continued to experience anxiety in the sessions because there was no mutually acknowledged desire. With my fiancé I feel intact when I'm with him, and then when I'm alone during the middle of the week, my anxiety begins to rise. The only way to maintain cohesion is to be in a mutually desired sexual relationship. Otherwise I lose cognitive skills. I can't think. I only regain them when I have a relationship. I've always thought that I had a learning disorder or, worse, some brain damage. (Schwartz-Salant, 1989, pp. 149–151)

Without doubt, this is a singular and extreme example of imaginal dynamics in the consulting room. Schwartz-Salant (1989) was aware of how charged and troubling such an exchange might seem to other professionals; he acknowledged that "the expression of erotic desires in the therapeutic process has long been recognized to be extremely dangerous" (p. 151) and understood that his publishing the exchange would "not be universally welcomed" (p. 151, n. 7).

Paula had a history of sexual involvement with her therapists. So Nathan's[3] open expression of sexual desire was perhaps doubly troubling—and also in its way understandable. In this context, the client's powerful, unreconciled inner conflict appears and draws in the therapist. In a sense, he cannot help but feel the desire. He can, however, refrain from enacting it.[4] What does it mean to enact the desire? Might not voicing the desire itself represent an enactment? What meaning might his expression have for the client? Might it confuse her and irrevocably damage the treatment process?

His expression of desire is the most explosive element of this exchange but it also reinforced our theme of the overlay of material and psychic experience. The imaginal couple between Nathan and Paula was two couples at once: Paula and her father, and Paula and Nathan. Whose desire did

The law of the (imaginal) land   141

Nathan feel: his own or Paula's father's? It is an unanswerable question: both and neither. Nathan was aware of the idiosyncratic way that Paula affected him unconsciously. He moved through this exchange intuitively, with an awareness of the multiple meanings and levels of experience as well as some awareness that he did not know everything and could not control the situation.

He also was aware of the laws that governed this moment. Although his professional code may not explicitly proscribe against the expression of desire, he knew that erotic feeling is powerful and difficult to regulate. In his book on sexual enactments in psychotherapy and their consequences, Rutter (1989) argued that "suggestive speech ... should be seen as sexual behavior. The way a man speaks to a woman can in itself become an act of sexual invasion" (p. 41). By voicing desire, Nathan risked imposing new violation on Paula. The transferential dynamic amplifies this. He was a male in power; she had an erotically charged and traumatic series of encounters with her father, who was the first and most important man in her life. Nathan's expression of desire would evoke this early trauma in deeply unconscious ways.

Regardless of whether Nathan expressed his desire, these dynamics were inevitably present. His theoretical point was that it would be dishonest to avoid expressing his desire, and it would take Paula out of this vital experience of an early trauma. His imaginal experience was his and Paula's and Paula's father's, all at once; her speaking it was a way to help Paula experience its objectivity and affirm what her father could not.

The interaction that acknowledged/created the imaginal couple is worth reviewing. Nathan suggested the idea that there "is an imaginary couple here composed of you and your father" (Schwartz-Salant, 1989, p. 149). Paula then spoke to the man of the couple and to Nathan: "I am lying over *your* lap on my bed" (p. 149, emphasis added) rather than "his lap." Paula assigned Nathan the imaginal role of her father, and he responded. The question is: Who responds through him?[5] Nathan's reflection on his experience of the imaginal dynamics suggests that there is not a clear answer. He noted that he was seeing double; he was watching the couple that appeared imaginally between them while also watching himself and Paula. Of the two couples, one was a co-creation of the other.

Nathan had seemingly sound theoretical reasons for what happened next. My projection and expectation is that he was not thinking about a *transference couple* when he asked her, "What do you want to do?" (Schwartz-Salant, 1989, p. 150). He was responding intuitively and without clear understanding of the intention of the speech. He acknowledged that his sense of boundaries were at stake in the moment. He let slip the safety of traditional ethical codes and professional conduct, with the hope that the shifted boundary would allow Paula a pivotal imaginal experience. I expect that he also knew

142 The law of the (imaginal) land

that he was transgressing. His question intensified the erotic charge of the interaction. Paula responded with her desire to see him naked and aroused.

At this point, Nathan took a decisive leap into the shared fantasy (Schwartz-Salant, 1989). He reported that a "fantasy emerged in me" (p. 150); he chose to report it to her with the statement, "I want to penetrate you from the rear." He did not report dispassionately; his desire was present too. Did Nathan want to penetrate her? Was he feeling the father's unconscious desire? The answer to this question will always involve an interpretation, even (or perhaps especially) for Nathan. I believe that both are true, but I do not have grounds other than my intuition. Even if we theorize that Nathan consciously became a vessel for the unconscious of the father, Nathan was still the one who felt the desire. In the exchange, it remains important that he did not objectify the man in the imaginal couple but took him on and spoke in his voice. "He" did not want to penetrate Paula; "I" did. Nathan abandoned the protective construct of ethical distance to participate fully in the experience with Paula.

He reported that he was "engaged in the thoughts and feelings of the couple" (Schwartz-Salant, 1989, p. 150) as his fantasies emerged. From the vantage of traditional ethical codes, there is no way to evaluate this statement; there is no observable behavior but only interpretation. Indeed, Nathan's reflections were all interpretations, after the fact, of his experience in the moment: they could not have been anything else. As we have discussed, ethical action is always an interpretation. It raises an important and likely unanswerable question: To what degree are Nathan's theoretical reflections also fictions imposed after the fact? Did he *know* what he was doing? Was he conscious of the complex relational dynamics in the moment? Alternatively, was his intuitive, spontaneous response to the emerging fantasy only later contextualized and legitimized using theory?

Theory plays an intriguing role in the transcript. Not only does it appear where one would expect, in Nathan's reflections on the experience, but it also appears explicitly in Paula's interpretive commentary. She understood herself through the construct of psychoanalytic theory. She described the "loss of the oedipal father" (Schwartz-Salant, 1989, p. 151) and discussed her history of "acting out" (p. 151) with therapists who had "unresolved mother complexes and unresolved father complexes" (p. 151). This kind of psychoanalytic self-reflection suggests that Nathan had good reason to believe that the risks he took could be understood by the client and the experience metabolized. In addition to her long-term psychoanalysis, she had been in treatment with Nathan for two years before this session. His decision to allow the fantasy to proceed and to participate in personal ways was not made in a vacuum.

It is worth commenting on the act of writing about clinical experiences. At points, the dialogue sounds inauthentic, particularly in Paula's reflections on the conversation. She told Nathan, "The only way I

The law of the (imaginal) land 143

could remain integrated was to be engaged in a mutually acknowledged sexual relationship" (Schwartz-Salant, 1989, p. 151). Perhaps she was spontaneously articulate. Nathan did not suggest that the transcript was based on anything other than his memory, which would have been influenced by his desire to make certain theoretical points. I do not want to digress into the ethics of writing about clinical sessions, but it is worth noting the blurry relationship between the session as reported and as experienced by each of the participants. We cannot imagine that we are getting an objective picture of what happened but only Nathan's fantasy of it. This transcript is a fantasy of the session or a fantasy about fantasies.

Nathan displayed respect for what I have called the *gravitational pull* of fantasy. After moving into this highly charged terrain, he used interpretation as a way to shift both of them from the experience of the imaginal couple back to the clinical setting. His allowing the fantasy to develop further might have led to enactment in the traditional sense. He told her, "I think that is just exactly what happened to you with your father" (Schwartz-Salant, 1989, p. 150). The meaning of the experience was created, or at least articulated, in that moment, and the experience also came to an end. It also included an ambiguity about the experience shared between Nathan and Paula. His statement can be read to mean that the experience they just had together reflected the same dynamics as those between Paula and her father; that is, Nathan and Paula had an experience that mirrored but was separate from those early ambiguous spankings. It also could be read as a precise enactment of the original, with Nathan experiencing and expressing a desire that was not his but Paula's father's. It is "just exactly" (p. 150) what happened.[6]

My initial reaction to this transcript was anger and revulsion. Nathan pushed it too far: he used the container for sexual gratification, he risked its integrity, and he took advantage of Paula. His listening to Paula's fantasies, holding them imaginally with her, interpreting them (i.e., stripping them of their erotic power), all would have been acceptable. His joining her in the fantasy, however, is fraught with complication and risk. I am also aware, however, of how fear of my own desire influences such a reaction. I doubt my ability to hold the container as Nathan demonstrates. I would have become disoriented, lost perspective, and retreated hastily, or perhaps even enacted the desire with her. It is not simply a matter of trusting that one's own analytic or introspective work will have made one aware of the hazards that would need to be avoided. Nathan knew that his theory and experience might not save him: "I felt as if I might lose my boundaries" (Schwartz-Salant, 1989, p. 150). His ethical stance in this instance was to value the integrity of the shared imaginal space, which is a commitment that echoes Haule's (1996) "partial dissolution and interpenetration" (p. 85) in the analytic container.[7]

My significant unease aside, I do not make a final judgment regarding Schwartz-Salant's (1989) work. Wrong and right are complex matters, and in any case, he regarded the treatment as successful. It is certainly safe to say that I cannot imagine taking the risks he took. I fear my own unconsciousness and how I might delude myself in service of my own desire. I wanted to illustrate the multiple layers of ethical discernment that can and perhaps should be applied to the imagination in a clinical context. We could say that the imperative to be ethically attuned to imaginal experience is greater in a clinical relationship. Regardless of how we might want to construct the therapeutic container as a meeting of equals that are mutually influenced, we must always acknowledge that ethical and legal responsibility for the experience rests on the therapist's shoulders. Therapy may be the only occasion in clients' lives when they experience and express their desire without shame to an accepting other. Therapists' ethical attunement to their own imaginal experience makes this extraordinary encounter possible. In reflecting on the role of the therapist as critic of desire, Neu (2002) suggested, "It takes a strong and accepting mother to help her child face, survive, and overcome the nightmares" (p. 155). Although his paternalistic tone reflects an unfortunately limiting conception of the therapeutic relationship, it reflects our first ethical responsibility as therapists: to accept the Otherness of the Other unconditionally.

Notes

1. See Preface, p. xx.
2. An excellent documentary about the case, *Thought Crimes: The Case of the Cannibal Cop*, was released by HBO in 2015 and is available to view on YouTube as of this writing.
3. To emphasize his role as an equal, personal partner in the clinical excerpt, I refer to Schwartz-Salant as Nathan.
4. An enactment is "a pattern of nonverbal interactional behavior between the two parties in a therapeutic situation, with unconscious meaning for both" (Plakun, 1998).
5. To be clear, I am not suggesting that Nathan might somehow have been channeling Paula's father or employing some kind of metaphysical connection with the actual person. The unconscious experience of the father was present unconsciously to Paula and thus present in the analytic transference. This situation suggests the kind of complex considerations we face when working with the imagination.
6. One wonders, too, whether it was not an example of both therapist and client succumbing to a repetition compulsion.
7. See the brief review of Haule's position in chapter 1, and my objections to his conclusions.

References

Caputo, J. (1999). Reason, history, and a little madness: Towards an ethics of the kingdom. In R. Kearney & M. Dooley (Eds.), *Questioning ethics: Contemporary debates in philosophy* (pp. 84–104). New York, NY: Routledge.

The law of the (imaginal) land 145

Ek, K. (2015). Conspiracy and the fantasy defense: The strange case of the cannibal cop. *Duke Law Journal, 64*, 901–945. Retrieved Oct. 20, 2018 from http://scholarship.law.duke.edu/dlj/vol64/iss5/3

Engber, D. (2013a). Free the cannibal cop. His fantasies are sick. His prosecution is even sicker. *Slate*, Feb. 6, 2013. Retrieved Oct. 20, 2018 from slate.com

Engber, D. (2013b). The cannibal cop on trial: A dispatch from Gilberto Valle's strange first two days in court. *Slate*, Feb. 27, 2013. Retrieved Oct. 20, 2018, from slate.com

Engber, D. (2013c). He didn't eat anyone. He's still guilty. The 'cannibal cop' has been convicted of a crime he only dreamed of committing. *Slate*, March 12, 2013. Retrieved Oct. 20, 2018 from slate.com

Engber, D. (2014). The cannibal cop goes free, but what about the murderous mechanic? One thought-crime conviction has been overturned. Three others have not. *Slate*, July 2, 2014. Retrieved on Oct. 20, 2018 from slate.com

Engber, D. (2015). An exclusive interview with the "cannibal cop." *Slate*, Dec. 10, 2015. Retrieved online Oct. 20, 2018 from slate.com

Foucault, M. (1978). *The history of sexuality: An introduction, Vol. 1.* New York, NY: Random House.

Goldstein, J. (2012). Officer plotted to abduct, cook, and eat women, authorities say. *New York Times*, Oct. 25, 2012. Retrieved Oct. 20, 2018 from nytmes.com

Haule, J. (1996). *The love cure: Therapy erotic and sexual.* Woodstock, CT: Spring.

Neu, J. (2002). An ethics of fantasy? *Journal of Theoretical and Philosophical Psychology, 22*(2), 133–157.

Plakun, E. (1998). Enactment and the treatment of abuse survivors. *Harvard Review of Psychiatry, 5*(6), 318–325. Abstract retrieved from http://www.ncbi.nlm.nih.gov/pubmed/9559350

Rutter, P. (1989). *Sex in the forbidden zone.* Los Angeles, CA: Jeremy P. Tarcher.

Schwartz-Salant, N. (1989). *The borderline personality: Vision and healing.* Asheville, NC: Chiron.

Valle, G. (2018). *A gathering of evil.* N.p.: Comet Press.

Whitfield, N. & Strong, B. (1971). Just my imagination (Running away with me).

Chapter 8

Conclusions

How do psychological ethics apply to the imagination? Perhaps a better question is: Should they? What do we gain by talking about the imagination in ethical ways? What do we lose? Jung warns us in *The Red Book* that "[t]he floodgates will be opened, there are inexorable things, from which only God can save you" (Jung, 2009, p. 324). If we take seriously the work of knowing ourselves, we face significant risks. And Richard Kearney evokes the dangers of one-sided approaches to these powerful imaginal experiences: "Ethics without poetics leads to the censuring of imagination; poetics without ethics leads to dangerous play" (Kearney, 1998, p. 236). To conclude our reflections, it is worth an attempt to summarize this constructed discourse and also to look for its shadow; that is, to begin to notice what has been excluded and how an ethical orientation to the imagination might serve, among other purposes, as a shield against important but troubling experiences.

In chapter 5, I articulated eight principles of an ethical approach to imagination. They are products of a moment in time and of my particular scholarly and cultural context and personal and ancestral histories. I understand them to be a fantasy in the narrow and provisional sense articulated earlier: fantasy is an imaginal experience that becomes conscious of itself as imaginal. These eight principles are a fantasy of a theory that hopefully will have some utility and that will need to be critiqued and discarded at some point. These principles should serve as a particular moment in an ongoing conversation. As we conclude, I want to pause for a moment with each of these principles and consider what they are intended to create and what they might exclude or attempt to destroy.

1. *Ethical codes are provisional and temporary expressions of an ethical impulse that serves a developmental purpose.* Ethical training for mental health professionals emphasizes adherence to ethical codes determined by licensing and accrediting bodies. In the profession, ethical discernment tends to involve interpretation of the existing codes and measurement of our behavior against our interpretations. The existence

of these codes does not keep clients from being harmed by therapists; ethical rules are broken regularly, and therapists can inflict emotional violence on clients without violating written codes or putting themselves at risk of professional consequences. An ethical education that focuses primarily on one's learning codes and understanding consequences fails to communicate adequately the dimensions of the therapist's responsibility for the client.

Ethics—specific lists of guidelines—may be put to institutional uses and may reinforce existing power structures, but they remain images of psychic processes. When we locate in the unconscious an ethical impulse that naturally reflects structural necessities in the psyche, we make the psychological nature of ethics explicit. We are not ethical because we have introjected ethical codes; we have ethical codes because we have an impulse to express the ethical imagination.

One danger in this position is that it might seem to minimize ethical codes, which is not my intent. They are a form of communication and help to establish patterns of conduct that allow the profession to take collective action when confronted by clients harmed by professionals. Another more serious objection involves the possible implication that humans are inherently ethical. Returning to a passage quoted at the end of chapter 2, Jung (1964/1958) argued, "Because we are still such barbarians, any trust in the laws of human nature seems to us a dangerous and unethical naturalism" (para. 357). We rid ourselves of this barbarism only "when the basic root and driving force of morality are felt by the individual as constituents of his own nature and not as external restrictions" (para. 357). Jung's fantasy was that we must become educated about the true root of our behavior and the means to guide it. It is perhaps worth noting that *barbarian* has been deployed in a variety of contexts historically, but the connotation of undifferentiated, unexamined Otherness pervades its usage. Fourth- and fifth-century Greeks referred to non-Greeks as *barbaroi* and used the same name to refer to slaves; as noted by Rosivach (1999), "When Athenians thought about slaves they habitually thought about barbaroi, and when they thought about barbaroi they habitually thought about slaves" (p. 129). By calling us *barbarians*, Jung (consciously or unconsciously) called attention to the heart of the problem: we are Other even to ourselves.

2. *The ethical impulse means we must respect and safeguard the experience of the Other and reflects the fundamentally relational nature of the psyche.* Both of these first two principles rest on a fantasy that humans develop relationally (more on this in a moment). Beneath that fantasy likely lurks another: the teleological unfolding of human development. Both fantasies can be seen as naïve and perhaps even unsupported. Certainly, they depend on Jungian and post-Jungian ideas about complexes and individuation. A significant lacuna in this discourse is any conversation

148 Conclusions

with contemporary cognitive or neurological research into moral development. Writing in a popular vein, the cognitive scientist Paul Bloom (2013) argued that contemporary research has suggested that morality is inherent in neural functioning and can be observed long before language acquisition or moral education. Further research would certainly benefit from a closer look at this significant contemporary discourse.[1]

The intent of this principle is to underline the intrapsychic value of ethical relatedness. If we are many within—a "team of rivals," as argued by neuroscientist David Eagleman (2012)[2]—it is reasonable to imagine that our ability to function involves the creation and maintenance of relationships among our parts. It is a further reach to imagine that to respect and safeguard the Other is a motive; as an initial goal for intrapsychic relationship, it is probably easier to imagine our keeping the Other from upending our agenda.

Again, this is not to make the obviously foolish argument that human beings always behave ethically or are always ethically engaged even when they make decisions that result in suffering for Others. Sociopaths cannot see past their transference, and most of us struggle mightily to see past our projections. Ethical conduct in the world may be a reflection of lessons learned internally about how to achieve a working equilibrium. That equilibrium, however, is difficult to attain; the ethical impulse is by no means the only driver of human behavior.

3. *Following Levinas (1985, 1989/1984, 2008), an ethical impulse involves recognition of pre-existent responsibility for our participation in the entire field.* A commonplace of dream interpretation involves one's understanding all elements of a dream to reflect different aspects of the dreamer. In this imaginal space, the dreamer is both the dream-ego—the element of the dream with which the dreamer identifies or a figure who often looks like the dreamer but sometimes does not (as when the dreamer reports "I am a wolf, running through the forest")—and the dream itself—the setting; characters; and most importantly, the process, the plot, the movement of energy. We experience ourselves as the king or queen in the chess game, but we are actually the board and all of the pieces.

This is the sense in which I understand our intrapsychic responsibility. We do not control the actions of intrapsychic Others, but we are responsible for them nonetheless. It may be a guiltless responsibility, in Levinas' (1985, 1989/1984, 2008) sense. It follows from this assumption, however, that the argument for individuation as an ethical process derives. We have an ethical responsibility to know ourselves, so that we will not inflict harm on Others as a result of our unconsciousness.

The specter of scrupulosity looms over this discourse. My grandmother's catatonic paralysis[3] derived from the impossible demands of her conscience. We can never be good enough; we literally must sacrifice our lives to fulfill our responsibility. It is an unlivable ethic. Yet I believe it reflects a fundamental human experience. As argued by Bauman (1993), *"The moral self is a self always haunted by the suspicion that it is not moral enough"* (p. 80, emphasis in original). Do we have to live our lives haunted by inadequacy and guilt? I believe that Levinas (1989/1984) did not intend this—thus his "guiltless responsibility" (p. 84)—and I certainly do not. I believe, however, that Levinas articulated an *is* and not an *ought*. He was attempting to bring into discourse our inextricable connections. We are always already related to each other and always already related within.

4. *Ethical response from a Jungian perspective is inherently interpretive.* We are called to engage our experience symbolically. To interpret is not to engage semiotically but to understand that multiple interpretations of a situation are correct and that multiple, contradictory actions could be required.

   This perspective has potentially frightening implications. How can we ever know how to act? We can never be assured that the course we have chosen is correct because there are no correct courses. There are many courses, each of which leads to a different future. We cannot attain perfection, and any fantasy of objectivity is untenable. We can only interpret.

   One definite shadow of this principle is its seeming attack on the notion of responsibility. If there is no true course but only interpretations, then can we be held responsible for our actions? After all, our interpretation is no less valid than the interpretations of concerned Others. The obverse of this is also a shadow: if we can only interpret, we can never act without fear of failing in our duty to Others. We are responsible for the outcomes of our actions without the certainty of a code to ensure correct action. Worse still, we can never be sure that our choices are not made for us by the unconscious.

   Yet this perspective also reflects the gray zone we all inhabit and resonates with our lived experience. To embrace our responsibility to interpret can release us from the burden of a life lived within artificial boundaries. As Jung (1964/1958) wrote, "The beast is not tamed by locking it up in a cage" (para. 357). When we move beyond rigid adherence to codes to the uncertain terrain of the symbolic, we open up the possibility of seeing through the phenomenon to a transcendent solution. Schwartz-Salant's (1989) narrative recounted in chapter 7 reflects the dangers and opportunities afforded us by this interpretive position. He risked his client's stability and his reputation, but he made room for a potentially healing experience that arguably would not otherwise have been possible. To recognize the interpretive nature of ethical discernment means acceptance of a greater burden of responsibility that we always already carry. This position also opens a frontier of creativity and freedom.

5. *The ethical response may directly contradict traditional ethical codes.* Although this perhaps is not true in the strictest sense,

Schwartz-Salant's (1989) narrative reflects the spirit of this principle. Our ethical impulse may put us into direct conflict with received wisdom and may threaten our security and livelihood. This is a truism of social activism. Sometimes, civil disobedience is the most compelling ethical option.

Within the domain of imaginal experience, this view is perhaps easier to understand and accept. Jung's (2009) account of eating the girl's liver[4] reflects the natural perversity of imaginal experience. In dream and fantasy, our experience is often perverse or turned the wrong way (Perverse, n.d.) from our expectations. We have to remain sensitive to the relational implications of the moment, regardless of the resistances we may bring with us. What does the situation require? How can I express my integrity in this moment? How do my ethical codes serve as a shield against necessary experience?

The shadow of this principle is the risk of significant harm to ourselves and those in our care. When we depart from our ethical codes, we lose the protection of collective wisdom. It becomes easy to understand ourselves as following a deeper integrity when in actuality we are meeting unconscious needs. This is no less true in the imagination than in clinical or personal experience. Just because a strongly felt urge to act in contradiction of an ethical code seems to align with a deeper purpose does not safeguard us or our others from harm. The risks are intense. Millennia of human grappling with paradox is embedded in our received ethical guidelines, and they should not be set aside without a full awareness of the worst consequences.

6. *We have an ethical obligation to bring into consciousness the intrapsychic violence we encounter.* Carl von Clausewitz (2013) famously suggested that "War is a mere continuation of policy by other means" (p. 127). Michel Foucault (2003) turned that thesis on its head, suggesting that "Politics is the continuation of war by other means" (p. 48). From Foucault's perspective, the institutions that furnish us imaginal and actual security emerged only as the result of violent conflict, and violence lies at the heart of human experience. In a passage that echoes Giegerich's (1993) comments on the blood that birthed our symbolic imagination,[5] Foucault (2003) argued that our ethical codes (i.e., our law) are "not born of nature, and it was not born near the fountains that the first shepherds frequented: the law is born of real battles, victories, massacres, and conquests which can be dated and which have their horrific heroes" (p. 50). This war continues:

> Peace itself is a coded war. We are therefore at war with one another; a battlefront runs through the whole of society, continuously and permanently. ... There is no such thing as a neutral subject. We are all inevitably someone's adversary. (p. 51)

Conclusions   151

It is naïve and dangerous to believe without questioning that we can achieve a bloodless peace. Foucault (2003) refused to let us avoid this fundamental reality of human existence. This view is at the heart of the American creation myth: a tyrant and a tyranny had to be overthrown. Negotiation failed; only the violent expression of power could bring about justice. When we confront the horrific suffering that attends violent conflict in the world, we at least have to consider that this violence mirrors a truth of intrapsychic functioning.

We also have the capacity to take responsibility for our violence and its effects. Ricoeur's (1999) more hopeful formulation in the first paragraph of chapter 5 suggests that we have an opportunity to bring our conflicts into discourse before they become violent or before their conceptual violence becomes actual. This principle reflects a fervent belief or the therapist's hope that further suffering can be avoided by an unblinking assessment of our conflicts. This hope that we can bring our conflicts into discourse also implies that we take seriously both (or multiple) positions in the conflict. The murdered girl's corpse presented to Jung an act already accomplished that could continue to happen if he were not able to accept and integrate it.

7. *The course of human psychological development can be described as the increasing integration of separate elements of the psyche.* Human development depends on our relating to intrapsychic Others with respect, compassion, and concern.

One shadow of this fantasy, which I referenced briefly in (2) above, is that it implies a movement toward wholeness, a common element of Jungian myths of individuation. Experiences of fragmentation might be understood not simply as psychic problems but as moral failures. If we struggle to navigate core conflicts, we do not need to complicate our situation further by judging ourselves for not finding our way. Some conflicts are insoluble; all we can do is bring them to our awareness and hold them. Wholeness, per se, is not achievable, and integration also suggests a definite conclusion. Will we ever experience ourselves as integrated?

If for Levinas (1985) ethics is first philosophy, this principle proposes that relationship is first psychology. To be perceived, energy must move between poles. Our intrapsychic poles express Otherness: we perceive them as possessing some degree of autonomy or as falling outside of our control. The fantasy that we might control the Otherness we encounter within creates conflict. Along with the myth of psychic integration, we also should offer the option of imagining our task as increasing psychic relatedness.

The values of respect, concern, and compassion should not imply capitulation to elements of psyche that threaten or inflict violence. In a *New York Times* article, Kershaw (2010) related the promising results

152 Conclusions

of a new treatment for sufferers of PTSD-related nightmares. The treatment taught dreamers ways to rehearse repetitive dreams that replaced horrifying elements with innocuous ones. Kershaw quoted a Jungian psychologist as bemoaning the treatment, arguing that "you really lose an opportunity to get some meaning out of [the dream]" (para. 9). This seems to me a wrongheaded and perhaps even unethical position. When the dreamer is overwhelmed and unable to process the experience because of its unrelenting violence, the healer's task is to give the dreamer tools to alleviate suffering. Meaning cannot be made in the face of such intrapsychic violence; first, we must end open hostilities.

8. *The* ethical imagination *is both a description—in that the imagination is inherently ethical, in the sense that it is a matrix of relationship—and an imperative—in that we need imaginative ethics that respond to the complexity of our experience.*

In chapter 1, I suggested that the goal of this project was not to enthrone a Big Brother of the imagination. That remains a shadow of this discourse: an implicit ethical code might lurk here. However well intended, does this line of thought stoke fear and moral anxiety rather than encourage growth and development? Will rules inevitably emerge to limit experience and provide some illusion of security in the dark caves of the unconscious? What aberrant wonder or what necessary monster might be hidden from our experience?

Monster is etymologically related to the word *monstrance*, which is the receptacle used to expose the host for adoration in the Roman Catholic tradition. The shared Latin root, *monstrare,* means to show (Monstrance, n.d.). The monster is also the vehicle for the sacred, the numinous, the awesome, and the terrible, which can transform or annihilate us. We must allow ourselves to imagine them, even as we must sensibly protect ourselves against their unrelated power. Once we have imagined them and protected ourselves against them, we can come into relationship with them and be shown what has been hidden within us.

How we imagine matters. It is from the imagination that we are reflective, conscious, and in fact human. When we grapple authentically with the human condition, we must speak in ethical tongues. Our codes have undoubted utility but are always provisional. Ethics dynamically interact in an imagination that thereby attains profound existential significance. To imagine ethics is the deepest human calling. In a Levinasian sense, the ethical imagination is who we are.

Notes

1. It is also worth remembering that science is one discourse among others and the integrity of scientific ways of knowing rests in rigorous insistence on constant revision. Truths are almost never definitively established. As the eminent

medical researcher John Ioannidis commented, "Science is a noble endeavor, but it is also a low-yield endeavor. ... I'm not sure that more than a very small percentage of medical research is ever likely to lead to major improvements in clinical outcomes and quality of life" (Freedman, 2010).
2. Eagleman (2012) borrowed the phrase from the title of historian Doris Kearns Goodwin's book, *Team of Rivals* (2006), which Goodwin used to describe Abraham Lincoln's cabinet. Lincoln selected his political rivals for cabinet positions so that his ideas would receive vigorous critiques.
3. See chapter 4.
4. See chapter 5.
5. See chapter 2.

References

Bauman, Z. (1993). *Postmodern ethics.* Malden, MA: Blackwell.

Bloom, P. (2013). *Just babies: The origins of good and evil.* New York, NY: Crown.

Clausewitz, C. (2013). *The essential Clausewitz: Selections from* On War. North Chelmsford, MA: Dover Courier.

Eagleman, D. (2012). *Incognito: The secret lives of the brain.* New York, NY: Vintage.

Foucault, M. (2003). Society must be defended. *Lectures at the College de France, 1975–1976.* New York, NY: Macmillan.

Freedman, D. (2010, November). Lies, damn lies, and medical science. *The Atlantic.* Retrieved from http://www.theatlantic.com/magazine/archive/2010/11/lies-damned-lies-and-medical-science/308269/?single_page=true

Giegerich, W. (1993). Killings. *Spring, 54,* 1–18.

Goodwin, D. K. (2006). *Team of rivals: The political genius of Abraham Lincoln.* New York, NY: Simon & Schuster.

Jung, C. (1964). A psychological view of conscience. *Civilization in transition: Collected works, Vol. 10* (pp. 437–454). Princeton, NJ: Princeton University Press. (Original work published 1958)

Jung, C. (2009). *The red book: Liber novus.* New York, NY: W.W. Norton.

Kearney, R. (1998). *Poetics of imagining: Modern to post-modern.* New York, NY: Fordham University Press.

Kershaw, S. (2010, July 26). Following a script to escape a nightmare. *New York Times.* Retrieved from http://www.nytimes.com/2010/07/27/health/27night.html

Levinas, E. (1985). *Ethics and infinity: Conversations with Philippe Nero* (R. Cohen, Trans.). Pittsburgh, PA: Duquesne University Press.

Levinas, E. (1989). Ethics as first philosophy. In S. Hand (Ed.), *The Levinas reader.* Malden, MA: Blackwell. (Original work published 1984)

Levinas, E. (2008). *Otherwise than being or beyond essence* (A. Lingis, Trans.). Pittsburgh, PA: Duquesne University Press.

Monstrance. (n.d.). Dictionary.com unabridged. Retrieved from http://dictionary.reference.com/browse/monstrance

Perverse. (n.d.). *Online etymology dictionary.* Retrieved from http://dictionary.reference.com/browse/perverse

Ricoeur, P. (1999). Imagination, testimony, and trust: A dialogue with Paul Ricoeur. In R. Kearney & M. Dooley (Eds.), *Questioning ethics: Contemporary debates in philosophy* (pp. 12–17). New York, NY: Routledge.

Rosivach, H. (1999). Enslaving "barbaroi" and the Athenian ideology of slavery. *Historia: Zeitschrift fur alte geschichte, 48*(2), 129–157. Retrieved from http://www.jstor.org/stable/4436537

Schwartz-Salant, N. (1989). *The borderline personality: Vision and healing.* Asheville, NC: Chiron.

Index

The Ability to Mourn (Homans) 57
abstraction 2, 9, 19, 31, 34–6, 40–2, 91, 102, 122
accreditation 146
active imagination 10, 21, 35–8, 40–1, 44, 46, 62, 96
adultery 1
Adverse Childhood Experiences (ACE) questionnaire 87
aesthetics 31, 82
"The Aims of Psychotherapy" 23
alchemy 10, 24, 58, 66, 103–7
alienation 18, 55
Allphin, C. 80–1
Alone with the Alone (Corbin) 37
amplification method 60–1, 104
analysts 8, 10, 42, 57–62, 67, 81, 83, 92, 98, 106, 138, 140
analytical psychology 3–5, 8, 10, 15, 19–20; analytic hermeneutics 58–63; and ethics 71–83, 89–92; and fantasy 57, 61; and imaginal 110; and imagination 35, 37, 40
anchorites 22
angels 33, 38–9, 105, 107
anima mundi 33
anima/us 125
animals 33
anxiety 8, 71, 85, 87, 90, 107, 114, 129, 140, 152
appropriation 55–6
aqua permanens 106
Aquinas, T. 52
arcanum 105
Archetypal Psychology: A Brief Account (Hillman) 30, 32
archetypes 16, 20, 26, 35–7, 39; archetypal background of experience

61–3; archetypal psychology 30–2, 73, 79; and ethics 72, 77, 82, 90; and fantasy 63; and imaginal 104; and imagination 41, 45; and law 136
archons 105
Aristotle 4, 16, 24, 36
artists 42, 80
ascesis 57
asceticism 22
assimilation 54
atonement 100
aurum philosophorum (philosopher's stone) 104–5
authenticity 7, 14–15, 17, 23, 30, 59, 77, 91, 117, 125, 142, 152
autoeroticism 23
autonomy 41, 102–3, 151
Avens, R. 3, 32
Averroes 36

Bachelard, G. 35, 40–2
barbarism 46, 147
Bartosewzki, W. 123
Baudrillard, J. 15, 19, 133
Bauman, Z. 81, 91, 95, 123, 149
Baydala, A. 58, 60–2
Beckett, S. 16
Beebe, J. 81
Being and Time (Heidegger) 53
bias 9, 51
Bible 1, 32, 52
Big Brother 4, 152
binaries 31, 71–2, 77–9, 110
biology 2, 6, 90–1, 107
Bion, W. 8
bipolar disorder 87
Black Books (Jung) 35, 97
Blake, W. 14, 40, 71

156 Index

blasphemy 4, 108
Bloom, P. 148
Bohman, J. 52
Brann, E. 18
Brinkmann, S. 10, 83–5
Brooks, R. 10, 85, 90
Buddha 102
Bultmann, R. 57, 65

cannibalism 10, 136–7
Caputo, J. 133
caregivers 7
Carter, J. 1–3
Casey, E. 15, 17, 31, 35, 40–2, 46
catatonia 70, 148
Catholics 70, 90, 152
celebrities 115
censorship 108
Central America 90
chat rooms 45–6, 51, 134, 136–7
Cheetham, T. 51
chivalry 120–1, 123, 125
Chodorow, J. 20
Christians 1–4, 16–17, 22, 24–6, 39, 58,
    60, 73, 78, 91, 100, 103–4
civil disobedience 150
Clausewitz, C. 150
Clifford, W.K. 71
clinicians 87, 107
codes of conduct 5, 7, 146–7, 150,
    152; and desire 114, 121–3, 125,
    129–30; and ethics 71, 74–5, 77–8,
    81, 83, 91; and imaginal 96, 101; and
    law 141–2
cognitive-behaviorism 76
Cohen, B. 10, 85, 89
Cohen, R. 86
Coleridge, S.T. 4, 17, 32, 43
Collected Works (Jung) 20, 58
Columbine High School 85
commedia dell'arte (Green and Swan) 118
compassion 5, 84, 102, 110, 122, 129, 151
The Conflict of Interpretations
    (Ricoeur) 64
conflicts of desire 5–6
conflicts of duty 5, 74–7
conscience 10, 71–6, 78–9, 148
consciousness 4, 6, 146–7, 150, 152; and
    desire 114; and ethics 75–7, 79, 82, 84,
    86, 88; and fantasy 51, 56, 61, 64–6;
    and imaginal 98, 101–2, 104–5, 110;
    and imagination 15, 18–19, 21, 25–8,
    30–1, 33, 35, 43; and law 142

conspiracy 134–8
Constantinople, Council of 32
Constitution 136
consumer culture 6, 84, 90
Copernicus, N. 32
Corbin, H. 4, 15–16, 24, 35–40, 44
cosmology 39
countertransference 7, 9, 83, 138
crime 10, 96–8, 100, 133–7
Cruise, T. 114

damnation 70
Dante 37
death 15–16, 36, 105, 107, 109; and
    desire 118–19, 123–4, 127–9; and
    ethics 71, 73–4, 77, 86, 88; and fantasy
    54; and imaginal 95–8, 100
dementia 70
democracy 77, 79
demons 22
depression 109–10
depth psychology 15, 46, 51, 76, 82, 85,
    95, 110
Depth Psychology and a New Ethic
    (Neumann) 76
Derrida, J. 4, 19
Descartes, R. 56
desire 6, 26, 41, 45–6, 113–32; and ethics
    71, 78, 90; and fantasy 51–2, 63–4;
    and imaginal 105, 107, 109; and law
    135, 140–4
devil 72
dialectics 8, 60, 81, 96
differentiation 29–30, 32, 77
Dilthey, W. 52–4, 65
dimensionality 2, 6, 33, 37–9, 44, 85,
    107, 136
discernment 8, 22, 72, 77, 92, 95, 103,
    109–10, 127, 144, 146, 149
distanciation 54–5, 96, 98–9, 113, 142
divinity 4, 16–18, 24–5, 34, 37, 39, 73,
    75, 86, 104
Djuth, M. 17
Doran, R. 54
Dream Story (Schnitzler) 10, 113–14, 119
dreams 96, 108, 148, 150, 152; and desire
    113–32; and ethics 74, 78, 80, 90; and
    fantasy 56, 66; and imagination 15,
    20–1, 27, 30, 35–6, 40, 42–3
dualism 30, 79–80, 103–5

Eagleman, D. 42, 148
East 80

Edinger, E. 103
ego 23–4, 28–9, 44, 46, 56, 62, 65–6, 74,
    76–7, 79, 104, 107
Einbildungskraft 2
Ek, K. 134–6
electroconvulsive therapy 70
Eliade, M. 65
empathy 7
Engber, D. 134, 137
epistemology 3, 53, 60, 90, 129
equilibrium 85, 110, 117, 123, 148
Eros 7
eroticism 5–7, 23, 102, 107, 110–11,
    113–14, 116, 140–3
eschatology 105
esoteric 36–8, 40
essentialism 85
ethics 2, 4–10, 14, 20, 28; among
    Bigs and Littles 44–6, 51, 137; and
    analytical psychology 71–83; and
    dreams 113–32; and eating the liver
    95–112, 150; ethics of discourse 97;
    and fantasy 52, 57, 62, 66; imaginal
    ethics 6, 8–9; and imagination 32,
    70–94; and killing the tortoise 95–112;
    and Neumann 76–80; new ethics
    10, 92; and postmodernism 85–90;
    principles of 101–2, 146–54
etymology 4, 38, 51, 100, 118, 152
evil *see* good and evil
existentialism 10, 18, 29, 37, 55–6, 70–1,
    83–4, 89–90
exteriorization 133
extraverts 26
Eyes Wide Shut (Kubrick) 10, 114

false consciousness 56
fancy 43
fantasm 25–6
fantasy 1, 3, 7–10, 51–69, 146–54;
    building containers for 102–11; and
    conspiracy 134–8; creative fantasy
    28–9, 83; and desire 113–17, 122,
    126–30; and ethics 71, 73, 76, 79–80,
    90; formal definition of 25–8;
    gravitation pull of 110, 143; and
    imagination 14–15, 19–24, 30, 32, 35,
    43–6; personal fantasy 5–6
Federal Bureau of Investigation
    (FBI) 134
Feldman, B. 7
femininity 74, 104, 106–7
fetishes 45, 134

First Amendment 135
fixation 55, 60
flirtations 114
Foucault, M. 133, 150–1
Freud and Philosophy (Ricoeur) 56–8,
    63–4
Freud, S. 27, 30, 46, 56–7, 59–60, 62–4,
    86, 113, 116, 138
"Further Notes on Image" 30
future research 10, 148

Gadamer, H.-G. 29, 53–5, 66
Gaddam, S. 122
Gantt, E. 10, 85, 89–90
Gaudin, C. 40
Gergen, K. 10, 66, 83–5
Germany 78
Giegerich, W. 35, 100, 150
Gjesdal, K. 52–3, 66
Goethe, J.W. von 32
good and evil 10, 71–6, 79–80, 82–4, 102,
    104–5, 109, 114, 135, 137
"Good and Evil in Analytical
    Psychology" 72
gray zone 80, 82, 96, 101, 149
Great Depression 70
Great Famine 70
Greeks 16, 52, 78, 82, 95, 105, 147
Guggenbuhl-Craig, A. 10, 80, 83
guidelines 10
guilt 6, 77, 82, 86, 96, 99–101, 103, 129,
    136, 138, 148–9

Harrington, D. 10, 88–9
Haule, J. 7, 143
Heidegger, M. 53–4, 61, 86
heretics 17, 60, 103
hermeneutics 9–10, 20, 29–30, 37–8,
    40; analytic hermeneutics 58–63;
    behind text 54–6; in front of text
    54–6; hermeneutic circle 52–3, 63;
    hermeneutics of suspicion 54, 56–7,
    64; and imaginal 95
Hermes 95–6, 104–5
Hewison, D. 57, 62
Hillman, J. 9, 15–16, 20, 28, 30–5, 37, 40,
    42–4, 79, 85, 96, 108
Hindus 25
Hippocrates 109
historicism 55
History of Sexuality (Foucault) 133
Hollis, J. 73
Holocaust 78, 82, 86

Homans, P. 57
hubris 4
Hull, R.F.C. 103
humanistic psychology 10, 18, 71, 83
Husserl, E. 41, 62

Ibn 'Arabi 4, 35–9
iconoclasm 30, 32
idealism 17
idols 24, 54
images 20–1, 24, 30–1, 33–5, 40, 42, 89, 96, 98, 102, 108–9
imaginal experience 9, 95, 97–8, 100, 108; and desire 130; and eating the liver 95–112, 150; and ethics 71, 74, 91; and fantasy 51–2; imagining the imagination 14, 21–3, 25–6, 28–9, 35–6, 42–4; and killing the tortoise 95–112; and law 136, 138, 141, 144; role of 146, 150
imaginal space 7–8, 14, 16, 20–1, 23–4, 31, 39, 42, 45–6, 66, 108, 148
imaginatio veram 24, 42–4
imagination 2–6, 9–10, 96, 101–2, 106–9; active imagination 10, 21, 35–8, 40–1, 44, 46, 62, 96; and desire 113–32; digitized imagination 134–8; and dreams 113–32; and ethics 70–94, 146–54; as experience 19–20, 22, 43–4; and fantasy 19–30; imaginal land 133–45; imagining the imagination 14–50; and law 133–45; metaphysical imagination 35–40; revisioning of 30–5; Western visions of 15–19
Imagining: A Phenomenological Study (Casey) 41
imperialism 57, 79
impulses 83–5, 101, 107–8, 110, 117, 134, 146–8
incest 45
individuation 5, 39, 76, 104, 106, 114, 130, 147–8, 151
infidelity 115–16
"An Inquiry into Image" 30
instinct 6, 27, 29, 33, 64, 67, 90
integration 10, 77, 79, 82, 84, 100, 102, 129–30, 140, 143, 151
internalization 5, 8, 86, 137
internet 45–6, 51, 111, 115, 133–8
interpretation 43, 51–8, 90–1, 146, 148–9; behind text 54–6; and desire 117, 121, 123, 127; in front of text 54–8, 66; and imaginal 95–6, 101, 103,

106–7, 109–10; and law 138, 142–3; and unconscious 63–7
intrapsychic relations 6, 10, 46, 96–8, 100, 102, 107, 109, 125, 129, 148, 150–2
introjection 78, 147
introspection 10, 20, 143
introverts 23, 26, 29, 70
intuition 19, 26–7, 31, 37, 61, 66, 76, 141–2
Iraq 99
Ireland 70
Irish Americans 70
"Is Ontology Fundamental?" 87
Islam 35–8, 97
Israel 78

Jackson, R. 135
jealousy 114, 128–9
Jesus Christ 1–3, 24, 58, 91, 100
Jews 16, 25, 78
Jones, A. 57, 65
Journal of Analytical Psychology 57
Jung, C.J. 3–5, 7–10, 146–7, 149, 151–2; and analytic hermeneutics 58–63; and dreams 113–32; and eating the liver 95–112, 150; and ethics 71–85, 89–91; and fantasy 53, 57; and *imaginatio veram et phantastica* 24, 42–4; and imagination 15, 18–30, 38, 40–1, 46; and killing the tortoise 95–112; and king in sweat-bath 103–7; and Neumann 76–80; revisioning of 30–5; and synthesis of insights 28–30; and unconscious 63–7

Kant, I. 4, 17, 22, 32, 63
Kearney, R. 4, 15–19, 24, 32, 57, 146
Kerenyi, C. 95
Kershaw, S. 151–2
Khidr 37
Kidman, N. 114
Kierkegaard, M. 18–19
Klein, M. 81
Kripal, J. 19
Kubrick, S. 10, 113–15, 121–2

The Lancet 99
Lash, C. 134, 136
law 10, 14, 46, 133–45, 150
Levi, P. 82
Levinas, E. 10, 71, 81, 85–91, 96, 101, 123, 148–9, 151–2

"Liber Secundus" 97
liberation theology 90
libido 21, 25–6, 29, 57, 60, 81, 88
lived experience 26, 79, 149
Llinas, R. 42
logos 33
lunacy 23
lust 1–3

mania 87
Manichaeism 103–7
Mardi Gras 113
Marx, K. 56
masculinity 9, 44, 106–7, 122–3
masochism 88
materialism 2–3, 5, 35–6, 38, 42, 108, 111
Matthew's Gospel 1, 3
media 6, 99
Memories, Dreams, Reflections (Jung) 35, 108
metaphors 3, 27–8, 33, 41, 65, 77, 109
metaphysics 6, 16, 18, 33, 35–40, 72
metapsychology 38, 56, 66
Middle Ages 4, 24
Miller v. California 135, 137
Milton, J. 118
mimesis 16–18, 81
modernism 15–17, 19, 85
monogamy 5
monotheism 79
monstrance 152
morality 1–3, 71, 74–8, 148–9, 151; and desire 123; and ethics 81, 84, 86, 90–1; and fantasy 62; and imaginal 95–7, 102, 106; and imagination 14, 17, 46
Morgan, M. 86
mortality 84–5
Mote, H. 91
Murdoch, I. 2, 14
Murr, P. 62
Mysterium Coniunctionis (Jung) 9–10, 22, 60, 103–4, 106
Mysterium Lectures (Edinger) 103
myths 2, 95, 106, 118, 151; and eating the liver 95–112, 150; and ethics 79, 82, 85, 89, 91; and fantasy 57–9, 65; and killing the tortoise 95–112; and king in sweat-bath 103–7

narcissism 6, 56, 81, 129
Nazis 78, 86, 123
necrophilia 100
neglect 7, 81

neo-Kantians 17
Neu, J. 113, 144
Neumann, E. 10, 76–80, 82, 86, 92, 95
neuroscience 42, 122, 148
neuroses 76
New Testament 1
Nicea, Council of 32
Nietzsche, F.W. 56

obscenity 135, 137
obsessive-compulsive disorder 70
O'Conner, F. 91
Oedipus complex 88, 138, 142
Ogas, O. 122
Ogden, T. 8
Old Testament 1, 52, 72
Olver, A. 53
online spaces 45–6, 51, 111, 115, 133–8
ontology 4, 22, 44, 53–4, 72, 85–7, 102
Origen 52
Ostanes 105
Other 134, 136–7, 144, 147–9, 151; and desire 119, 123, 125, 129–30; and ethics 81, 85–6, 88–91; and fantasy 62, 64, 66; and imaginal 95–6, 98, 101–2, 107–9; and imagination 17, 20, 28, 44–6

panic attacks 8
Pare, D. 42
parents 7, 45, 60, 62, 70, 75, 81, 83, 109–10, 124
pathology 46, 70, 76
patricide 57
phantasia 16–17
phantasma 16–17, 24
phantastica 24, 42–4
phenomenology 10, 16, 23, 41, 56, 62, 83–4, 104
Philo of Alexandria 52
philosophy 2–3, 5, 9–10, 14–16, 151; and ethics 71, 81; and fantasy 55, 61, 63; and imagination 29, 32, 36, 40–1, 46; and law 133; and postmodernism 85–90
Pietikäinen, P. 61
Plato 16, 32
play 29–30, 45–6, 55–6, 65–7, 96, 138, 146
Plotinus 31
pneuma 106
poetry 30, 32, 57, 118, 146
polarities 79, 104

160 Index

politics 4, 55, 97, 150
pornography 122
positivism 53
post-Jungians 9, 20, 28, 38, 62, 78, 80–3, 95, 147
postmodernism 3, 15–16, 18–19, 46, 57, 81, 85–91, 95
power 2–4, 104–5, 109, 147, 151–2; and desire 114, 117–19, 122; and fantasy 52, 54, 57, 61, 80, 83, 87, 89; and imagination 16–18, 40–2, 45; and law 136, 138, 141, 143
praxis 41–2, 46, 96
pride 2
prima materia 104–6
"Principles of Practical Psychotherapy" 60
privatio boni 102, 104
professional obligations 7–9
projection 9, 22, 37, 43, 58, 83, 98, 148
prostitutes 116
Proulx, C. 72–3, 75–6
psyche 9, 136, 140, 147, 151; and desire 114, 122–3, 125–7; and ethics 74–80, 82–3, 85; and fantasy 57, 63; and imaginal 97, 100–2, 104, 106, 108–10; and imagination 17, 19–23, 25, 27, 40–2, 44–6
psychiatry 3, 70, 87
psychoanalysis 8, 27, 57–60, 63, 71, 81, 88–9, 91, 116, 142
psychodynamic theory 5, 7
"A Psychological Approach to the Dogma of the Trinity" 76
Psychological Types (Jung) 9, 20, 25, 28, 59
"A Psychological View of Conscience" 74
Psychology and Alchemy (Jung) 24
psychopathology 46, 76, 134
psychotherapy 5, 9, 23, 60, 76, 82, 85, 88–9, 107–8, 137, 141
PTSD 152

Quinn, P. 70

Ramberg, B. 52–3, 66
"Re-visioning Psychology" 30
reciprocity 86
The Red Book (Jung) 28, 35, 73, 91, 97, 146
regression 60, 116–17, 123

reification 32, 40, 57, 88
"The Relations between the Ego and the Unconscious" 21
relativism 1, 23, 30, 64, 72–3, 76, 78, 83, 109
religion 4, 6–7, 97, 99–100, 106; and desire 119, 122; and ethics 70–1, 75, 78–80, 91; and fantasy 52, 57–8, 60
repression 8, 26, 78, 88
responsibility 101, 110, 144, 148–9, 151; and desire 116, 128; and ethics 74, 77, 80–2, 85–6, 89–90; and imaginal 96, 98–9; and imagination 23, 44–5
revenge 116–17, 123, 125–6
reverie 8
Ricoeur, P. 9, 29–30, 43–4, 52–8, 63–7, 95–7, 121, 151
romantics 17–18, 32, 40–1
Romanyshyn, R. 10, 62–7
Rosarium Philosophorum 24
Rosivach, H. 147
Rutter, P. 141

"The Sacrificial Murder" 101
sadism 88
St Augustine 16–17, 24, 52, 74, 78, 104–5
St Bonaventure 24–5, 44
Sartre, J.-P. 4, 18, 22, 41
Schelling, F.W. 57, 65
Schenk, R. 42, 98–9
Schiller, F. 25, 67
Schleiermacher, F. 52, 65
Schnitzler, A. 10, 113–14, 116–19, 122–3, 127–9
Schwartz-Salant, N. 8, 10, 138, 140–4, 149–50
scientism 2
scripture 1–2
scrupulosity 70, 73, 90, 148
Sebek, M. 80–1
"The Secret of the Golden Flower" 23
semiotics 30, 34, 59, 61–2, 66, 101, 149
sensation 8, 31, 33, 116
sense perception 22, 31, 33, 36–9, 41–3, 77
shadow 33, 45, 52, 56, 74, 81–2, 84, 146, 149–52
Shamdasani, S. 35
Shi'ism 24, 35, 37–8
sin 1–2, 4, 32, 70, 72
Smith, M. 105
Smythe, W. 58, 60–2

social constructionism 3, 10, 66, 83–5
social movements 52
sociopaths 148
software 134
solidarity 84
solipsism 22
Solomon, H. 10, 80–2
Sophia aeterna 37–8
soul 17, 22, 31–2, 35–7, 43, 45, 63–4, 73–4, 89, 98–101, 114, 138
specters 116, 148
Spinoza, B. 57
spirituality 3, 36–7, 39
Stanley v. Georgia 135
Stevens, W. 30, 32
Strong, B. 138
subjectivity 8, 19, 22, 29, 98; and ethics 72, 81; and fantasy 54–5, 58–63, 66–7; and hermeneutics of suspicion 56–7; and imagination 31–2, 35, 43
suffering 1, 6, 101, 148, 151–2; and desire 128; and ethics 70–1, 75–7, 82, 86, 89–91; and imaginal 105–10; and imagination 27, 40
Sufism 24, 35, 44
suicide 110, 118, 127
superego 86
suppression 75, 78, 104
Supreme Court 135
symbols 7–8, 54, 56–60, 65, 149; and desire 121–2, 127–9; and ethics 71, 81, 89–90; and imaginal 95–6, 99, 101, 104–6; and imagination 27–8, 30, 34, 36–40
synchronicity 36, 121, 128

taboos 45
Tan, H. 53
Taves, A. 19
Tavistock Lectures 24, 28
Ta'wil 37–40
teleology 61, 66, 73, 79, 82, 147
temptation 114, 125, 127
theodicy 86
theology 15–16, 32, 39, 52, 58, 90, 105, 133
theophany 37–9
therapists 5, 7–9, 14, 147, 151; and ethics 81, 83, 85; and fantasy 61; and imaginal 107, 109–10; and law 140, 142, 144

thought crime 134
totalitarianism 77
transcendence 18, 66, 72, 76, 91, 101, 122, 149
"The Transcendent Function" 9, 20
transference 7, 9, 138–9, 141, 148
transformation 18, 21, 43, 66, 96, 106–11, 133, 152
trauma 46, 81, 87–8, 90, 136, 141
triggers 8
truth 23–4, 30, 56, 60, 151; and desire 122, 126; and ethics 72, 83; and fantasy 62, 66; and imaginal 96, 99, 107, 110
Twyman, M. 80–2

Ulanov, A. 102
unconscious 5, 8–10, 147–8, 150, 152; and desire 114, 117, 122–3, 127–9; and ethics 73–7, 79, 84, 89; and fantasy 51–2, 56, 60, 63; and imaginal 101, 103–6, 109; and imagination 20–1, 23, 26, 28–9, 34, 40, 42, 45–6; and interpretation 63–7; and law 140–2, 144
United States (US) 1, 99, 135, 151
universalizing impulses 83–5
utilitarianism 55

Valle, G. 134–8
value for life 59–60, 62, 66–7
Van Hise, M. 134, 136
veram 24, 42–4
violence 21, 46, 87, 95–102, 110, 114, 117, 134, 147, 150–2
Voice of God 75, 78
voyeurism 115

The Wake of Imagination (Kearney) 15
war 2, 6, 78, 80, 86, 150
Weinberger, G. 119
West 1, 3–5, 14–19, 32, 52–8, 78, 97
White, V. 103
Whitfield, N. 138
Wilson, A. 53
Winnicott, D.W. 81
wish-fulfillment 6
Wordsworth, W. 18
World War II 78

Zoja, L. 10, 80, 82, 86, 89, 91, 96
Zoroastrianism 105

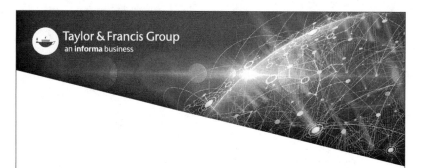